Letters from Elvis

Shocking Revelations to His Secret Confidante

Gary Lindberg

CALUMET EDITIONS

Minneapolis • London • Nuremberg

**CALUMET
EDITIONS**

Minneapolis • London • Nuremberg

FIRST EDITION NOVEMBER 2018

BIO005000 Biography & Autobiography / Entertainment & Performing Arts

Printed in the United States of America.

10 9 8 7 6 5 4 3 2 1

Cover and interior design: AuthorScope

ISBN: 978-1-7327944-8-1

This book is dedicated with love to my son
Brendan Lindberg (1972 - 2016)

Author's Note

Letters from Elvis consists of independent reporting and commentary about a collection of handwritten letters that appear to have been written by Elvis Presley, Marlon Brando, Harry Belafonte and Tom Jones. This book is not sponsored or endorsed by, and is not affiliated in any way with, the foregoing celebrities or their heirs and successors, including Priscilla Presley.

Table of Contents

Also by Gary Lindberg

Nonfiction
The Power of Positive Handwriting
(with Elayne V. Lindberg)

Historical Fiction
Ollie's Cloud

Thrillers
The Shekinah Legacy
Sons of Zadok
Deeper and Deeper

Letters from Elvis

Shocking Revelations to His Secret Confidante

Gary Lindberg

A Secret Cache of Letters

Imagine my surprise when one afternoon I was handed a cache of unpublished letters written by Elvis to a secret confidante. The letters revealed a life unexposed to the public and many of his closest aides. The letters explained many mysteries of Elvis's behavior and presented a wholly different personality than the façade created by the media and Elvis's handlers. As I read these handwritten letters, tears often came into my eyes. More than once, I was struck by disbelief. *This can't be true! This could not have happened to a celebrity like Elvis!* But the astonishing content of the Elvis letters would soon be corroborated by another collection of letters from three other well-known celebrities—intimate friends of Elvis.

The information in these letters has been like a ticking time bomb in my life ever since I became aware of it. After reading the letters, every time I come upon a new Elvis book or documentary I flinch because I'm reminded of the calling I've so far refused—a calling to reveal the startling truth about Elvis to a public that deserves to know and all those fans who were heartbroken at his rapid decline and early death.

According to the correspondence—which has been fully authenticated by world-renowned handwriting expert Charles W. Sachs—Elvis went through unrelenting hell during the five years represented in the letters, an almost unbelievable hell that has remained hidden from our view. The reason for the secrecy will

1

become obvious as each section of this book unfolds. Now, with the exposure of the events related in these letters, all previous books will have to be read within the context of this one. At first, I struggled to accept some of the events described. I can honestly say that I've often wished they were a massively elaborate hoax, the motivation for which is lost to us, but I'm afraid they are no hoax— not at all. The Elvis letters are clearly in his own handwriting, and what he writes, whether you're a fan or not, will sometimes create admiration, and sometimes horror.

A salient characteristic of contemporary society is to immortalize popular entertainers by transforming them into icons, thus stripping them of their privacy and humanity. Inevitably, society is shocked when the inner lives of these chosen ones are revealed to be chaotic and tragic—stars like Marilyn Monroe, Michael Jackson, Robin Williams, Prince, but perhaps none more so than the biggest entertainment icon of all, Elvis Presley. I'm sure that sociologists and philosophers can explain why few things advance a famous entertainer's career more than dying young and tragically. Just as absolute power seems to corrupt absolutely, so it goes that absolute fame and the complications that accompany it overwhelms many celebrities.

When the hidden lives of celebrities are exposed, we are often shocked to find that they are human. Unfortunately, it is usually a profound disadvantage for stars to be seen as such, so their handlers go to extreme lengths to preserve the Olympian status of their clients, especially after death when the value of the celebrity's assets can quickly collapse if mishandled.

Imagine, then, the risk of revealing the hidden life of Elvis Presley, one of the top-earning dead celebrities of all time. Imagine the resistance that might arise against anyone or anything threatening to change the status quo by revealing facts that might alter public perception of this supreme icon. Over two decades, the consequences of such resistance have frustrated all my attempts to reveal the astonishing information contained in these Elvis letters. Now that I've decided the time has come to go public with this story, I know that I'd better get it right.

I have a lot at stake in translating these letters into a book, including my reputation. I have worried for years that the letters may prove to be forgeries, and I carelessly missed the telltale clue. I've had nightmares that facts contained in the letters and reported by me would be proven by an astute reader to be untrue. I've been extremely anxious over the possibility that undetected contradictions may exist in the body of letters, destroying my reputation for thorough analysis.

As a necessary part of due diligence our team made requests for FBI documents pertaining to Elvis under the Freedom of Information Act (FOIA). We quickly learned that government agencies take their time in fulfilling these requests, sometimes many months, and then often deliver only a handful of available documents making additional time-consuming requests necessary. In our case, after scores of requests, we ended up with hundreds of pages of documents, many of them highly redacted for reasons of "personal privacy, national security, and law enforcement" according to the FOIA website.

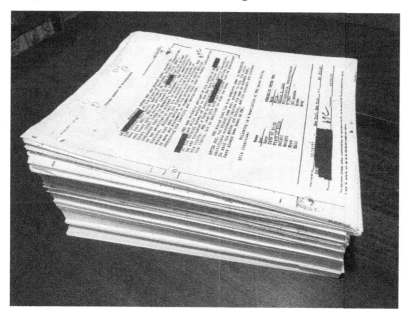

A stack of FBI documents related to Elvis and released to us under the Freedom of Information Act.

The FBI has reportedly documented hundreds of threats on Elvis's life, yet most of the pages delivered to us related to a single legal case in which con men attempted to swindle the entertainer out of millions of dollars in a plot involving a jet aircraft owned by Elvis. Either this case consumed a disproportionate share of FBI attention for some unknown reason, or the FBI withheld a lot of information from us.

After reading the hundreds of letters and surveying the cache of FOIA-released documents, I was dismayed at how the attempts to take advantage of Elvis seemed to never end. It took me a few years to appreciate the eerie timing of the attempted aircraft scam. I'll describe the mysterious details of this elaborate con later.

My fears of missing important details, failing to connect disparate but related facts, plus a touch of OCD, are the reasons why I have checked, rechecked and cross-checked everything that was checkable, including competing theories and alternate explanations for reported events, of which there are many. And then our obsessive fact-checkers did it all again. I do not want to be made a fool.

A Prince and the King

At noon on Thursday, April 21, 2016, I was shocked at the news on Channel 5. Superstar Prince Rogers Nelson had been found dead in Paisley Park, his home and studio complex in Chanhassen, Minnesota. The famously clean-living Prince had for years suffered from chronic, debilitating hip pain caused by injuries sustained during his gymnastic performances. Arguably, he was one of the most magnetic, sexy, theatrical singers and musicians to perform on stage since Elvis Presley had captivated the planet with his provocative, often-censored gyrations.

For years, mostly unknown to his fans, Prince had performed with intense pain. When the painkillers he relied on inevitably stopped managing the misery, he had turned to fentanyl, a powerful synthetic opioid that is up to fifty times more potent than heroin and one hundred times more potent than morphine. One microgram of fentanyl can kill the user. For Prince, the drug finally did. His lifeless body was found in the Paisley Park elevator.

I had met Prince a few times because of my work as a filmmaker. My wife and I had partied at Paisley Park. I knew Prince as a model citizen and a dependable but secret philanthropist in the local community. He was also a spiritual seeker, having become a Jehovah's Witness in 1975.

Then suddenly he was gone at the age of fifty-seven.

Watching the shocking story unfold on television at my home just a mile from Paisley Park, I was struck by how the Prince tragedy paralleled a similar event that had occurred thirty-nine years earlier. On the evening of August 16, 1977, the world was stunned by news that Elvis Presley, the "King of Rock 'n' Roll," had been found dead in his bathroom. Initially, the coroner had listed the cause of death as "hypertensive cardiovascular disease with atherosclerotic heart disease"—in short, a heart attack. But later, a toxicology report revealed that ten separate prescription medications had been found in Elvis's body. According to the toxicology report, one of these drugs, the painkiller codeine, was present at a level about ten times the therapeutic dosage. At forty-two, Elvis had been fighting a losing battle with weight for a few years and had suffered from various illnesses including hypertension, various cardiovascular compromises and a chronic colon condition diagnosed as Hirschsprung's disease.

Rumors persist that Elvis faked his own death, perhaps to escape the incessant pressures of being Elvis, or to enter the federal witness protection program after assisting in a drug sting. The possibility that his death was a suicide is seldom raised. But if you accept the fact that Elvis died in 1977, you must admit that it was a profitable though inadvertent career move. In 2016 his estate was worth three hundred million dollars. Forbes ranked Elvis as the second-highest-earning dead celebrity; the highest-earning star was Michael Jackson, who died in 2009 of an overdose and, ironically, was Elvis's son-in-law. Fifty-one years after his death they're still using his songs for television ads, making new documentaries, sticking his face on the cover of popular tabloids and magazines, and discovering unauthenticated and so-called suicide letters.

Since Elvis's death, over sixty books have been published about him, the most successful ones authored by people who knew him—relatives, colleagues, friends, employees, entertainers, and hangers-on. There is a book by his wife, bodyguards, hair-dresser, brother-in-law, even a personal nurse who cared for him in the hospital. Many of these books contain some truth, some merely perpetuate an Elvis mythology, a few contain numerous half-truths, and some contain

6

outright lies. Because there are few documents written by Elvis in which he describes his innermost thoughts and emotions, all these books attempt to reconstruct his inner life based on his behavior and spoken words. None of the authors can faithfully describe some of the most pivotal events in Elvis's life that occurred in private. Now, however, I can.

* * *

I was not an instant fan of Elvis. In 1956, I was thirteen years old and learning to play the guitar from my father, a talented guitarist, songwriter, magician and housepainter. One day after school a recording by a performer named Stan Freberg came on the radio. At first, I thought Freberg was just a singer, but quickly realized he was spoofing another singer. The song was "Heartbreak Hotel."

I had heard of Elvis Presley, but honestly could not have named a single song by the man who would become a "king." It turned out that "Heartbreak Hotel" was his first gold record. The hilarious Freberg parody contained a slight echo effect that mushroomed into a baffling, Escher-like reverb that threatened to swallow the singer whole. Sixty years later I still laugh when I think about it.

A few days later, I heard the authentic Elvis version, which suffered from the lack of Freberg's biting humor. But I had to admit, Elvis's voice was really something. I became an admirer. Over the years, as the singer's fame exploded, and his persona devolved into a Freberg-like caricature of an entertainer, I drifted away. His musical departures from rock and gospel left me disappointed, his movies became cheap and absurd, his Las Vegas shows embarrassingly campy. Still, now and then I heard Elvis sing a number that shivered my bones. *Such talent*, I remember thinking… *such emotion. Such a waste.* How could such a powerful entertainer seem so adrift?

Then in 1977 he dropped dead, still a young man, just seven years older than me. Suddenly, I realized that he had contributed a lot of music to the soundtrack of my life. I was going to miss him. We had grown up together; he had been like an older brother—

7

not a close one, really, but always present in the background, like a memory of someone close. I was shaken, like I was when Prince died so suddenly in my hometown.

The death of Elvis became a conspiracy bonanza. Elvis became a "jumpsuit Jesus" who never died, an unwitting cult leader whose mythology inspired countless novels, movies, lonely hearts, impersonators and after-death sightings. A global society seized on the mystery of Elvis and wouldn't let go because Elvis symbolized all the dreams and heartbreak, the power and humiliation, the fame and insecurity that we all covet and fear.

I had many questions for Elvis, and I was angry that he had so suddenly left them unanswered. But after a time, I decided to let him rest in peace.

And then, thirteen years later, like a voice from beyond, Elvis decided to answer.

A Late Night Call

Bill Mack is an immensely talented artist who developed a new technique for reproducing bas-relief sculptures. Calling his works *bas-relief* is technically incorrect because the term refers to *low* relief sculpture. Mack's work in many ways is beyond high relief, with elements of it rising from the background in full-round form to extend into space. His work is in the collections of presidents, celebrities, international business leaders and galleries.

Bill Mack is an internationally renowned relief sculptor and painter.

Bill recognized early in his career that a strong brand was necessary to make it in the cutthroat art world. He decided that *he* would be that brand. As Salvador Dali and LeRoy Neiman had done earlier, Bill established a vivid, distinctive identity out of a hundred little details ranging from a dramatic signature to the ever-present rosebud that decorates his lapel wherever he goes. This persona, coupled with true artistic genius, made Bill a rich man, and wealth allowed him to indulge his other passion—collecting memorabilia of historical figures and celebrities, including Elvis.

My mother, Elayne Lindberg, proprietor of arguably the most well-known art gallery in Minneapolis at the time, had given Bill his first big art show. My sister, Bonnie, managed the gallery. I got to know Bill when Bonnie recommended me to produce a promotional film. Bill loved my work, and we became good friends. Both Bill and I had degrees in journalism from the University of Minnesota, so we shared an appreciation for communications strategy and execution.

Late one evening in 1990, I received a phone call from Bill that would send me on an unexpected journey. "Gary, sorry to call so late," he said.

"No problem," I replied. "It's been a while since we talked—over a year. What's up?"

"Well, I have a proposition for you—I'd like you to develop a book based on some letters I came across."

"So, these letters…" I replied, "they must be important. Who wrote them?"

"I can't tell you right now. I've got quite a bit of money invested in them, and I really don't want news leaking out until the right time."

Suddenly, for the first time with Bill, I felt mistrusted.

My silence must have betrayed my feelings because Bill said, "Nothing to do with you—just that I promised my partner I wouldn't reveal the source until we both agreed it was time."

"I assume the letters are by someone famous."

"Yes, of course."

"A politician?"

"Is this going to be Twenty Questions?"

"I'm just trying to get a sense of scale."

"Definitely not a politician," Bill answered. I could tell he wanted to reveal the letter writer to me and was frustrated that he couldn't.

"A historical figure then?" I knew he had collected numerous letters in the hand of famous people from history.

"Well… not in the sense you mean."

"So more contemporary than historical… maybe recently dead?" There was no answer, so I knew I was getting close. "Can you give me a clue?"

"Think royalty."

I ran through a list of kings and queens and princes and princesses. None seemed to be worthy of such secrecy. But then I had a hunch. I knew that Bill loved to collect letters and signatures by celebrities.

"So, could the writer be considered a king of sorts?"

Bill laughed. "I never should have started playing this game with you. But since you guessed it…"

"How many Elvis letters do you have?"

"Nearly a hundred—all authenticated. And about two hundred more by three other celebrities, all to the same person."

"And what kind of letters are they?"

"Deeply personal. Deeply."

"Anything in them that we haven't heard before?"

"If you're in, you can read them and make up your own mind."

"OK, but it's hard to imagine anything about Elvis that hasn't been revealed by someone."

The next day I drove to Bill's studio, and we settled into a conference room. From a banged-up banker's box he extracted a collection of papers and envelopes of many sizes and colors, some of them folded and ragged, a few stained. He set them in front of me.

"These are the original letters," he explained.

The first letter, dated June 3, was written with a blue ballpoint. It began "Dear Sister." I glanced at the signature. "Sincerely, Elvis."

Was I really holding in my hand an original letter penned by the King of Rock 'n' Roll?

"This is confusing," I said. "I'm no Elvis scholar, but I'm pretty sure Elvis had only one sibling, a twin brother who died shortly after birth. But this letter is addressed 'Dear Sister.'"

Bill nodded. "That's a pet name for his secret confidante. I think it shows how close he felt to her. All the letters begin pretty much the same way—*Dear Sister, Dear Sis, For my Sister…*"

The June 3 letter was clipped to an envelope postmarked June 4, 1969 and was addressed to a woman at 2255 Cahuenga, Apt. 37, Hollywood, Calif. 90068. I waved the envelope at Bill. "The confidante's name was Carmen Montez?"

Bill nodded.

"And do all the letters have postmarked envelopes?"

Bill shook his head. "Many were delivered by courier, probably trusted people who worked for the authors. I think you should just read through the letters. A lot of your questions will be answered… and a lot more will be raised."

I read the first paragraph of the June 3 letter. "This will take some time," I said. "It's kind of hard to decipher his handwriting."

Bill pushed a second stack of papers toward me. "We all had the same problem, so I had my secretary type them up."

I began to read the transcripts. They didn't always make sense because they were out of sequence. Some had the month and date written on them but no year. Some had no date at all. Many referred to comments or questions by Carmen Montez, but of course I did not have Carmen's side of the conversation. It was like listening to only one side of a telephone call with the conversation scrambled. But even read as separate letters, the content was at times astonishing, hair-raising, bewildering, and deeply moving. The portrait of Elvis that emerged from those pages was inconsistent with the freakish, out-of-control Elvis that had been portrayed by the media, but instead portrayed a confused, intensely spiritual man who was brutally abused and betrayed, maliciously manipulated, and deserving of compassion. After reading the letters, I felt like apologizing to

Elvis for not having understood the purgatory of his life and the circumstances of his tragedy.

By the time Bill came back to the conference room, my mind was whirling with questions, just as he had predicted. "I need to know about this Carmen Montez," I said. "Understanding more about who these letters were written to will make it easier to understand the content. I assume she's your partner who doesn't want word of the letters to get out."

"No, she's not." Bill sat down next to me. "Unfortunately, Carmen Montez is dead. But her best friend is still alive, and she's my partner. Her name is Carmen Rayburn."

"*Two* Carmens? Quite a coincidence."

"Not really," Bill said. "But an amazing story."

The Confidante's Confidante

I didn't meet Carmen Rayburn, the owner of the Elvis letters, until six years after signing on to the project. Finally, in 1993, I was about to meet her face-to-face. My wife, Gloria, and I flew into the Ontario, California airport on Good Friday, rented a car and drove to the high desert where we found Carmen's ranch. It seems amazing now, but after many years of researching Elvis Presley and rooting around Memphis and Tupelo, Mississippi, I knew a lot more about the King than I did about the owner of the Elvis letters.

Carmen Rayburn, who had come to possess the letters, still fascinates me. Born in 1926, nine years before Elvis, she was sixty-four when I first spoke to her on the telephone. During the following years, when it seemed impossible to legally publish a book based on the Elvis letters, Carmen continually begged me to keep up the effort.

We arrived at the ranch at twilight. There were two structures—a main building where Carmen lived and another made of cement blocks that looked like a motel with a line of guest rooms that are still in use today. Gloria and I stayed in one of those rooms, and ranch hands lived in the others.

We pulled up to the main building, tires crunching the stony driveway. A young man named Nathan greeted us with a grin. He was one of the "Lost Boys," as Gloria came to call them—young men with troubled pasts who had found a generous soul in Carmen, who had become their employer and second "Mom."

14

"Welcome to Carmen's," Nathan said. "Let me show you around back… that's where the shop is. We can put your bags into your room later."

We couldn't see the backside of the main building from the road, but it contained a dress shop and a restaurant/bar that overlooked the town of Apple Valley.

We were ushered into a dress shop—"Carmen's pride and joy," Nathan explained. The dresses and gowns Carmen had selected for sale were bold and colorful, some of them downright flamboyant. They reminded me of some of the gowns my mother wore to gallery openings. I wasn't sure if women in high desert country were in the market for such garments, but the variety was dazzling.

After about ten minutes, we finally met Carmen face-to-face. For me it was like meeting a second mother. She exuded warmth and sincerity as she made her entrance in a flowing purple gown that shimmered with her movements. Still in my travel jeans and a denim shirt, I felt wholly underdressed for the occasion. I could imagine how Gloria felt, though I didn't ask in front of Carmen. Almost instantly, though, Carmen dismissed any discomfort we may have felt with a broad, heartfelt smile and that low, comforting voice I had heard so many times on the telephone.

"My dears!" she said, making us feel as if we were family arriving at a reunion. Then, turning to Gloria, she said, "I hope you enjoy my dresses. These are just playthings for special occasions. Jeans are always appropriate on the ranch. But if you want to try anything on… just let me know. I'll bet you're hungry after your long trip." She looked around for Nathan, who was right behind her. "Nathan! Please show our guests to the restaurant."

We followed Nathan up a flight of stairs to the restaurant, which was empty except for one of the Lost Boys who stood behind the bar. I wondered if Apple Valley residents ever patronized Carmen's restaurant. After a delicious steak dinner, I was sure they did.

Carmen Rayburn holding great-niece McKenna Rayburn.

We had a lot of small talk and laughter that evening, but Carmen eventually diagnosed travel fatigue and sent us off to our room, where we found our suitcases and bottles of water. "You can get pretty dried out up here," Nathan said. "If you go out, just beware of the coyotes. Usually they don't bother no one, but you never know."

I abandoned my idea of an evening walk.

Saturday morning, Gloria and I woke up early and went for a walk in the morning sunshine, dodging cacti and scaring jackrabbits along the way. Before breakfast I recorded my impressions of the previous evening in my journal.

Carmen did not join us for breakfast. "She gets pretty worn out sometimes," Nathan told us, "and doesn't have the appetite she used to. But she'll join you later this morning."

About ten thirty, after Gloria and I had returned from a long hike, Nathan found us. "Carmen is ready to get started," he said. "I can show you into the study now. It'll be private in there."

March 27, 1993 Saturday

I'm at Carmen's Ponderosa Ranch. After 5 years I've finally met Carmen Rayburn. She's not what I imagined but I'm convinced she believes everything about the Presley letters. She's unfocused but entertaining. The ranch is her little empire which is sufficing until she becomes "Empress" of her own Fiji island. A great sense of humor. We just had an enormous steak dinner at her restaurant and met her nephew. Carmen said I was one of the most interesting people she had met — because I was interested in her, I am sure. We've started taping interviews with her to form the basis for a Presley book. There are dogs everywhere here — and four cats. And stray humans she's taken in who seem to treat her as "Queen". In her own words, this place is a world unto itself. It's extremely windy here and quite cold tonight. The wind is whistling through the windows. I wonder if this strange place is the beginning of our book or just another memory? Time will tell.

A page from the author's journal.

Our plan was to start recording a series of interviews to document Carmen's experiences and knowledge of events to date as well as to reconstruct years of conversations she'd had with the other Carmen—Carmen Montez. These recollections, corroborated by the handwritten letters, would provide the material I needed to write the book with minimal legal peril. I'll explain the risks later, but this trip was intended to begin the final stage of project development.

Nathan ushered me into the study where Carmen sat in an upholstered chair. I sat down at a wooden table and pulled out my voice recorder.

"Before we start," Carmen said, "can I show you my island?"

I had no idea what she was talking about. She had never mentioned an island before. "Sure—I'd like to see it. Do you have pictures?"

"First a map so you can see where it is."

With great effort—she seemed tired and fragile that morning—she rose from her chair, unrolled a large map on the table and traced her finger to a small dot in the Pacific Ocean. "There it is—my Pacific isle."

"You own an island in the Pacific?"

"Not yet. But it's for sale, and I'll own it as soon as the book is published and becomes a bestseller."

In a drawer below the table's surface she found a larger map and several photos of the island showing an airstrip, a water tower, a small building that seemed capable of supporting life, and a hut she said contained a generator.

"This is what keeps me going, Gary. It's why I keep bugging you to get this book published. I don't know how much longer I have left, and I need to spend some time on my island before I go."

I was alarmed at this sudden twist to our conversation. "Carmen, you didn't tell me you were ill. What is it?"

"Oh, sometimes a person just knows that something's wrong. I don't feel well. Pain… you know. But please, dear—help me get to my island, will you?"

I remember being confused. I wasn't sure if Carmen was fatally ill or if she was just manipulating me to speed things up. I also remember feeling ashamed that I doubted this woman to whom I had grown so attached. To soothe my emotions, I chose a reality to believe in—that Carmen was ill, but not fatally, that she had reason to complain and worry, as we all do, and that it really was time to double-down on my effort to get the book written and published.

It would be wonderful, I thought, if the generous Elvis I had come to know—the Elvis who gave friends Cadillacs and money to pay their debts—would also be a source of great joy and support for my friend Carmen.

The following day was Easter Sunday, and Carmen's house was soon overwhelmed by family members and friends. I could not keep the names and relationships straight, and I never knew for sure if all those guests were gathering as an annual Easter tradition or because Gloria and I, the link to the publishing of the Elvis book—which everyone seemed to know about—had come to visit. The food was prepared mostly by the Lost Boys, and a more hilarious show of culinary chaos we had never seen before. A large ham refused to be ready until two hours after the turkey was done. The side dishes all had minds of their own, "finishing on God's mysterious schedule," as someone said. But no one seemed upset at the delays, everyone happily chatted away, and Gloria and I felt like part of this boisterous and loving family.

Half the people I met seemed eager to make it in the movie or music business—this was California, after all. Some of the guests, however, had found success. I had a wonderful visit with Richard Henrick, whose submarine thriller *Crimson Tide* had been made into a movie starring Denzel Washington. He offered to make some introductions to publishers when the Elvis manuscript was ready. I never learned his connection to Carmen, or that of almost anyone else.

Most memorable, however, was the house itself. I had been so anxious to dig into work on the book that I had not explored the adjoining living and dining rooms. Now I had a chance, and I found the home's innards to be a museum of Elvis kitsch—coasters and tumblers, calendars and ashtrays, napkins, place mats, mobiles—virtually everything adorned with Elvis's likeness, name or signature. My two favorites were a nearly life-size image of Elvis in a Vegas jumpsuit hand-painted on black velvet, and a larger-than-life bust of Elvis with magical eyes I discovered staring at me no matter where in the room I stood. Even today, when I am working on this Elvis book, I sometimes feel him staring at me, prodding me to get the work done.

Easter at Carmen's ranch was an exhausting, exhilarating, highly entertaining experience. That evening I slept soundly for the first time in weeks, and the next day Carmen and I went back to work. I checked, and Elvis was still watching.

* * *

"Even today, when I think of Elvis I think of fiery flamenco guitar music. That's because I can't think of Elvis without seeing the face of my best friend, a beautiful Spanish woman named Carmen Montez."

Those words were spoken by Carmen Rayburn during one of my interviews. That was the first time I had heard the full story of the woman on the other side of Elvis's secret letters—his confidante. In truth, Carmen Montez never physically met Elvis, but she had come to know him perhaps more intimately than many of his closest friends. She had learned his innermost thoughts and feelings, many of which he expressed only to one secret confidante, a woman he seldom referred to by name but lovingly called "Sis." As a product of the "guru culture" of the sixties, which today seems quaint, Elvis had previously attached himself to other centers of influence as well.

Elvis loved his "Sister," not in a romantic way, but in a deeply spiritual and needful way. That Carmen Montez loved Elvis is also a certainty because she had told her best friend that Elvis had become her "brother in spirit" and the "child I feel compelled to protect and nurture."

The secret relationship between Elvis and Carmen Montez was based on that terribly old-fashioned tool of communication, written correspondence. What passed between them, though, was a continuous flow of candor and emotion that described in intimate detail the hauntings of a troubled life, the betrayals of friends and allies, the physical traumas and emotional scars that would shape one of the most famous lives of the twentieth century.

Almost everyone who knew Elvis has commented on his life in minute detail. Millions have read the "inside" stories about the King's escapades, his eccentricities, his successes and foibles. It is always hard to sort out fact from fiction. In many cases the authors help us by telegraphing their motives and biases.

Does anyone believe that Priscilla was always as sweet and kind and understanding as she portrayed herself in *Elvis and Me*? After reading Albert Goldman's body of "biographies," all of them hatchet jobs on major celebrities, it is not hard to see a marketing theme emerging when we go back to his sensationalistic and one-sided book, *Elvis*. Illicit sex sells, or so Goldman thought before disappointing sales revealed a disbelieving public that obviously saw through his long-form tabloid diatribe (which I believe revealed much more about the author than the subject).

After being fired, it is not difficult to imagine the sense of betrayal that brought bodyguards Red and Sonny West to write their scathing "tell all" story of life with Elvis. Was it really to wake up Elvis to the peril of his ways, as they claimed? Was there no bias at all in that book? Oddly, in a phenomenal bit of good fortune for book sales, it was published on August 1, 1977, just fifteen days before Elvis died.

So many people, so many books. Books by his nurse, his hairdresser, his doctor, his bodyguard, his stepbrother, his uncle; the list goes on.

* * *

Carmen Rayburn met the mysterious Carmen Montez because of a quirk of nomenclature: they were both named Carmen by their parents. Carmen Rayburn met Carmen Montez because she advertised her name. As she explained to me, "I ran a small boutique on Wilshire Boulevard in Los Angeles called Carmen's. Even today, many years after meeting her, I can still recall our first encounter."

From her description, I envisioned it as a precursor of her dress shop in Apple Valley. Carmen's offered a bold collection of the exotic and the unusual. The clothing and jewelry reflected her love of vibrant, Hawaiian patterns.

That particular morning, Carmen recalled, had been very slow. No sales, only a few bored browsers. She was fidgeting with a display in the front of the boutique when a shopper opened the door. Carmen Rayburn's first impression of the woman would stay with her forever—dancer's legs, shapely hips, large bosom, black hair. The body was fabulous, but its presentation was what stood out. This woman wore a gown and necklace nearly identical to what Rayburn had chosen to wear that day. Had they both been outfitted by JCPenney it would not have been so curious.

The shopper spoke first. "I was just driving by and saw the sign on your shop. I had to stop in and see who this other Carmen is. That's my name too."

"I'm Carmen Rayburn. Happy to meet you, Carmen...?"

"Carmen Montez," the woman replied.

For Rayburn, these were clearly happy memories—a chance encounter with a woman who would become a close friend and who was always full of surprises. "I could not have guessed how well I would come to know Carmen and her husband, George," she told me.

Although I've been unable to locate her immigration records, Carmen Montez told Rayburn she was born in Barcelona. As a teenager she fell in love with American movies and set her compass for Hollywood, determined to let nothing stand in her way of gaining fame and fortune. Somehow she made it to Los Angeles by the age of twenty or so—the exact history is largely undocumented. With long, black hair and pale, iridescent skin, she turned heads wherever she went. Beneath the 100 percent natural packaging, however, lay her major assets: confidence, steely nerves, a quick mind, and an intuition that bordered on supernatural according to those who knew her.

She was already a woman of robust appetites with a compulsion to indulge them. Wherever Carmen was, there was a party. Men were drawn to her, and unsurprisingly women both envied and loathed her. The explosive mixture of sex appeal, talent and intelligence was a recipe for disaster or success. Whatever the outcome, Carmen was determined to have fun.

Carmen Montez in her later years with her beloved dog Marlon.

She ultimately caught the eye of casting directors, the kind who were more interested in set decoration than acting. Carmen's legs scissored their way into a handful of forgettable films, sometimes dancing, sometimes merely brightening the landscape. It was not high art, but it was work, and on the movie sets Carmen met actors, producers and directors. Few could ignore her, and fewer still were *not* surprised when she talked to them with wit and intelligence. Her career was progressing at a miraculous pace.

At one of the Hollywood parties, Carmen met George Ramentol, a man she would have quickly forgotten except for his humor and charm. A Cuban-Russian, George had a wonderful smile and seemed genuinely more interested in her mind than her body. George was not in the movie business; he was, well... Carmen was not quite sure what he did for a living. But she was immediately impressed with his energy and zest for life.

George was a transplant from Long Island, New York. He had served in the United States Army during World War II, experiencing many battles and campaigns: Ardennes, Central Europe, Naples -Foggia, Rhineland, and Rome-Arno. He loved flying and volunteered for The Parachute School, Airborne Command, and finally got his chance to jump from a plane in the summer of 1942. Seventeen months later he was wounded in battle and received a Purple Heart with one oak-leaf cluster. He had lots of war stories, and he told them well. For the rest of his life he indulged his passion for planes by flying remote control miniatures.

After her first encounter with George, Montez found herself thinking about him. The Hollywood pretty boys she met, the power brokers with their slippery promises—these she forgot quickly. But George, the only one who didn't seem to step right out of *Gentleman's Quarterly*, was definitely... well, *different*. She wished he would call.

He did, and after a whirlwind romance they were married in 1952. She was twenty-two, and he was eight years older. Legally, in the California Marriage Index she became Carmelita Ramentol Montez even though she continued to use her professional name, Carmen Montez. Her official death record refers to her as Carmen Ramentol Montez.

It was not long before Montez discovered George's secret career. He gambled for a living. Occasionally he made some investments in parking lots, but mainly he gambled. For Carmen, it took some getting used to. George would disappear for stretches of time, and Carmen would dip back into the party scene. But then came a turning point.

Late one evening, returning home from a party, Carmen's automobile careened out of control and struck a tree. The experience shook her. With time to heal came time to reflect, to think about her life. It occurred to her that the accident may have been a wake-up call, that perhaps her life had some greater purpose. These thoughts journeyed through uncharted territory for Carmen because she had never seriously thought about such things. The accident drove a wedge between Carmen and George. She found it difficult to continue overlooking his vices, and after fourteen years of marriage they divorced in April of 1966.

Even though they were no longer married, they stayed close friends, and neither remarried. George later told Carmen Rayburn that after the accident and divorce he noticed a *pivot* in her personality. She seemed more introspective, more *luminous*. That was the word that came to him... *luminous*, as if light were originating deep within her. He began gambling less, or at least for shorter periods of time, and this gave him more time to spend with her as a friend. The pressure of marriage was off, and this new Carmen Montez was even more attractive to him than the old one.

Montez told Rayburn that she was sometimes remorseful that she and George had divorced, but she still felt married to him "in spirit"—closer to him than she was even when they were married. While in marriage they had come to live mostly separate lives, in divorce they had become nearly inseparable. She could enjoy his company without feeling responsible for him.

Carmen often told her friend Carmen Rayburn, when they talked years later, that her world indeed had changed with the accident. The desperate need for a good time had been replaced with something different, something warm and peaceful, something she recognized as the "love of God." Though George remained a gambler, Carmen, the party animal, became an ordained minister in the Universal Church of the Master (UCM), an organization that was begun in 1908 by spiritualists on the west coast. Its beliefs were founded on the teachings of Andrew Jackson Davis who claimed to be a medium who had successfully interacted with Emanuel Swedenborg, a sixteenth-century Christian Scientist who struggled to understand the world of spirit through investigation of the physical world. For many years UCM remained a small regional body, but in the 1960s, when Carmen was searching for a spiritual home, the organization had begun to grow nationally, and by 1980 it had three hundred congregations, thirteen hundred ministers (mediums) and over ten thousand members.

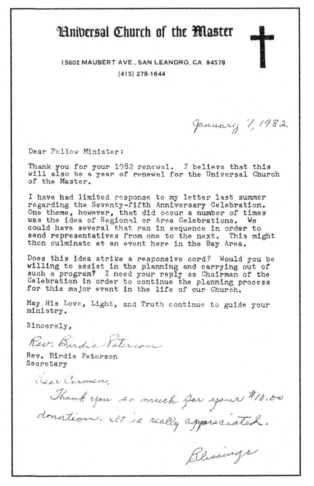

Carmen Montez continued to renew her ordination, at least through 1982. This letter from Rev. Birdie Peterson is dated four months before Carmen's death.

Carmen Montez began a back lot ministry, serving a troubled hodgepodge of humanity in the movie business. She was astounded at the problems that plagued the same crowd she used to party with— actors, producers, directors, agents—and how desperately they sought a personal peace. Many in her "congregation" were astonished at the remarkable change in this woman, but few would discount the gift she seemed to have been given to calm and heal the spirit.

She attracted many followers, "students" who were attracted by her methods and their results. She always discredited ownership of her own gifts, attributing them to a "higher power" and resisting the enticement to become herself the object of worship. To the movie crowd, her confident but self-effacing manner was startling at first. Some didn't believe it was honest, but most were drawn to her sincerity and spirituality in whatever way they recognized it.

One of her students, Christopher Stone, wrote the book *Re-Creating Your Self* in 1997. In the introduction to that work he presents her as "the woman who was to have the most important influence on my life… Carmen was a spiritual teacher, and the most loving human being I have ever met… Wise, compassionate and humble, with a delightfully dry wit, Carmen was highly spiritual but equally down to earth… Carmen maintained that it wasn't as important to believe in an 'afterlife' as it was to make the most of life in the 'here and now.'"

From my conversations with Carmen Rayburn I learned that throughout the ministry of Carmen Montez she maintained a strong desire to make an impact on the world. Montez knew that helping individuals could do this indirectly, but in a moment of great clarity her destiny became suddenly clear. Her life prior to the accident had not been a waste after all; it had been a time of gestation. Her abilities, her professional contacts, her experiences—all these things now existed for a reason, and that reason was to help Carmen Montez illuminate the world with God's message. And what better way than through movies?

She discovered that her unusual clientele was tailor-made to assist the mission that God had assigned her. Of the people to whom she ministered, a select few had become close enough for her to confide in. There was the actor with the penetrating gaze and hawk-like nose, one of the most famous profiles in Hollywood. Called by some the greatest actor in the world, Marlon Brando was also deeply troubled and compassionate about the well-being of his surprisingly small circle of friends. Brando became a close confidante of Carmen Montez.

There was a caramel-skinned Caribbean crooner with a deep and intense spirituality. This charming but often brooding man named Harry Belafonte was possessed of a fierce intuition; Carmen called it a "spiritual connectedness." At times he seemed possessed, so deeply felt were his insights. He would suffer great psychic pain when the spirit of one close to him was wounded by another. He would fret over the prophesied difficulties of his friends and family. He would muse endlessly over plans to help his loved ones avoid any future injury. And he was fiercely dedicated to the advancement of civil rights. Early on, Carmen and Belafonte became business partners.

There also was the passionate Welshman named Tom Jones who sang rhythm and blues like an African American. His swiveling hips and sweat-soaked shirts projected a raw kind of sexual energy that was just beginning to whip American women into a feeding frenzy fanned by his full-throated, emotional sermon-songs. He was a British Elvis.

Finally, there was the enigmatic, impossibly handsome rock 'n' roller with a honey-kissed drawl and an unmistakable spark of genius. Still a young man, Elvis Presley was the greatest paradox: already successful beyond imagination, he now felt alone, oppressed, frustrated, and frightened; he was the sexual fantasy of millions of women around the world, yet he was incapable of a genuinely intimate and trusting relationship with any woman other than his mother… until Carmen Montez.

Few of Carmen's clients could see her as often as they wanted. They had business trips to take, long tours, location shooting schedules, homes in other lands. There was also a fear among some clients that it might be discovered they were seeking *help*. In a few cases, there were jealous wives who might find it difficult to understand frequent liaisons with a woman who looked like Carmen Montez. Many of the meetings, then, were held in secret. At least one "student" never met Carmen in person.

Carmen disliked the telephone for serious conversations. She greatly preferred letters handwritten by the client because, as she explained often, she liked to reread the content and could detect emotional cues from the fluctuating strokes, slants and pressures of their script. Only occasionally, during "spiritual emergencies," as she called them, would she meet face-to-face. There were protests at first from some of her clients, particularly Elvis, who seldom wrote anything but an autograph and maintained a secretarial staff to sign most of the pictures and letters that were sent to fans. Soon, though, the intimacy and practicality of personal correspondence won them all over. Elvis eventually came to think of letter writing as a form of therapy. Writing about his feelings provided an outlet whenever he needed one, which was often. And passing along the secret messages, often by a trusted courier, may have added a captivating element of intrigue.

Carmen's ministry became a complex web of intrigue as her clients increasingly turned to her for help, and she in turn began to court their influence. Her communication with them more frequently relied on letters, notes, and cards, yet the intimacy of the relationships seemed to grow.

Carmen began to carry more heavily the emotional burdens of her clients. Despite her help, Elvis seemed to be spiritually and emotionally declining. She could sense the end coming even as his career was launching toward a second peak. In the end, she suffered secretly with his startling death. Having failed to save him with her best efforts over the years, Montez began to doubt her mission.

Before meeting Carmen Rayburn, Montez had never talked about her clients, never revealed their secrets, never betrayed their confidences to anyone, including her husband. After about a year, however, Montez began to tell Rayburn about her involvement with many of Hollywood's elite. As their friendship grew, the trust between them increased.

"Even psychiatrists need psychiatrists," Montez told her friend one day, "if only to unburden some of the emotional baggage that they've been carrying for their clients." Carmen Montez chose Carmen Rayburn as her emotional outlet.

Rayburn was understandably shocked the first time the name Elvis Presley came up in conversation. While not particularly an Elvis fan, she was certainly aware of him. One day, after seeing an article about Elvis in a popular magazine, she made a disparaging remark to Montez about self-indulgent stars who probably get what they deserve.

"I remember that Carmen suddenly grew very still and quiet," Rayburn told me during an interview. "She was so quiet I thought she might have become ill. Then she looked at me and said, 'I've been carrying around a lot of secrets about Elvis, and it's time to put them out into the universe.'"

Rayburn was alarmed when her friend mentioned exposing the celebrity's personal revelations. She knew Montez as a person of the highest integrity. The confessions of Elvis had been delivered to her with the expectation of confidentiality. Was she contemplating making them public? Montez was an ordained minister, which made the ethical issue seem even more relevant.

"You mean exposing his secrets?" Carmen asked.

Montez nodded.

"Seems like you'd be violating his trust."

"I've thought a lot about that. Elvis has been gone for a year, but we've kept in touch."

In Montez's church, a minister was a "medium" believed capable of communicating with the spirit world. Rayburn took her words to mean that she was still communicating with Elvis.

"It's time," Montez said, "for the world to know what Elvis went through. While he was alive, Elvis could never have survived the public humiliation of the truth being revealed. And today he can't tell his story by himself. But now he's in a different place. I'm sure he agrees that it's time."

Rayburn pledged herself to secrecy as they embarked on a mission to tell Elvis's story. Montez began to reveal things that Elvis had told her. In time, those sessions evolved into a plan to develop a book about the "true" Elvis and the difficulties he had endured. Carmen Rayburn accepted the role of recording secretary. Step one, thcy agreed, was to simply "get it all down and worry about the writing later."

* * *

Over the next nine months the two women met frequently and worked on their secret project. Montez had a detailed recollection of everything Elvis had told her. Some of these talks probed deeper into things Elvis had written down in letters. It was clear that these conversations had played themselves over and over in her mind. As Montez would tell her things, Carmen Rayburn often felt uneasy, like a voyeur.

"Listening to Carmen was almost like eavesdropping on intimate sessions with Elvis," Rayburn told me. "She would become very emotional. Sometimes she cried. This was all a real emotional release for her. I became very aware of how close she and Elvis had become."

During the time that Carmen Montez was confiding in her friend, she became ill, and the sessions stopped. On May 8, 1982, at the age of fifty-two, Montez died of cancer and was buried at Forest Lawn Memorial Park in Hollywood Hills.

Rayburn thought that she had enough material for a book that would "set the record straight" but knew that without Carmen's first-hand testimony the incredible story would lack credibility. After all, Carmen Rayburn was only the secretary. With deep regret, she shelved the idea of the book, expecting that the story would never be made public.

Montez had left no heirs. Despondent, George declined to act as executor of her will, as she had requested. The state of California collected Montez's belongings and put them up for auction in Los Angeles.

Carmen Rayburn didn't want to drive that far alone, so her nephew, Ralph, agreed to drive her. As she looked over the remnants of her friend's estate, it didn't seem like very much: some furniture, boxes of personal effects, and several unopened suitcases. Those pale objects were a poor representation of a life that had been full and rich.

One object stood out—a three-section mirror she had given to Montez on a special occasion. When the auctioneer from Norm Sulflow & Sons began barking out a base bid for the mirror, she knew she had to get that mirror back. It had witnessed so many wonderful things in Carmen's home and had some fascinating stories to tell.

Strangely, bidding drove the price of the mirror up to over $185. Twice she almost dropped out, but something pushed her on. Finally, for the sum of $190, the mirror was hers.

She waited listlessly while the other small pieces were quickly sold. In the spirit of bidding, she bought more than she intended: nine small tables, two of George's remote-control airplanes, two cartons of clothes, a blender, and a ring. At last she decided to leave, and as she was getting up to collect those objects and figure out how to get them into her vehicle, the auctioneer frantically picked up the pace. The audience had grown small and unresponsive, and he was trying to inject some excitement for the next inconspicuous piece. He hoisted a well-traveled suitcase onto the auction block.

"All right," he said. "Next, we have this sturdy suitcase, and two more like it, all full of experience, of proven construction, *plus* whatever's in it." He lifted one of the suitcases again, feigning great weight. "Who knows? Maybe it's filled with hundred-dollar bills, maybe old *National Geographics*. Who'll give me one hundred dollars for all three suitcases?" He began a mesmerizing chant.

Guarding her horde of merchandise near the doorway, Carmen Rayburn turned back and recognized the suitcase. Carmen Montez had brought it with her every time she had visited overnight. The crowd was wholly disinterested.

"Seventy-five dollars, just seventy-five for the suitcases and everything they contain. Who'll give me seventy-five dollars?"

She pictured the suitcase years ago on the bed in her guest room, in the trunk of Carmen's car, and being carried in the hand of her dear friend who never traveled without it. All at once, she knew what the suitcase contained—memories of a friendship, dreams of adventure, and at least some of the love that exuded from a woman she would remember as the most loving person she had ever known.

The auctioneer was growing despondent. "All right, do I have *any* bids for the damn things? No minimum. Who'll make a bid?"

"Sixty dollars!" Carmen Rayburn heard her own voice call out the figure, then immediately wondered why she'd bid so much. Somehow, she had managed to pay a substantial amount for those small pieces of Carmen's and George's lives. Exhausted by the event, she gave the payment to her nephew to complete the transaction.

The receipt for Carmen Rayburn's purchase of the suitcase (written as "suitcases clothes"). Address has been blurred for privacy reasons.

At home after the long drive, she remembered sighing as she entered the house. The day had been unusually draining. A peculiar, undetected tension was now beginning to knot the muscles in her neck and back. She lugged her new possessions into the house and set them down. Having these scraps of Carmen's life felt comforting, almost like having Carmen pay a last visit.

And then suddenly she cried, and it mystified her. She had not cried at Carmen's funeral or the reception. She had not cried in the following months, even in the two years since. Had it really been that long? She had felt a profound loss, a desperate sadness, a hot crampy lump in her throat at times, but she had not wept.

In tight, staccato gasps she tried to stop, but the sobbing was too deep, too intense. She couldn't remember how long she had wept, but she told me it seemed like hours.

At last she carried the heavy suitcases into the bedroom, tossing them under the bed where they lay unopened and forgotten.

Six months later she came upon them while cleaning and decided to open the one she recognized. As she raised the lid, the yawning case gasped with a faint breath of mustiness. There was no gold inside. No stacks of hundred-dollar bills. Only a heaped mass of letters and envelopes.

She picked up a letter. "Dear Carmen," it began. The closing simply read, "Love, Harry."

She rummaged and picked another one. "Carmen," was scrawled at the top. Flipping over the letter she saw the closing words, "Love, Tom."

She lifted another one addressed to "Carmelita" and ending with "Marlon."

And then she chose a pastel-blue letter and brought it closer. "Dear Sister," it began. The letter closed, "Elvis."

As she read the letters, a slowly growing wave of astonishment overtook her as she discovered in these handwritten letters and notes the same story that Carmen had revealed to her years earlier. Here was a detailed accounting, in the words of Elvis and others, of the meetings, events, emotions, and thoughts of the King of Rock 'n' Roll.

With new resolve, Carmen Rayburn decided to complete the project she and her friend had begun together, but this time with the words of Elvis himself. Montez most likely had saved this collection of letters as support for her future book. Rayburn did not know why Carmen Montez had never mentioned that she still had these letters or suggested publishing them, but it didn't seem to matter, for here they were.

All she had to do was put them into a book.

* * *

George, Montez's ex-husband, simply floated for a time. His wife had been his compass, and now he felt directionless. He began gambling more heavily, dabbled in land investments, and bought another parking lot. But his life was unbearably hollow. At last he decided to do something about it. He drove to visit an old friend in the high desert of California with a bizarre offer in mind.

Carmen Rayburn was astounded at his proposal of marriage. How could she marry the ex-husband of her best friend? George had been a good companion over the years, but not a lover, and picturing him as a husband... well, it was impossible. She loved her independence and was not prepared to squander it. Besides, marrying George would have seemed like a betrayal of her special relationship with Carmen.

George took the rejection with a stoic face and feigned understanding, but now he seemed even more lost. He bought a motorcycle and threw himself into his gambling and his parking lots. He made new friends, some of them of questionable integrity.

On Tuesday morning, November 10, 1983, George left home, climbed on his motorcycle and rocketed off to check on a particularly lucrative parking lot in Los Angeles. A car suddenly shot out of an alley and sideswiped the motorcycle. Hit and run. George was dead on arrival at the hospital. Rumors swirled that his parking lots were a money-laundering scheme tied to the mob and that the "accident" was in fact a "hit."

Author, Author

Nearly a hundred Elvis letters littered Carmen Rayburn's desk, and over two hundred more handwritten letters still lay mostly unread in the suitcase. Taken separately, the countless disjointed stories and confessions in Elvis's letters were a jumble of unraveled threads and disconnected references. Yes, there were sensational revelations scattered throughout the unsequenced collection, but connecting all the dots to comprehend the multiple and often interrelated storylines would be a difficult slog. If everything could be put into the context of Elvis's life, the value of this information could skyrocket.

From a cursory survey of the correspondence by Tom Jones, Harry Belafonte and Marlon Brando, Rayburn knew that these letters also provided meaningful insights into the Elvis material and frequently corroborated claims made by Elvis, some of which described criminal activity.

On her first read-through of the letters, she was struck by the deep friendships between Elvis, Tom and Marlon. That these celebrities had met each other was widely known, but that they frequently communicated, shared secrets and advice, even helped each other out of perilous jams was virtually unknown by the public. In fact, ugly comments about Elvis had been attributed in the tabloids to Marlon, so the fact that Marlon and Elvis had once been best friends was a revelation, impressing Rayburn with how little of the lives of celebrities was visible outside of their inner circles.

Rayburn's thought of publishing the Elvis letters with a simple introduction quickly gave way to the concept of adding value by properly organizing them and adding thoughtful commentary. This would require a writer, of course. At a dinner party a few months after discovering the letters she met a charming and bestselling author/screenwriter who seemed to have just the right credentials to write the Presley book.

In 1974, Robert Slatzer reviews a hardback copy of his book, *The Life and Curious Death of Marilyn Monroe.*

Robert Slatzer had compiled a colorful career in the entertainment business that began inauspiciously as a literary critic for the *Columbus Dispatch* in Ohio before relocating to Hollywood in 1946 to write about the film industry. He went on to direct two low-budget B movies—*The Hellcats* in 1968 and *Bigfoot* in 1970. Neither received any Oscar nominations but earned him an unfortunate reputation as a Hollywood hack. As an author, he had greater success with two biographies—*Duke: The Life and Times of John Wayne*, and *Bing Crosby: The Hollow Man.*

In 1974, he gained the media spotlight with his book *The Life and Curious Death of Marilyn Monroe,* in which he notoriously claimed to have secretly married actress Marilyn Monroe in Mexico but agreed to have their 1952 marriage dissolved three days later under pressure from Darryl F. Zanuck, head of 20th Century Fox Studios. According to Slatzer, he and Marilyn returned to Mexico and paid fifty dollars to the attorney who had married them, and who then destroyed the marital paperwork at the courthouse. Slatzer's marriage claim was roundly denied by Monroe's biographers and many others, but the marriage was never fully disproved, which kept the mystery alive.

The cover of Robert Slatzer's international bestselling book.

The Life and Curious Death of Marilyn Monroe became a highly controversial bestseller. In it, Slatzer also claimed that Marilyn was murdered because of an alleged affair with John F. Kennedy. While many readers and critics called the theory rubbish, many fanatical Monroe fans supported his assertions.

In Hollywood, of course, truth never gets in the way of a good story. In 1991, the ABC network broadcast a Movie of the Week called *Marilyn and Me* based on the Slatzer/Monroe marriage. Ironically, the role of Robert "Bobby" Slatzer was played by actor Jesse Dabson, who had played the role of Elvis's guitarist Scotty Moore in the 1990 TV series *Elvis—Good Rockin' Tonight*.

Carmen Rayburn was captivated by Slatzer's experience writing celebrity biographies, his bestseller credentials, and his apparent contacts in the movie business. But even more appealing was Slatzer's comfortable relationship with controversy. She knew that the highly contentious material contained in the letters would be explosive when revealed to the public, so Rayburn approached Slatzer, who eagerly read the letters under a non-disclosure agreement.

Smitten by the prospects of writing another bestseller, Slatzer was eager to move things along. He introduced Rayburn to a well-regarded agent, Andrew Ettinger of Los Angeles Literary Associates, to represent the property to publishers. A few months later, in March of 1985, Rayburn signed an agreement in which Ettinger, as exclusive agent, would receive 10 percent of all proceeds and Slatzer would pen the book and share with Rayburn "as equal partners (50%-50%) in any and all income or proceeds derived from all sales, rights, licensing or any other use of The Letters."

The project, it seemed, was about to launch.

Slatzer had personal issues that undermined his work on the book. After nearly a year, little progress had been made because of "financial difficulties," as he benignly put it. He had finally determined that it would take much too long for relief to come from a royalty windfall.

Slatzer contacted Bill Mack, an active collector of celebrity memorabilia whom he had met regarding some Marilyn Monroe collectibles. In 1986 Mack agreed to pay Slatzer to work on the Presley book in exchange for 50 percent of Slatzer's interest in the project and 100 percent of Slatzer's interest in any sale of the original letters. This made Mack a 25 percent stakeholder in the letters and a 50 percent owner of any proceeds from selling the physical letters.

Excited by the potential of the project, Mack negotiated a buy-out of agent Andrew Ettinger's contract for a combination of cash plus valuable Bill Mack artworks. Mack became the exclusive literary agent for "The Letters" and gained an additional 10 percent interest for those responsibilities.

By 1990, despite infusions of cash from Bill Mack and constant prodding from Rayburn, Robert Slatzer still had made little progress on the work. That's when Bill made his late-night phone call to me. When I was finally read into the project, I was both excited and disappointed—excited by the astonishing facts and the celebrity of the letter writers, but disappointed that Robert Slatzer was contractually guaranteed author credit for the book along with Carmen Rayburn.

"Bob has proven that he can't do his job," Bill told me. "I need you to work with him and find a way to get this project going. Maybe you can ghostwrite it."

* * *

Knowing I'd be laboring in anonymity, but transfixed by the outpouring of celebrity secrets, I signed on to coax a manuscript out of a seemingly incapable author. Slatzer had agreed that an early step in preparing the manuscript was to study the details of the letters and verify the information, a tedious and time-consuming task. He had not begun this work. He had also agreed that the content of the letters should be analyzed and organized into a chapter outline for the book. This job also had not begun. Neither had he done any original research to plug informational gaps or explain factual inconsistencies. Nor had he made any attempt to date and sequence the letters so the many interweaving storylines could be better understood. He had not done any interviews with Carmen Rayburn, who had useful information about Montez and her relationships with the letter writers. And finally, he had not cross-checked the letters by each author against letters by the other authors to discover common themes, events, perspectives, and much-needed corroboration.

Obviously, these tasks would now fall onto me. If I could complete this work, I hoped that "Bobby" could at least offer his version of a chapter outline.

After a few months of correspondence with Slatzer, I knew that our collaboration was likely to go nowhere. He was often late in responding to my questions or suggestions and sometimes didn't reply at all. I was concerned by comments Carmen Rayburn made about Bob's "heavy drinking." I finally suggested to Bill that we fly Bob in for a week to work with me face-to-face. Maybe I could steer him into a work routine. At least I might be able to figure out why he was behaving so erratically.

In our first meeting, shortly after arriving in Minneapolis, I made a joking comment about alcohol on Bob's breath. "Fear of flying," he told me. "A drink or two calms me down." He was cordial, alert, and cooperative. I liked him. He had no disagreement with my plan to do the grunt work and provide him content with which to organize an outline. He offered to make a list of factual issues that, he said, "need to be looked into because they're kind of mysterious or suspicious. I've been meaning to do that but haven't gotten around to it. That's something you could do for me."

The next morning, I arrived at his hotel, but he failed to come down for breakfast. We had planned to work together that day. A heavy night of drinking had left him incapacitated. After a few hours, he was awake. With bloodshot eyes, he informed me that he was not used to collaborating so closely, but promised that if we came up with goals for him each day, he would do his job.

It was very sad to witness Bob's daily dissembling and excuse-making. In the end, after a week of futility, Bob flew home. I never received the list of facts he needed me to check out, or any other work he promised to do.

When it was all over, I met with Bill. "The book is never going to happen as long as you're relying on Bob to do any part of it," I told him. "I thought I could manage him, but he's beyond my ability to wrangle."

"I pretty much knew that," Bill said. "Now we know for sure. Unfortunately, his contract is ironclad, so we can't just fire him. Except for the author credit, I think the book is yours to do right now. Carmen will be fine with that—she likes you. We just won't be able to rely on Bob for anything. He'll just fade into the background."

Somehow, I had managed to assume even more work for no credit. And the complications were just beginning.

Family Matters

Seventeen centuries before Elvis was born, during a period of civil war between different Roman factions, a Roman general and would-be emperor named Constantine led an army toward Rome to battle the forces of Maxentius. Before the conflict began, Constantine had a vision of the sign of the cross emblazoned in the sky with the words *in hoc signo vinces* (in this sign you will win). Recognizing the significance of this message, he ordered the Christian cross to be inscribed on the armor of all his soldiers. Although his army was outnumbered, he vanquished the enemy, victoriously entered Rome, and became emperor.

Crediting the power of Christianity, Constantine the Great issued the Edict of Milan, which legalized Christianity and permitted religious freedom throughout the empire. He became a patron of the church, and over time Christianity became the official religion of the empire. It seems that Constantine found it difficult to stay true to Christian principles, however. In 324 AD, Constantine had his son executed on suspicion of adultery with Constantine's second wife, Fausta. A short time later, Fausta was murdered by slow-cooking in an overheated bath chamber.

Without miraculous prophetic vision, Constantine could not have known that exactly fifty generations later a descendant would arise that, like him, would become the king of a conquered realm, would embrace Christianity, and whose faith would often waver because of overpowering passions and bouts of penitence.

It is unlikely that Elvis Presley had ever heard of Constantine the Great, or had known that the emperor, referred to as Saint Constantine and called Equal-to-the-Apostles by the Orthodox Church, was his forty-eighth great grandfather. This was not known until a landmark genealogical work by Lorina Bolig, *Ancestors of Elvis Aaron Presley: 50 Generations*, was first published in 1994. When I first encountered this eight-hundred-page work, I was awestruck by the effort invested in researching and organizing the thousands of details.

The reason I sought out Bolig's book was to help solve a genealogical mystery that had perplexed me immediately after reading the Presley letters. Of the nearly one hundred documents, one stood out because of a startling claim written by Elvis about his parentage: "Vernon is not my real father."

Coming from Elvis Presley, those words carried impact. To the world, Vernon Presley was not only the father of the King but one of Elvis's closest confidantes. After the death in 1958 of Gladys Love Presley, Elvis's mother, Vernon became perhaps the most important figure in Elvis's life. "Daddy," as Elvis usually called him around friends, often advised Elvis on business affairs. The popular version of Vernon's colorful history made him famous in his own right.

On January 28, 1968, Elvis was awaiting the birth of his child but was profoundly troubled by his deteriorating relationship with Priscilla. He sent a long, rambling note to Carmen Montez in which he vented his feelings and then, two days later, realized the letter might not make much sense. Secretly, he placed a telephone call to explain.

Years later, Montez told her friend Carmen Rayburn, "When I received the letter I was terribly confused and concerned for Elvis. He was in a terrible state of mind. Even now I'm not sure he was thinking clearly. Elvis told me that Vernon was really his uncle."

"I'm not sure I understand how that's possible," Rayburn had replied.

"Well, he tried to explain it to me. He seemed very convinced about what he wrote—that Vernon was his father's twin brother."

The 1930s in the South was a long time ago. Family secrets were locked up tightly then, not openly discussed on Oprah.

Elvis explained to his "Sister" that his biological father was named Virgil and worked as a conductor on a railroad that ran between Memphis and Nashville. I have checked numerous Presley family trees, but none lists a "Virgil Presley" born the same year as "Vernon." The only official brother of Vernon is Vester, who is three years younger. But "official" does not always mean "complete" or "accurate." Official records—if kept at all—were often filled out sloppily or lost altogether. Memories faded.

I traveled to Mississippi looking for records of any kind that might shed light on this mystery. I visited schools, churches, cemeteries, even newspaper offices and archives. If Virgil had ever existed, no record of him has survived.

Elvis's paternal family tree—the part we are concerned about—begins in 1886 with the birth of a boy in Itawamba County, Mississippi, whose name was recorded as Jessie D. Mcclowell Presley, more often called "J.D." This grandfather of Elvis was the illegitimate son of Rosella Presley and an unknown male partner. J.D. had at least three brothers: Calhoun, Noah and Joseph. There were probably others, but history has lost their names as well. Even the US Census misses some people.

Official records are further sullied by the fact that J.D.'s name was scribbled carelessly in the early records. According to genealogist Julian Riley in *The Roots of Elvis Presley*, "Rosetta could not read or write. There was no Mcclowell in Itawamba County, Mississippi." But there was a Jessie Dee McDowell Presley. Riley proposes that "writing McDowell with a small 'd' could make it appear as a 'cl.' This error would have been repeated over and over for all his life."

From a young age, J.D. was a scoundrel. He lived fast and drank hard. For J.D., nights were for prowling and carousing, usually with a lively young woman. Too often, though, days were spent nursing a hangover in the town jail.

When he was eleven, he left school and started taking odd jobs to make a quick buck. By the time he turned seventeen, he had enough street smarts to know a good thing when he saw it, and he saw it in Minnie Mae Hood of Fulton, Mississippi, whose family had lots of money. When they married, Minnie Mae was eight years older than the teenage J.D. Interestingly, their marriage license seems to have vanished along with a son.

J.D. gained a dowry but soon spent it. With his striking good looks and carefree manner, he was an enigma to the people of Fulton. Even when family income was meager, and J.D. was drifting from job to job, he found a way to dress like a fashion shop mannequin. He was never caught making or running moonshine, but many believed it was illegal booze that paid for his wardrobe.

J.D. and Minnie Mae had at least six children including daughters Nasval ("Nashville"), Delta Mae, and Gladys Earline (who would come to be called "Little Gladys" to distinguish her from Gladys Love, Elvis's mother), and Lorene ("Dixie"). According to the record there were two sons. Vernon was born in 1916 and Vester in 1919. Elvis believed that there was a third son, Virgil, who was Vernon's twin brother.

After thirty years of marriage and at least six children, J.D. surprised his wife one day. He walked out and filed for divorce, claiming that she had deserted him. Incensed, Minnie Mae wrote to J.D.'s lawyer explaining that J.D., in fact, had deserted *her*. But this was the forties, and the judge granted J.D. the divorce.

J.D. quickly married another woman, Vera Leftwich (some histories give her last name as Pruitt), and settled in Louisville, Kentucky. Perhaps to cover his trail, or maybe simply to revert to an older spelling of the family name, J.D. changed "Presley" to "Pressley," confusing some public records. On the marriage application, J.D. lists his father's name as John Presley and his mother's as Rosie Wesson, both lies. J.D.'s father was John Wallace, and his mother was Rosie (Rosella) Presley. He gave his parents' first names accurately but swapped their last names, probably so his new wife wouldn't know he was the illegitimate son of John Wallace. Naturally, this has led to numerous genealogical errors.

Always looking for a fast buck, J.D. tried to ride his grandson's coattails after Elvis made it big. Reverting to the "Presley" name for his new career, J.D. cut two songs—"The Billie Goat Song" and "Swinging in the Orchard"—which were released by Legacy records. They were never played on the radio.

Julian Riley has found many photographs of the Presley family and Minnie Mae Hood's family of this period, but as he writes in *The Roots of Elvis Presley*, "we have not found one picture of Jessie Dee or Vernon at any of these gatherings. We have not found any picture of Minnie Mae and Jessie Dee together." J.D.'s brother Noah and his wife Minnie Mae are pictured at these gatherings, but not J.D. or Elvis's father, Vernon. The photographic evidence seems to have been wiped clean. Or maybe J.D. just didn't like family gatherings.

J.D.'s brother, Noah, married Susan Griffith in 1910 and lovingly took in her three existing sons, raising them as his own. Whitford and Eackford simply took the Presley name as their own, and Sumpter kept the last name of Griffith. The descendants of these sons consider Noah to be their grandfather. One of Noah's grandsons is listed on official records as Sales Presley, though "Sales" was a nickname. His given name was Persell.

Creating fraudulent records that would muddle history seemed to run in the Presley family. When J.D.'s brother, Noah, was going to be married for the second time, he falsely declared his father's name to be Tom Presley and his mother's name as Mrs. Tom Presley. Noah's mother's name was Rosella Presley, but we know she was never married, so who was Tom Presley?

He is a work of fiction. Noah knew a man named Tom Hussey who helped keep him out of the draft. It appears that Noah invented a father who did not exist from the names of a man (*Tom* Hussey) and a woman (Rosella *Presley*) who did.

Not all problems with official records were caused by human intervention. Sometimes, the records were simply incomplete. Noah's youngest brother, Joseph Warren Presley, disappeared from the 1910 Census and then miraculously reappeared again in the next one.

Besides the loss of individual identities to history, such as J.D.'s father, there were also family secrets in the Presley clan. In his book *The Boy Who Would Be King*, Earl Greenwood—Elvis's second cousin and press agent—explained how one of J.D.'s daughters was all but erased from the family tree. Dixie Presley apparently had contracted syphilis and was left untreated. She survived but grew mentally unstable and eventually was put into an institution. Family humiliation was immense.

According to Greenwood, "Dixie simply ceased to exist to her family. Period. J.D., Minnie, Vernon, and Vester never spoke about Dixie after she left, nor did they include her in any family remembrance. Vernon and Vester never acknowledged they had a sister named Dixie and, in fact, preferred to deny it rather than reopen the wound."

Greenwood claims that Dixie was secretly moved to a mental ward in nearby Jackson; neighbors were told she was visiting friends.

Was Vernon's twin brother "Virgil" more successfully erased from the family tree than Dixie? Or was he a figment of Elvis's imagination?

As we've seen, records are often an imperfect window on the past. If there are no records, or the records are lost or inaccurate, the window slams shut. Add to this the confusion of overlapping family branches and you have a thick fog shrouding the truth.

The family branches in Elvis's tree do get quite entangled. Take Vester Presley, for example. Vester, son of J.D. Presley and brother of Vernon and Dixie, married Clettes Smith in 1935. Clettes is the younger sister of Gladys Love Presley, Elvis's mother. This means that Vester is Elvis's double uncle.

But did Vester have two brothers who were twins, Vernon and Virgil? Twins do run in the Presley family tree. J.D.'s brother, Noah, fathered fraternal twin sons, Sales and Gordon Presley. Sales and his wife, Annie, became the grandparents of twins. Gladys Love Presley and her mate—Vernon or Virgil—also gave birth to twin sons, Jesse Garon and Elvis Aron Presley.

The story of Elvis's birth takes on a new dimension when considered in the light of his belief that Vernon's twin brother was his biological father.

There are many conflicting accounts of Elvis's birth, which is not surprising considering the times and fading memories. In his scathing and one-sided biography, *Elvis*, Albert Goldman made at least one contribution to clearing things up. He discovered that Sara Potter, the daughter of the physician who delivered Elvis, had found detailed notes written by her father.

Dr. Bill Hunt practiced in a small office above Riley's Jewelry Store in downtown Tupelo, Mississippi. On the cold and blustery night of January 7, 1935, Dr. Hunt was summoned to the home of a young couple he did not know to supervise a midwife, Mrs. Edna Robinson. Gladys Presley had been enduring a long and hard pregnancy and was losing a lot of blood. Even though they had no money to pay him, the Presleys finally called for the doctor. The rest we know from Dr. Hunt's notes.

Since he had begun practice in 1913, Hunt had kept a Physician's Record Book for every year containing the circumstances of each "labor case" he attended. His Record Book for 1935 straightens out the record. Gladys did not give birth at noon on January 8, 1935, as reported by many sources, but at 4:35 a.m. on that dark winter morning. Her son was stillborn. Thirty-five minutes later, Dr. Hunt witnessed the delivery of the dead son's twin brother, who survived. The family never paid for Hunt's services; welfare covered the fifteen-dollar bill.

The tragedy deeply affected Gladys, who distorted the true events of that evening in her recollections. The stillborn son became Elvis's *identical* twin, which cannot be proven. And Gladys managed to instill in Elvis the belief that he had been born first.

In his retelling of the story to Carmen Montez, Elvis explained with a pang of guilt that his brother had been born not only second, but *alive.* He had died because the doctor had been so busy trying to save the frail firstborn, Elvis. This was clearly untrue according to the 1935 Physician's Record Book discovered by Sara Potter in 1980. Elvis, nevertheless, lived his life with the conviction that he was somehow responsible for his twin brother's death.

Typical of the times, the official records are filled with errors and contradictions. Beginning with the marriage of twenty-one-year-old Gladys Love Smith to J.D. Presley's seventeen-year-old son, the records lie. Perhaps embarrassed by the disparity in their ages, Gladys listed her age as nineteen; "Vernon" Presley added five years, becoming twenty-two.

The birth certificate for "Elvis Aron Presley."

The birth certificate for Elvis and his dead brother, Jesse, was not filled out by Dr. Hunt for two days. On January 10, 1935, Hunt misspelled Jesse Garon Presley's middle name, making it "Garion." In the Physician's Record Book, he spelled Elvis's name the way it was pronounced in Mississippi: "Evis," without the "l." While Hunt correctly listed the father's age as eighteen, Hunt erred again by reporting Gladys as twenty-one rather than twenty-two years old. In his Record Book, Hunt called the father a "white," eighteen-year-old "laborer." He listed the father's name as "V. Presley," as if he was not sure of the actual first name (all of J.D.'s sons had names beginning with "V").

Dr. Hunt's Physician's Record Book.

To further confuse the record, V. Presley filled out a *second* birth certificate (they must have been easy to obtain in those days). It is not known how much later this certificate was completed. Remarkably, Elvis's father also messed up the record. Mr. Presley lied about his age for the birth certificate, listing it as twenty instead of eighteen, and made Gladys one year younger for good measure. He also spelled Elvis's middle name "Aron," conflicting with Hunt's correct spelling, "Aaron," in the Physician's Record.

Elvis's middle name was in honor of Aaron Kennedy, a friend of the Presley family who was staying with Elvis's grandfather, J.D. Presley. Kennedy was a Sunday school superintendent whom everyone admired greatly. Elvis officially changed the spelling of his misspelled middle name in later years to "Aaron."

The official records of marriage and births in this family are highly suspect. The confusion often appears deliberate but is sometimes due to ineptitude. While Jesse Garon Presley was buried in an unmarked grave in Priceville Cemetery on Feemster Lake Road northeast of Tupelo, the plaque bearing his name in the Graceland Meditation Gardens is misspelled. "Jesse" has become "Jessie"; if not the identical twin of Elvis, he at least has become the identical namesake of his grandfather.

The twins theme recurs throughout Elvis's life, even in ways that have no bearing on the Virgil mystery. Priscilla Presley, for example, has two twin half-brothers, Tim and Tom. Gladys Love Presley's great-grandmother bore twins, Jerome and Martha Tacket. James Kingsley, staff reporter for the *Memphis Commercial Appeal* and the reporter closest to Elvis, had a twin brother named John.

Even in Elvis's professional life, a visitation of twins would continue to be upon him. On April 3, 1956, Elvis appeared on the Milton Berle Show. Uncle Miltie played Elvis's twin brother in a comedy sketch (and inadvertently called Elvis by the name "Elvin"). Because of strict child labor laws, three sets of twins were hired to play Rick and Marla's baby in the Elvis movie *G.I. Blues*. In the 1967 film *Double Trouble*, twins—played by real-life identical twins Marilyn and Melody Keymer—appear in a London nightclub. *Kissin' Cousins*, Elvis's 1964 movie for MGM, required Elvis to play the dual role of cousins who are physically identical—except for their hair. In a blonde wig, Elvis plays hillbilly Jodie Tatum; as clean-cut air force officer Josh Morgan, Elvis looks like his usual self.

I have often wondered what emotions in Elvis may have been stirred up by these odd twin-based acting roles; after all, he was a young man who believed his father and uncle were twins

51

who swapped real-life roles and believed himself at least partly responsible for the death of his own twin brother.

The beat goes on. Was Elvis merely obsessed with the idea of twins, or has history lost the record of a matched set named Vernon and Virgil? Which of J.D. Presley's sons fathered Elvis? Who looked on as Jesse and Elvis were born in a small house on North Saltillo Road? Which Presley brother was the "V. Presley" named in Dr. Hunt's birth certificate? Elvis believed his father was Virgil, Vernon's twin brother. Real or imagined—by Elvis or Gladys—Virgil was a flesh and blood resident of Elvis's memory. In all his conversations and letters to Carmen Montez, he consistently referred to Vernon as "my uncle" or "Uncle Vernon." In front of everyone else, however, Vernon was "Daddy."

According to Elvis, Virgil was a railroad conductor and part-time evangelist. Elvis claimed to remember attending many tent meetings and church sessions with his father, Virgil, and Gladys. He loved to sing at those meetings. But Elvis claimed that when he was still young, Virgil fell off a moving train and was killed. Vernon moved in to help out. He was like a father to Elvis, who called him "Dad" because he liked it. But Vernon lacked the energy and moral certitude of his twin brother and quickly wound up in jail. Before Elvis was four years old, his real father had died and his "new" father had been taken away.

Following the slippery tradition of fraud, begun with falsified ages on official documents, Vernon and two friends concocted a truly stupid scheme. Vernon had sold a hog to Orville Bean, his landlord and employer. Bean was a local dairy farmer and broker of cattle and hogs. He was also Vernon's brother-in-law. According to Elvis, Vernon had sold Bean a hog that he considered to be worth more than the meager amount Bean had paid for it. Along with a local friend named Lether Gable, Vernon and his twenty-three-year-old brother-in-law Travis Smith altered the sum of Bean's check from four dollars to forty. Bean immediately detected the fraud and lodged an accusation. The evidence was brought to a grand jury.

The *Tupelo Journal* for November 17, 1937 ran a short news story stating that the three men were "indicted for forgery and placed under bonds of five hundred dollars." The story misspelled Vernon's last name, making it "Pressley," and spelled Lether "Luther."

The three young men originally pleaded not guilty, and their families unsuccessfully tried to get Orville Bean to drop the charges. Of the three men, only Vernon remained in custody until trial. Lether Gable was bailed out by his family. Surprisingly, the bail for Travis Smith was put up by Vernon's father Jessie and another man, J.G. Brown. For reasons we can only guess, J.D. Presley left his son in jail.

Faced with a trial and the prospects for a harsh sentence, the three changed their pleas to guilty. According to a notice under docket number 9756, Vernon and his two accomplices were each sentenced to "serve a term of three (3) years in the State penitentiary, and they are hereby remanded to the custody of the sheriff for safekeeping in the county jail until called for by the proper officer or agent for transportation and delivery to said institution."

The state institution was a concentration camp in Mississippi known as Parchman Farm. Located in the steamy delta, Parchman was a twenty-thousand-acre prison farm where two thousand convicts toiled in chain gangs overseen by harsh, horse riding bosses toting shotguns. Half the plantation was planted in cotton, the other half in corn, sugar cane and other foods necessary for the feeding of the prisoners. Cotton was the money crop, though, and the profits from it were deposited into the pockets of clever businessmen in Jackson who had concocted a plan to replace slave labor with prisoners. The penalty for any convict failing to deliver two hundred pounds of cotton per day was severe; a long leather belt dubbed "Black Annie" would be used to flog a laggard's back. Vernon became a motivated worker after experiencing the lashes first-hand. According to some sources, both Vernon and Travis were whipped for offenses, and both carried the scars of "Black Annie" for the rest of their lives. In the book *Elvis: His Life from A to Z*, authors Fred Worth and Steve Tamerius claim that the humiliation of the scars on Vernon's back prevented him from ever going shirtless at Graceland.

Back in Tupelo, Gladys and Elvis were thrown out of their two-room shack by Orville Bean when Vernon pleaded guilty. Gladys moved in for a time with Ben and Agnes Greenwood, relatives on the Presley side. At first Gladys took in ironing and did other jobs to pay bills. Like her sister, Gladys also took in a fair share of booze. When drinking, which was often, her favorite trick was to eat large pieces of onion to mask the odor of alcohol. Ben's nephew, Earl, wrote that "Gladys was merely in keeping with the rest of the Smiths, all considered alcoholics."

Vernon eventually pleaded family hardship, and the governor commuted his three-year sentence. Many reports claim that Vernon only served seven to nine months of his sentence, but the official date of his discharge was January 4, 1941, a few months shy of a full three years. When he returned home in freshly laundered clothes with two dollars of state-supplied cash in his pocket, he found Gladys in a sorry state. She was bloated, and her skin was splotchy. The dark circles that he saw beneath her eyes would never go away. And her lustrous, black hair was peppered with gray.

To Elvis, "Daddy" was home. But as Elvis explained to Carmen Montez in 1967, this man was not his real father even if he was the next best thing. Vernon's prison record clearly embarrassed Elvis, but they never talked about it at home. After Elvis became a star, efforts were made to conceal it. Some members of the "Memphis Mafia," Elvis's inner circle, have said that Elvis was unhappy during the entire filming of *Jailhouse Rock* and avoided the movie afterward. Perhaps the image of a Presley in prison was too painful for him. When the movie was released, the musty records of Vernon's incarceration had not yet been accidentally discovered and made public. Until they surfaced, it has been said that Colonel Parker's knowledge of the prison term gave him a powerful hold over both Elvis and "Uncle" Vernon.

I wonder what must have been going through Elvis's mind during the shooting of the movie *Speedway* when he sang the song entitled "He's Your Uncle, Not Your Dad."

The Smith side of Elvis's family tree has been more carefully researched than the Presley side. Research conducted by Elaine Dundy for her book *Elvis and Gladys* turned up verification for one of the claims that Elvis consistently made to Carmen Montez.

Over the years, many people speculated that Elvis's dark good looks suggested Indian ancestry. Elvis believed himself to be part Native American. In talking to Montez, he would often call himself "this wild Indian," or refer to his intuition as "my Indian sixth sense" or by saying "an Indian knows these things." The prospect that he had Indian blood was important to him. Some of his most flamboyant costumes during the Las Vegas years used Indian motifs. Once, in a telephone call following up on remarks in a letter, Carmen probed Elvis's desire to tattoo his body with something that no one would understand or decipher—perhaps his army serial number, or his name in Indian signs and symbols. Elvis told Carmen Montez that his name in "Indian" meant "in God complete." He told others that it meant "one with God."

Montez understood the importance to Elvis of his Indian blood and the connection between his ancestry and his spirituality. Carmen Rayburn remembers Montez explaining it this way: "To Elvis, Indian blood transfused him with spirituality, which he desperately sought. Through his unstable early years, living as 'white trash' in East Tupelo with a felon for a 'father,' Elvis seized on the idea of being an outcast, just as Indians had become outcasts in their own land." The idea would affect many of his choices in life.

It turns out that Elvis was right about his Indian roots. Elaine Dundy's genealogical research discovered Native American ancestors on the maternal side of the family tree. A woman named Morning Dove, a full-blooded Cherokee, was Elvis's great-great-great-grandmother. Born around 1800, Morning Dove married Bill Mansell in 1818. Mansell was a Tennessee farmer who had previously fought under General Andrew Jackson in the wars against the native Indians. Morning Dove apparently won his heart. A few years after they were wed, Mansell moved his family to Alabama where he staked a claim to some fertile land and built a home. Morning Dove died in 1835 after giving birth to her third child, James Mansell. Her firstborn, John, was Gladys's great-grandfather and a scoundrel rivaling J.D. Presley.

Like Elvis, John Mansell was born in the family home, a farmhouse in western Alabama. In the late 1840s he married Elizabeth Gilmore and fathered nine children. He also had children with his wife's sister, Rebecca, who lived with them. As the oldest son, he had inherited the family farm, but by 1880 he'd lost it. At the age of fifty-two and no longer tied to the land, John transported his wife, her sister, and all his minor children to the doorstep of his adult son, White Mansell, and left them there. With a lovely young woman on his arm, he set off for Oxford, Mississippi, never to be heard from again. Somewhere, I am sure, there are records.

Elvis's professional life would continually reverberate with echoes of his family's past. Ironically, he would play the part of a "half-breed," like his great-great-grandfather John Mansell, in the 1960 movie *Flaming Star*. In December of 1960, Elvis was inducted into the Los Angeles Indian Tribal Council by Chief WahNeeOta in honor of his "constructive portrayal of a man of Indian blood." The public at that time had no idea how heartfelt Elvis's performance was in this movie. In 1968, Elvis revealed to his "Dear Sister" the emotion he had felt playing a character who was part white and part Indian like himself—like John Mansell. The movie was fiction, but Elvis's empathy for the character he played helped him transcend his own acting abilities and turn in one of his finest and most convincing performances. In three words of Elvis's choosing, the movie "was a mess" after the producers cut some scenes, tinkered with the ending and even cut some lyrics in the title song. But the character of Pacer Burton had given him a chance to work out some of his own feelings about being a "half-breed outcast."

There is no doubt that Elvis's family history and heritage—whether true or merely believed to be true—significantly shaped the rest of his life. As Carmen Montez told her best friend Carmen Rayburn, "It's not surprising that Elvis was troubled. The only stable influence in his life was a hard-drinking mother who had a very loose grasp on reality. Everything else was shifting sand—smoke and mirrors. His need to keep an extended family together was based on the fear that someone might leave, even someone he disliked, because losing family was painful. That's why friends and relatives and their families were part of his entourage." For Elvis, life was a constant search for family and stability.

Every year since I was brought into this mystery I have futilely searched the numerous online family tree sites for any clues about the enigmatic Virgil Presley. And every year I became more convinced that Elvis's evangelist father was a vivid invention of a boy's imagination, or maybe the product of myths told to him by an alcoholic mother. No Virgil Presley fathered by J.D. and Minnie Mae Presley in 1916 ever made an appearance in any Presley family history.

When finishing this manuscript, I conducted another search and discovered a site I had never visited before. The website wikitree.com is attempting to merge everyone's family trees together into one universal tree. For the first time, I found what I had spent many years looking for. Virgil at last had made an appearance as the brother of Vernon and Vester Presley.

A family tree established at wikitree.com shows the largely unknown
Virgil Presley as the brother of Vernon and other siblings.

Clearly, someone other than Elvis knew about Virgil. He wasn't just a figment of the King's imagination. If you have more information about Virgil Presley, please contact me at elvis@calumeteditions.com.

Authenticating Elvis

The letter in which Elvis disclaims Vernon Presley as his biological father is a small part of the reason it has taken so many years to write and publish this book. There are serious issues of authenticity, credibility and legality. Let me explain the dilemma posed by the sources of my information.

While I have documented the remembrances of verbal conversations between Carmen Montez and the authors of the letters, including Elvis, those recollections were retold to me by Carmen Rayburn. The most generous characterization of this information would be "hearsay." Such information might be credible enough for posting in the tabloids, but my view is that it lacks credibility until it is corroborated by other sources. After all, the reliability of Montez's testimony is dependent on her memory and her integrity. She could be lying, or her memories could be muddled.

The only first-hand record of Montez's conversations with Rayburn is in Rayburn's memories of them, or in the incomplete written summaries of those conversations in Rayburn's journal. Because of the celebrity of the letter writers, Montez had a potential profit motive to establish a relationship with Elvis, and Rayburn could have shared a similar motive to enhance the credibility of the information she had acquired.

Undoubtedly, there is a great deal of uncertainty. Three facts about the sources of this information can be established, however.

First, it was known to a few of Montez's friends that Elvis and the other letter writers were "students" of Montez, though none except Carmen Rayburn seems to have known about any written correspondence. Second, the two Carmens were close friends and Rayburn legally purchased the suitcase of letters at an auction of Montez's and her husband's personal belongings. Third, Rayburn kept a journal that included some of the information revealed to her by Montez about conversations with Elvis and the others. By her own admission, however, these contemporaneous accounts are incomplete because of Rayburn's self-professed "lack of discipline."

Let's be honest about something else. Most of the books about Elvis rely almost entirely on the distant memories of the authors who generally had a relationship with Elvis but also had a potential motive to achieve fame and monetary gain by publishing their accounts. Some books were written by professional historians or biographers, but these, too, rely on interviews with living witnesses whose memories may be unreliable and on written documents such as newspaper articles, historical records, and personal letters, all of which are difficult to corroborate. In all these books, reconstructed anecdotes—even detailed dialogue recalled decades after the fact—are often treated as historical facts, though they almost certainly are merely reminiscent of the truth. Here are some examples.

In *Taking Care of Elvis*, Letetia Henley Kirk, a private nurse who took care of Elvis, wrote a book about their relationship, including multiple stories in which Elvis and Kirk were the only persons present, thus no corroboration is available for those stories. Priscilla Presley's book, *Elvis and Me,* is filled with unverifiable anecdotes and personal conversations. Can she remember the precise dialogue between Elvis and Vernon before the wedding reception at Graceland as she offers in the book? Of course not. These same issues plague all such books, including *Caught in a Trap: Elvis Presley's Tragic Lifelong Search for Love* (as told by his stepbrother Rick Stanley with Paul Harold); *The Boy Who Would Be King: An Intimate Portrait of Elvis Presley By His Cousin* (written by Kathleen Tracy, based on the recollections of Earl Greenwood).

There arc many other examples, of course. But perhaps the best illustration of the credibility issue surrounding recollections and third-party interviews is another book by author Kathleen Tracy, *Elvis Presley: A Biography*. In the book's introduction, she states that, unless specified, all quotes in the book are based on many hours of interviews with Elvis's cousin and friend Earl Greenwood, who later worked for Elvis. She goes on to explain:

> The quotes are Greenwood's personal recollections of conversations he participated in, overheard, or was directly told about by Elvis and other family members. Additionally, the thoughts attributed to Elvis are based on conversations he had with Greenwood during which Elvis expressed his opinions and feelings on his career, fame, family, and women.

In other words, *Elvis Presley: A Biography* is an assemblage of first-hand, second-hand and sometimes third-hand recollections supported by doses of hearsay but unsupported by any contemporaneous notes to improve the accuracy of details.

If you think about it, personal memoirs—a popular genre— rely almost entirely on one person's recollections, most of which have not been contemporaneously documented, and all of which are subject to the emotional bias and reporting integrity of the author.

If all we had were Carmen Montez's recollections, some of which were recorded in Rayburn's journal shortly after hearing them, we would have a more credible batch of documentation than most Elvis books can claim. But readers could still justifiably question the credibility of the information and the sources.

Fortunately, we have a large collection of handwritten letters by Elvis Presley—his thoughts and description of events in his own words—the facts of which are often corroborated by other authors in handwritten letters. Naturally, the value of these letters in establishing credibility is only as good as the authenticity of the letters. The obvious question is: could the letters be forged? In other words, were the Elvis letters actually written by Elvis Presley?

Handwriting is a unique and distinctive individual behavior. The patterns of handwriting that distinguish one person's script from another's have been attributed by researchers to a variety of influences including perceptual abilities, physiology (musculoskeletal and nervous systems), intellectual development, emotions, motivations, education, occupation and the writer's unique collection of personality traits. The effect of these influences is an individual handwriting pattern that may be impossible to duplicate in its entirety by another writer. E. J. Smith in 1984 computed the likelihood that two writings by different authors would be identical in just twelve of the five hundred characteristics found in a typical page of handwriting to be 1 in 241 million.

While individuals usually don't vary their writing, an individual for a variety of reasons may deliberately change a handwriting style to create a different appearance. Also, handwriting may occasionally be altered unconsciously by such factors as mood states, physical well-being, or even the qualities of the writing instrument and writing surface. Characteristics of the writing situation can also exert a powerful influence on the appearance of the written specimen—a signature written at a busy check-out when the author was rushed, tired or distracted may vary considerably from a signature written on personal correspondence when the author was relaxed or attempting to create a positive impression. Despite a variety of influences, however, handwriting is a relatively enduring and automatic behavior that is reliable and consistent once the author achieves maturity, unless influenced by chemicals, injury or poor health.

The pattern of handwriting produced by a mature individual is sufficiently unique to be distinguished from the handwriting patterns of another person by a highly trained examiner. The single exception is the existence of similarities in the writing of some very closely related persons. Even when individual samples of handwriting from one person exhibit markedly different patterns of writing, expert analysis may conclude that the writing styles share enough critical identifying features to be authenticated as the same author. Such detailed analysis, however, may require the use of specialized microscopes, optical equipment, calipers, and grids and devices for measuring the slant of the writing and the pressure applied to the writing surface.

As a first step in authenticating the letters, Bill Mack commissioned the world-renowned handwriting expert Charles W. Sachs of THE SCRIPTORIUM in Beverly Hills to authenticate sample "Elvis" letters from the Montez/Rayburn collection. Sachs was the expert analyst called in to authenticate the celebrated will of Howard Hughes when it was challenged. In court, he pronounced the document a fake, and in time the jury agreed.

In his authentication letter to Bill Mack, Sachs wrote:

> In the normal course of THE SCRIPTORIUM'S business, a good deal of ELVIS PRESLEY memorabilia passes through my hands, most of which is the product of secretaries or celebrity fan mail services. Some of it, of course, is genuinely signed by Presley himself. Accordingly, I am quite familiar with his handwriting, even from different periods of his life.

In his opinion, Sachs outlined the authentication process:

> I have spent several hours comparing the photocopies and the original letters you sent me to known exemplars of holograph specimens of ELVIS PRESLEY's hand. From the study, I have concluded that the hand that wrote the letters represented by your photocopies and the two (2) original letters you allowed me to examine is that of the singer, ELVIS PRESLEY.

Gary Lindberg

The Scriptorium

427 NORTH CANON DRIVE
BEVERLY HILLS, CA 90210

Mailing Address: Box 1290
Beverly Hills, Calif. 90213

Mr. William S. Mack
4656 Nine Oaks Circle
Minneapolis, MN 55437

19 November 1988

(612) 831-6580

Dear Mr. Mack:

You have retained me to authenticate certain letters
believed by you to be hand-written by ELVIS PRESLEY, the late
singer and performer.

To that end, you placed in our hands photocopies of
six (6) holograph letters or fragments thereof, variously
dated "Sept. 5," "April 12," "May 22," "Nov 12," "Mar.
24," and "March 2, 1969." In addition, you have allowed me
to examine two (2) original holograph letters together with
envelopes on which there is additional handwriting.   The
original letters are dated "April 14," and "Nov. 3rd."
All of the letters are addressed either to "Dear Sister," or to
"Dear Carmen."

I have spent several hours comparing the photocopies and
the original letters you sent me to known exemplars of holograph
specimens of ELVIS PRESLEY's hand.   From the study, I have
concluded that the hand that wrote the letters represented by
your photocopies and the two (2) original letters you allowed
me to examine is that of the singer, ELVIS PRESLEY.

My expertise in the field of authenticating handwriting
is well-established.   As the owner of THE SCRIPTORIUM, which
has been in business for two decades, I must guarantee the
authenticity of every document we agree to sell.   I am happy
to say that this firm enjoys a reputation for probity second to
none.

As a nationally recognized authority in the authentication
of handwriting, I am asked from time to time to testify in

BUYERS, SELLERS, APPRAISERS
of Original Letters, Documents & Manuscripts of Famous People
(213) 275-6060 • 278-4200

Page 1 of the Sachs authentication letter regarding the Presley
letters.

Sachs - Mack   -2-   19 Nov. 88

court as a "questioned documents expert."   As an example,
when the celebrated HOWARD HUGHES will was challenged, I was
invited by the court in Las Vegas to examine the document
first hand and to render my expert opinion as to its genuineness.
I did so, of course, and pronounced the document a fake, which
judgment, in time, was the same conclusion the jury arrived at.

    In the normal course of THE SCRIPTORIUM's business, a good
deal of ELVIS PRESLEY memorabilia passes through my hands, most
of which is the product of secretaries or celebrity fan mail
services.   Some of it, of course, is genuinely signed by
Presley, himself.   Accordingly, I am quite familiar with his
handwriting, even from different periods of his life.

    Please let me know if I may be of further service to
you.

                        Cordially,

                        Charles W. Sachs

Page 2 of the Sachs authentication letter regarding the Presley
letters.

It was hard to dispute the opinion of an expert like Charles
Sachs, but I knew something about handwriting analysis and the
difficulties of discerning fact from fiction when a document has
been executed by a truly skilled forger. I also knew that an expert
forger might be able to duplicate a signature. But to successfully
forge the contents of a hundred handwritten letters without a telling
error somewhere? Highly unlikely.

Nevertheless, I felt compelled to delve even more deeply into
the handwriting. Fortunately, I was blessed with a brilliant, multi-
talented mother who could assist. Not only did Elayne Lindberg own
and manage the largest art gallery in the Twin Cities of Minneapolis

and St. Paul, but she was also a certified art appraiser and restorer. She was qualified to authenticate the paintings of many famous artists as well as to restore priceless, museum-quality artworks. Those were not the skills I required, however.

Elayne was also a certified graphoanalyst, qualifying her to perform character analyses based on handwriting as well as examination of questioned documents for police departments and the FBI. She frequently testified in court as an expert witness. Mother and I had collaborated on a book, *The Power of Positive Handwriting*, which explained how handwriting was really "brainwriting," and how the tiniest strokes could decode one's personality traits. The book went on to explain how this could be applied in reverse— how a person could reduce or eliminate a trait like procrastination by changing specific strokes in his or her handwriting. Because of my uncertified knowledge of Graphoanalysis™, I couldn't help but see parallels between its purpose of revealing personality and mood through analysis of handwriting and Carmen Montez's self-proclaimed belief that she could do the same thing in the letters written to her by her "students."

I asked my mother to examine the Elvis letters. She did not have a proven authentic exemplar of Elvis's handwriting for comparison, and the handwriting samples we found currently for sale were not all written by the same person, so it was difficult for her to say the handwriting truly was Elvis's. Fortunately, Charles Sachs had provided a couple of "genuine" Elvis exemplars. My mother did not know the provenance of those samples as Sachs did, so she was reluctant to categorically state they were genuine. But she did tell me that the Montez/Rayburn letters purportedly written by Elvis were indeed written by the same hand as the person who created the exemplars used by Sachs to prove authenticity.

I have much more to say in the next chapter about Graphoanalysis and the personality traits it has uncovered in the handwriting of Elvis, Marlon, Tom and Harry. But at the time, I took my mother's findings as further confirmation that the letters were authentic.

Bill Mack had also asked Charles Sachs to evaluate letters written by Marlon Brando. In his authentication letter to Bill Mack, Sachs wrote:

> You have placed in our hands photocopies of some sixteen holograph fragments representing portions of various letters ... I compared the various fragments with exemplars known by me to be genuine reproductions of Mr. Brando's handwriting. As you can see, I have paid particular attention to several idiosyncratic characteristics of Mr. Brando's holograph ... I have concluded that the handwriting contained in the fragments you have shown me and the handwriting of the known exemplars of Mr. Brando's hand are the same.

Mr. William S. Mack
4656 Nine Oaks Circle
Minneapolis, MN 55437

(612) 831-6580

Dear Mr. Mack:

   Once again you have asked us to authenticate certain letters in your possession, this time those believed by you to be handwritten by the actor, MARLON BRANDO.

   You have placed in our hands photocopies of some sixteen holograph fragments representing portions of various letters. I have numbered the fragments as Exhibit 1, Exhibit 2, and so on, through Exhibit 16.

   Next I compared the various fragments with exemplars known by me to be genuine reproductions of Mr. Brando's handwriting. As you can see, I have paid particular attention to several idiosyncratic characteristics of Mr. Brando's holograph. Many of the positive similarities you, yourself, have identified.

   Accordingly, I have concluded that the handwriting contained in the fragments you have shown me and the handwriting of the known exemplars of Mr. Brando's hand are the same.

   Do contact us if we may be of further help to you.

                              Cordially,

                              Charles W. Sachs

The Sachs authentication regarding the Brando letters.

I had noticed, however, that Mack had not submitted to Charles Sachs some very unusual Brando content. In well over twenty letters, Brando's handwriting would abruptly change as he would allegedly became possessed by the "spirit" of another person, or so the writer claimed. Some letters were executed solely by this other "spirit," but more often the body of the letter would shift between the "spirit" writer and Brando.

Reading these letters was a spooky experience. Information unknown to Marlon Brando would be communicated to Carmen by these "spirits," which would also occasionally issue stern warnings. Since Sachs had not been shown handwriting samples of these "spirit" passages, I asked my mother to evaluate them.

Elayne definitely stated that Brando *could not have written those passages*. Even if a person tried to disguise his or her handwriting, she told me, a trained expert can detect the ruse. Not only were these "spirit" passages written by two different individuals—the two "spirits"—but the personality traits revealed by the handwriting of those two writers were entirely different from Brando's and *from each other*.

In other words, either Brando was truly possessed by these spirits and their personalities when writing, or two human "confederates" had conspired with him to create letters with composite handwriting styles.

Neither my mother nor I could imagine any possible motive for a conspiracy of this nature.

I was satisfied that the letters in our possession were genuine. Despite the expert opinions, however, Bill Mack and I knew that many readers would not accept handwriting analysis as adequate proof of authentication. I decided, then, to switch gears and adopt the attitude of a total skeptic. It became my job to prove that the letters had been forged. This meant I had to find a plausible motive for the fraud, discover a method for perpetrating it, and uncover contextual evidence of fraud such as telltale inconsistencies or factual errors.

Motive

If the letters were fakes, there had to be a reason for faking them... a motive. The most common motives for forging documents are fraud-for-profit (such a forging checks), and fraud-for-reputation (such as forging a degree from college).

The recipient of the letters—Carmen Montez—could have made money by selling original handwritten letters signed by the four celebrities. The letters were dated and, in some cases, postmarked before Montez even met Rayburn, so Montez and/or her husband, George Ramentol, are the likeliest suspects in a letters-for-profit scheme.

The problem with this theory is that up until her death, Carmen Montez never made any attempt to publicize the existence of the letters or make money from them. In fact, except for Carmen Rayburn, even her friends knew nothing about the letters. She seems mostly to have kept the confidence of the letter writers.

It also appears that her ex-husband may not have known about the letters. In her will, which Carmen signed less than four months before dying, she named George as executor of her estate. But four months after Carmen died, George legally waived any right to act in this capacity. It certainly appears that he was not part of any conspiracy with his wife and that he didn't even know about the letters. During George's brief courtship of Carmen Rayburn, neither of them ever mentioned the existence of the letters.

If Carmen Montez had somehow faked the letters to gain notoriety or enhance her reputation, she appears to have lost interest or become discouraged with that strategy because she never revealed their existence to anyone except Rayburn. It would have taken an enormous effort to fake three hundred letters in handwriting that could fool expert document evaluators, so it makes little sense that Carmen would have undertaken such an extraordinary effort only to forfeit the potential spoils.

Who else might have had a reason to fake the letters, and what would that reason be? I've come up with a blank. Since the letters were written, no one has benefited from them, and no one in the chain of custody except Carmen Rayburn has had the opportunity to make money from their existence, and she has since died. Robert Slatzer is also dead. Bill Mack has relinquished his interest in the letters. This makes me the last one standing, and I was the last one to join the party.

Method

The method of faking the letters is another potential line of investigation. How could such a massive undertaking be accomplished? This was not just a handful of forged letters or a forged signature on a contract or a check. Consider the scale.

In all, there are nearly three hundred handwritten and signed documents, most of them letters but a few of them cards for Christmas, Easter and other occasions. Many of the documents seem to have been delivered by courier, but some were mailed. The postmarks range from 1966 to 1972, the earliest ones from Harry Belafonte.

A letter from Belafonte to Carmen Montez at her Hollywood address
was mailed on August 24, 1966, according to the postmark.
Interestingly, the special delivery letter arrived with $0.05 postage due.

Besides the letters, there were other documents in the suitcase such as signed contracts, which are also dated. If there was a conspiracy, it was a patient one that endured for nearly five years.

70

Imagine the effort to create and then draft hundreds of letters forged in the hand of each purported celebrity author. Imagine coming up with scores of intertwining storylines that weave throughout all four sets of letters with thousands of details and facts that can be checked—the listed date of a concert in a certain city, a TV show that played in Las Vegas on a specific evening, a news event that occurred on a specific date, an event that would only be listed on a police report, *et cetera*. It boggles the mind.

Then imagine the number of conspirators required to pull this off. Each of the batches of letters needed one skilled forger to simulate a celebrity author. The Brando letters required three forgers, one for Marlon and two for the "spirit" authors, which we've learned could not be the Marlon forger. That's six skilled forgers to produce the letters for a motive we cannot fathom. Imagine the difficulty of finding such a talented crew and managing their efforts over a five-year period. And if there were such a crew, what are the odds that none of its members would ever squeal?

Fact Checking

To prove the letters fake, the final step I undertook was the most time-consuming. I decided to check and cross-check the details of the content in the letters: dates, places, events—everything that could be factually checked had to be validated, and if the same facts were mentioned in several letters by different authors, the consistency of those facts had to be verified.

Some events or details could not be verified because they were private and not part of the public record. But thousands of facts could be checked online, in newspaper archives, in published books and reference works, through on-site historical research, and through interviews. In some cases, because some letters were not dated, researching the date of a specific concert mentioned in a letter helped me put a date on that letter.

The chronological sequencing of the letters turned into another monumental task, but it was the only way I could capture the meaning of all the oblique references to information contained in previous letters. Each group of letters written by an individual author was like a jigsaw puzzle that had numerous pieces hidden in the box of another puzzle.

The most frustrating part of this capture-the-meaning phase was that I only possessed letters received by Carmen. I had none of Carmen's responses. Even after sequencing the letters, reading them was like listening to one side of a phone call during which I could not hear Carmen. But by reading the letters in sequence, I could also determine if the various "stories" that wove through them made sense and were consistent from author to author and date to date.

Authentic and Consistent

The fact that I have written this book reveals the conclusion of my task of authenticating the letters. There is no doubt in my mind that the letters are authentic to each of the authors and were written to Carmen Montez, and that Carmen Rayburn legally bought the letters at a California state auction. While I found minor inconsistencies and a few small factual errors (the spelling of a name, the name of a casino, a future concert date, *et cetera*), these errors were the kinds of casual mistakes that normal people make when they write letters to each other.

The Credibility Issue

One other issue intrigued me. A few of the letters describe events of criminal activity, physical and emotional abuse, and other cruel actions that almost defy belief. Elvis claimed to have been the victim of atrocities by named assailants that are so horrible it is hard to imagine that they actually occurred or that they could have remained secret until now. These events are reported in this book, and the details I describe are faithful to the specifics provided by the authors of the letters.

Because I struggled with the credibility of these passages, I felt compelled to explore alternative explanations for how and why

Elvis and his friends might have embellished, or exaggerated, or even invented incidents of such ugliness and brutality, and then reported them as completely true to an audience of one woman, Carmen Montez. The puzzle was made more complex as reported details were corroborated by other Elvis friends who claimed to have been participants, observers, or nursemaids attending to Elvis's emotional and physical wounds.

I was confronted again by the need to identify a motive and a method—why and how could a group of individuals create, perpetuate and even actively participate in a sequence of myths? Was Elvis experiencing male rape fantasies due to homophobia or homosexual desire? This could explain the vividness of his reporting but falls apart when we read Marlon's descriptions of finding and freeing a bound Elvis who had been bloodied in his own living room. If such an event were a hallucination or a delusion, Marlon would have either been lying to Carmen or sharing the delusion.

From the letters, I knew that Elvis and Marlon had troublesome psychological issues including numerous fears and phobias, bouts of depression and severe anxiety. They openly confessed many of their problems to Carmen Montez and repeatedly told her that her spiritual guidance helped them get through tough patches. But is it possible that Elvis suffered from delusions and somehow infected his close friend Marlon with the same delusions? Is this even possible?

After reading the Presley and Brando letters in question, research by fact-checker and researcher Lynn Karin Ness turned up a psychological condition called shared psychotic disorder, or *folie à deux*. This is a rare delusional disorder shared by two or more people with close emotional bonds, sometimes even entire families. According to the *Diagnostic and Statistical Manual of Mental Disorders, Fifth Edition (DSM-5)*, the diagnostic criteria for *folie à deux* are threefold:

1. Two people share the same delusion or delusional system and support one another in this belief.
2. They have an unusually close relationship.

3. Temporal or contextual evidence exists that indicates the delusion was induced in the passive member by the active member.

There are two competing theories, then, that explain everything described in the letters. The first is relatively simple: bad guys with clear evil intent brutally assaulted Elvis in various ways over a period of several years. This would make a good movie. The second theory of *folie à deux* is more complex and harder to understand but remains a possibility. It would also make a good movie.

After spending three decades with this material, I have made up my mind. I'm sure you will make your own judgment. According to the scientific and philosophical rule known as Occam's razor, however, the simplest of competing theories is usually the correct one.

Brainwriting

Many people think that handwriting analysis, such as Graphoanalysis, is little more than fortune-telling. This misconception was compounded in the past when a buyer looking for a book on "graphology" found it in the occult section of a bookstore. Despite this unfortunate misclassification by the book trade, handwriting analysis is a proven science, and today even the Library of Congress has changed its classification to reflect this fact. Extensive research has determined the correlation of individual handwriting strokes to specific personality traits. Every "stroke"—which is the smallest part of a single letter written by hand—has a specific meaning.

In 1939, the American psychologist Lawrence K. Frank first spoke of "projective methods" of personality study. "Projection" is behavior that exposes the basic tendencies of a personality. In other words, projections are outward expressions of inner events. We all project ourselves. We "express" our personalities when we speak, act, and react to any stimulus.

When using projective methods of investigation, a scientist provides carefully selected methods for subjects to express themselves. Examples include the "word association" techniques used by Jung, the spots and splotches used by Rorschach, and the so-called "Thematic Apperception" tests. These various methods each encourage subjects to express themselves. The results give the psychologist insights into a subject's personality.

Graphoanalysis is an excellent alternative investigative method because the act of handwriting is another way we express ourselves—a complex set of gestures that originate not in the hand but in the brain. That's why Elayne Lindberg, my mother, called it "brainwriting." When we write, we are aided by visual perceptions (which take place in the brain's occipital lobe) and auditory perceptions (which take place in the temporal lobe.) Put another way, we write words that have been "read" or "heard."

Because handwriting is so directly controlled by the brain, it can be compared to the charts produced by electroencephalography (EEG), which requires a trained neurologist to "read" the recorded squiggles and properly interpret what is going on in the subject's brain. Brain waves, of course, provide an entirely different kind of information than handwriting, but within the highly individual strokes of a person's script is a subtle but revealing personal message communicated by the brain. A trained graphoanalyst can "read" this message and accurately interpret the personality traits it expresses.

Handwriting is the most common permanent record of the personalities and inner lives of people everywhere. Though not commonly known, psychiatrists use handwriting analysis to uncover issues that may remain masked by other techniques. Many companies use handwriting analysis to find people with traits that indicate a good fit for certain jobs. Forensic handwriting experts work for law enforcement agencies to determine the validity of "questioned documents" that may be forgeries. In authenticating the letters on which this book is based, we used the services of such an expert, Charles Sachs, and my mother was a charter member of the World Questioned Documents Association.

Even the courts have confirmed that handwriting is a form of behavior in public—an open display of personality—so the interpretation of personality based on handwriting does not violate privacy. In United States v. Mara, the Supreme Court rejected the assertion that a witness's Fourth Amendment right against unreasonable search and seizure was violated by a grand jury directive requiring product of handwriting exemplars. The Court stated: "…

there is no more expectation of privacy in the physical characteristics of a persons' script than there is in the tone of his voice." In Gilbert v. California, the Supreme Court ruled that compelling the production of handwriting exemplars does not violate the Fifth Amendment privilege against self-incrimination. These opinions allow us to investigate the letters by Elvis and the other celebrities not just for factual content, but also to unveil the personality traits of the writers, and, in some cases, their temporary emotional states as events intruded on their lives.

To assist in a deep analysis of the letters, we recruited a uniquely skilled woman, Jane Hollis, who has worked for many years as both a clinical psychologist and a certified Graphoanalyst, a rare combination of skills and experience. She is the owner of Career Development Consultants, LLC, in St. Paul, Minnesota, through which she consults on anxiety management in the workplace, employee career development, and the use of graphotherapy with business executives.

We gave Jane authenticated letters handwritten by Elvis, Marlon, Harry, Tom and Carmen Montez, then asked her to prepare a personality profile for each. Throughout this book we will reveal relevant portions of her analyses to provide deeper insights into these complex and often mystifying personalities. In a conversation with me, she revealed a summary of her investigation into Elvis Presley.

Jane Hollis points out some important details in the handwriting of
Elvis Presley to author Gary Lindberg.

Elvis Presley

Jane Hollis analyzed and compared the handwriting in two letters signed by Elvis. The first letter (designated EP1) was dated March 9, 1969. It contained rather routine reporting of recent personal details about his relationship with Priscilla, his "Dad Presley's" second marriage, his belief that he was part Indian and part Welsh, and his memory of a beating in 1957 that left him with facial scars. The content was communicated without the use of emotional language.

The second letter (designated EP2) was written shortly after an alarming home invasion in which he and his wife were physically assaulted. The content of this letter to Carmen Montez was delivered in highly emotional language, as one would expect.

"In Elvis's first letter," Jane told me, "he shows an organized personality with roots planted firmly in reality. He clearly has the ability to create both short-term and long-term plans. He also has a well-developed ability to concentrate on important things, shown by his small writing, and to pay close attention to details, revealed by crossing all his t-bars and dotting all his 'i's.'"

"Would this make him a reliable reporter of facts?"

"Let's say that these traits—particularly the ability to focus and observe details—are essential to being a useful witness. In this letter, Elvis showed that, despite numerous travails, he remained basically an optimist, indicated by the upward slope of the lines of his writing. He used his optimism as a tool for encouraging himself and others. He could be rather impatient at times, and very strong-willed—he was not afraid to take the initiative—but instead of directly confronting people he would have tended to use tact and persuasion to steer them into conforming to his will.

Elvis occasionally dots his "i's" with jabs instead of round dots,
indicating impatience. Jabs made from right to left show impatience
or annoyance with something in the past, perhaps a mistake, an
opportunity missed or a relationship that went wrong. This jab is left
to right, revealing impatience with others.

"Elvis would have softened any directness with humor and generosity. I don't necessarily mean Elvis was generous in the outward way, like giving Cadillacs to friends, but in the more important way of listening to other people—which he could do in a limited way—and genuinely considering their perspectives. His writing shows that he has a strong tendency to consider the feelings and needs of others. This is his innate nature. He may not have explicitly understood how his consideration for others helped him pursue his own goals, but undoubtedly it helped rally contributors to his success.

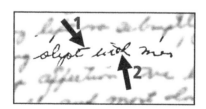

Arrow 1 points out a characteristically thick t-bar applied with
pressure on paper, indicating a strong will. Arrow 2 indicates a t-bar
that slopes downward, revealing a desire for control.

"There is some handwriting evidence that Elvis is clannish, trusting only a few people to know and keep his secrets. This may also help to explain why so few people knew about his relationship with Carmen Montez or his close friendships with Marlon and Tom."

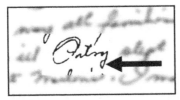

Small lower loops in Elvis's handwriting, either round or squared off, reveals clannishness—a tendency to be exclusive in his relationships.

Jane continued. "The way a writer sculpts the personal pronoun *I* can reveal a lot about the influence a mother and father have had on an individual's personality. Elvis's writing shows that his mother's influence was very strong while his father's (or father figure's) influence is weak or shallow.

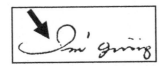

The large upper loop of Elvis's personal pronoun indicates strong influence by his mother, and the lack of a bottom loop indicates weak or shallow influence from his father.

"There is limited research on this topic, but studies suggest that exaggerated female influence is correlated with an individual who has a greater need to establish same-sex communication, perhaps as a counter-balance. Combined with a tendency toward clannishness, this could help explain why Elvis found it important to bond with a small group of trusted male friends with whom he could share even volatile secrets. And it could also help us understand why Carmen—a woman he called 'Sister' but in reality was more of a 'mother' figure—was able to influence him so profoundly.

"Regarding his goals, his handwriting demonstrates a person who set rather high goals and had faith in himself to reach them. He embraced challenges in his work and prized the feeling of 'moving ahead.' Reaching any kind of stasis, such as a plateau in his career, would have been intolerably frustrating, and this frustration could easily be amplified by his impatience.

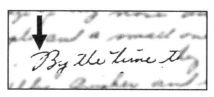

Long lead-in strokes provide another indication of Elvis's strong
controlling nature.

"The EP1 letter clearly shows that Elvis was his own boss. His writing shows a strong desire to control his own destiny. It must have been terribly difficult for him to have his life and career controlled by the overbearing Colonel Parker, which probably explains their perpetually combative relationship."

"How does this writing sample compare to the later sample written when Elvis was in a highly emotional state following a physical intrusion?" I asked.

"The second letter is clearly authored by the same writer," Jane said, "but the handwriting is radically different in many ways from the first specimen."

"In ways that could be attributed to his mental state?"

"Well, let me give you some of the details. Most obviously, the writing is larger than in the other letter. Larger handwriting shows a need to see a bigger picture or a striving for broader surveillance to help better protect the writer from more threats. Writing in various sizes like this is quite rare for an individual, and as most of Elvis's letters are written in a much smaller size, I suspect that the trauma of the event he is reporting may have influenced the size of his writing.

"In addition, the lines of writing often get mixed in with each other, showing restlessness and confusion of interest, most likely contributing to questions of 'What do I do next?'

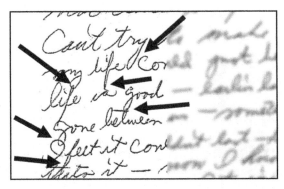

The six arrows show points where the lines of writing intrude on each other, showing restlessness and confusion of interests, perhaps the emotional consequence of the recent home invasion.

"Elvis's organizational skills, ability to make plans, and his attention to details—traits that were very pronounced in the first letter—are decidedly lower in EP2. This writing also shows greatly diminished confidence. At the time he wrote this letter, he was showing a lot of sensitivity to criticism of his personal life and career. His goals, which were once high, have been lowered, as if he no longer believed he could reach his previous goals. He now exhibits a tendency to worry and a sense of being overwhelmed and restless, as if he can't decide what to do next."

"I would expect those kinds of changes," I said, "considering the traumatic home invasion that he'd just experienced."

"And yet he shows some fascinating coping skills," Jane replied. "This second letter shows less anxiety than the first sample does."

"How can that be, after such a trauma?"

"He still shows some worry but has lessened his anxiety by virtually giving up any attempt to control the situation.

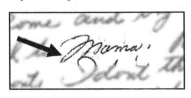

The unnecessary loop on the downstroke of the "M" in "Mama" shows that Elvis is worried.

"The far forward slant of Elvis's writing, showing a degree of emotion, has become erratic in this letter. At times the letters suddenly slant too far to the right revealing emotional volatility and a lack of impulse control. His heightened impulsiveness could lead him to do just about anything to shed his responsibility for bringing on this terrible event. He may just want to flee to a different life that is free of these persecutions. He seems suggestible to any plan to *emotionally* escape through medications, alcohol, mind-altering drugs, sex—or *physically* escape through travel or hiding out, even seeking another life altogether.

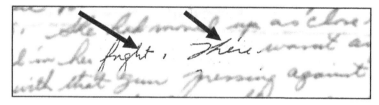

Notice the sudden change of slant in the two lower-case "h" letters. The one on the right is slanting much farther to the right, indicating emotional volatility.

"The pressure he applies with the pen on paper is lighter in the second letter, showing that he was already easing up his mind, perhaps by writing his report of the incident and getting it off to Carmen. As a psychologist, rather than a graphoanalyst, I would say this may be how he is able to relate the ugly details of the home invasion to Carmen. His language is less guarded, and he even names one of the persons assaulting him."

"I noticed that the bar crossing the letter "t" in some instances floats above the stem," I said. "That's not how he normally places his t-bars. What does that mean?"

"Well, in Graphoanalysis, that indicates that his thinking has become separated from reality. He's become a bit of a dreamer, perhaps even finding mental escape from reality to a place he'd rather be."

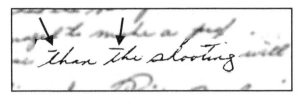

The arrows point out t-bars crossed very high on the t-stem, showing
high goals. T-bars that are above the stem reveal that his thinking
has become separated from reality, as if he were seeking escape.

"Maybe he was thinking about a different life as a means of coping?"

"Maybe. In this case it also could be why his nightmarish descriptions show some ambiguity, some lack of expected details, while reporting an unusually detailed account of other aspects. What's really interesting here is that this second letter shows a rather pessimistic attitude for the future. The writer repeatedly tries to pick himself up, to encourage himself, but becomes exhausted by the attempt and falls short. He tries to gain some degree of control, but that doesn't work, so he becomes increasingly devastated and emotionally tired. You can see how lines of writing that start out sloping upward as he struggles to lift his emotions suddenly slope downward signaling that he has abandoned the attempt and become discouraged.

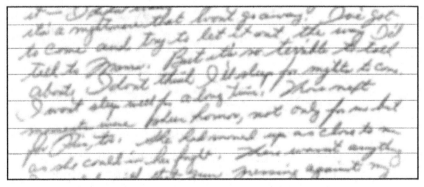

The up-and-down slopes of the handwritten lines in the second
letter indicate attempts to stay optimistic and then, perhaps from
exhaustion, giving in to discouragement and depression.

"Elvis's anxiety, once lessened, starts to increase again, as seen in the muddiness of the letters in some places. This leads to depression."

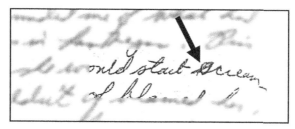

Notice the muddiness indicated by the arrow. In handwriting, this shows loss of impulsive control. In this written sample, this is perhaps due to his emotional recollection of his wife's wanting to scream during the home invasion he is describing.

Harry Belafonte

Jane Hollis also analyzed the handwriting of Harry Belafonte to help me understand the man whose letters to Carmen Montez I would be studying for many years. "In my opinion," Hollis told me, "Harry has the strongest personality among the authors of letters in your collection. When Harry enters a room, he captures everybody's attention and then takes up most of the space. When he corresponds, he is forceful but not off-putting.

"Among the group, he has the sharpest, quickest mind of the letter writers—the ability to reason, plan, solve problems, think in abstract terms, quickly comprehend complexity and learn from experience. He shows the 'acquisitive' hook in his writing which, when combined with traits identified by other strokes, shows that his acquisitiveness is for knowledge more than material things. He is intellectually active.

This inscription is on the cover page of a letter written by Harry Belafonte. Arrow 1 shows an initial hook in the capital "C," indicating acquisitiveness; in Harry's writing this means he has an interest in acquiring knowledge. Arrow 2 points to a large loop that shows Harry is thinking about behaving responsibly; but the loop is not closed, meaning he remains undecided.

"There is much more revealed in Harry's writing than the acquisition of knowledge, or test-taking smarts. Harry also has high emotional intelligence—the ability to identify and manage his own emotions and the emotions of others. Emotional intelligence includes three skills—emotional awareness, the ability to harness emotions and apply them to thinking and problem solving, and the ability to manage his own emotions and those of other people by persuading them to cheer up or calm them down.

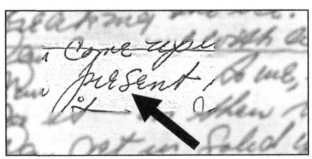

"Figure 8" shapes in Harry's handwriting indicate that he is very persuasive and resourceful.

"Harry is a crafty, skilled debater and seldom loses an argument unless losing serves his purpose. Usually he can persuade others to agree with his side. He is both highly persuasive and very persistent. Because he seldom gives up, he can seem quite dominating at times. He wants control but can usually be tactful and fair in gaining it. He's probably learned over time that he usually has the best ideas and would be the best leader of an endeavor rather than wasting time as a follower.

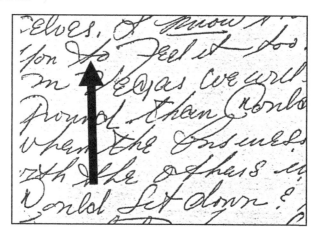

A "t" that "ties off" the t-bar to make a star shape out of the letter reveals the trait of persistence. This brief sample of Harry's writing contains nine such "t's." Can you find them all?

"His handwriting shows a person who is imaginative and creative with an understanding of art across different cultures. He is not only artistic, but the "e's" in his writing, which look like Greek epsilons, show that it's important to him that Carmen sees him as an artist.

The frequent cultural "e's" in Harry's writing reveal an artistic bent and the desire for people to view him as artistic.

"Harry's handwriting shows a number of 'cover' strokes. According to Graphoanalysis, a 'cover' stroke is a retracing of a portion of a letter. This stroke indicates that the writer can sometimes mislead others to get what he wants or to protect himself from the kinds of pain he had experienced in the past. At times Harry may use this trait to mislead himself, such as when he feels threatened, which causes him to 'cover' or protect himself, or when an untested opportunity arises that he instinctively wants to pursue.

Frequent "cover" strokes in Harry's writing indicate that Harry is capable of misleading himself or others about what he really wants.

"Harry is always alert to new opportunities and quick to take advantage, which may be why he so easily connected with Carmen and her movie project. He has such an agile mind that he sometimes jumps into action rather than taking time for a fuller analysis. Usually, though, his quick thinking is on the mark.

"The way that Harry writes the personal pronoun 'I' suggests to me that his father, or some other important male in his life, negatively influenced Harry so profoundly that he can become easily dejected whenever similar circumstances arise. This can sometimes cause him to sabotage himself through depression. Because this male influence only shows up in the way he writes a capital 'I,' it's likely that this influence only applies to personal goals, not career goals. I haven't researched his early years, but it's possible that a strong male figure once told him that he would never make it in life. Seizing opportunities, particularly if there is some financial gain involved, could be one way that Harry is telling that condescending male influence, 'I'll show you!'

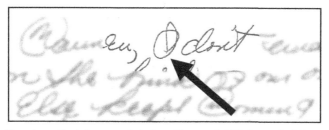

The strong final downward stroke of the capital "I" shows that Harry
has a high level of dejection regarding his father.

"Harry's active mind would make it extremely difficult
for him to relax because his mind is such a busy intersection of
thoughts, ideas and emotions. It is so busy, in fact, that he may have
invented a second 'Harry' to carry some of the load. This could be
one explanation of letters to Carmen in which he called himself the
'other Harry.' More likely this was simply an off-ramp for many
of the thoughts going around in his head, not a case of dissociative
identity disorder. Even so, when writing as the 'other Harry' just
hours after writing as the 'real' Harry, he displayed a personality
shift, becoming far more dominant and forceful, revealed by the
many downward-sloping t-bars in his writing."

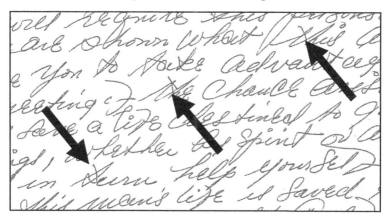

A thick, downward-sloping t-bar displays a desire to dominate others.

Gary Lindberg

Marlon Brando

Jane Hollis reviewed with me the highlights of the personality profile she developed from Marlon's handwriting. The first letter she analyzed (MB1) contained routine personal correspondence, providing a typical specimen of Marlon's handwriting without the emotional influence of extraordinary events in his life. The second sample (JENI) was a letter written by Marlon but signed "Jeni," an example of Marlon's "spirit writing" in which he appeared to be possessed by the spirit of a deceased girlfriend of Elvis.

"Marlon Brando's handwriting in MB1 shows him to be a basically optimistic and hopeful individual," Jane told me. "The strong rightward slant of his writing reveals that he has high empathy—an ability to understand, even vicariously experience the feelings of another person—which helps him relate easily to others."

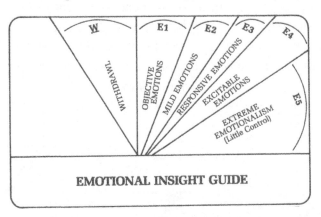

The slant gauge aids the graphoanalyst in the measurement of emotional response as displayed by the slant of a person's handwriting.

Thinking back to the early years of Marlon as depicted in Peter Manso's exhaustive tome, *Brando: The Biography*, I recalled an incident reported by Marlon's oldest sister, Jocelyn, that described a very sensitive Marlon beneath a tough, hyperactive exterior. Marlon "was walking along by the beach with his bike," his sister recalled, "and he saw this woman in trouble. She was drunk—whether or not

90

she was fainting, I don't know—but he went over to her and said, 'Can I help you?' He dipped his handkerchief in the lake and came back and put it to her face, and then brought her home with him."

I remembered another event during Marlon's early years. Marlon's childhood friend, Wally Cox—who became famous later in life as the actor who played Mr. Peepers on TV—was being bullied by a gang of students because of his small size, horn-rimmed glasses and high intellect. Marlon, a sturdy young man who was not afraid of a fight, immediately stepped in to defend his buddy. Numerous anecdotes attest to his passion for protecting underdogs and have-nots.

"Despite his compassion, he is strong-willed and craves being in control of his own life," Jane continued. "At times, this tendency toward willfulness creates a desire to control others, too, especially in areas where the conduct of others would affect his own life. His controlling nature can go undetected by others because he tends to lead through persuasion, convincing others to do what he wants them to do. Interestingly, his empathy sometimes causes him to do things that are good for other people but not so good for himself. On the other hand, he can convincingly feign interest in something—a movie project or a social activity—to prevent hurt feelings.

"Marlon has great initiative, the energy to back it up, and the analytical ability to make sense out of complex issues and situations. He's such a quick study and has such keen comprehension that he is sometimes catapulted forward in reaching conclusions, then becomes impatient with those who are not as insightful or quick to understand.

Notice the first "n" in the word "insane." The "V" shape at the center of the letter displays high analytical ability. The two sharp points making up the humps of the "n" indicate quick thinking. The second "n" has rounded humps showing logical thinking.

"He puts his quick-witted intellect to frequent use with a tendency to be argumentative. He likes a good debate and usually wins, unless he's debating Harry Belafonte.

The upper stroke on the letter "p" in Marlon's writing shows he loves to argue a point. He knows when a fight is worth having, but also when to yield strategically to obtain something of greater good.

"The 'responsibility loop' he makes when writing the name 'Elvis' indicates that he is capable of taking on responsibility for another person, in this case his friend Elvis Presley. When analyzing handwriting, I usually don't read the content of the handwriting because it has little bearing on what the handwriting strokes are telling me. But in this case, I confess that I read the letter by Marlon Brando for its content. The letter was filled with statements demonstrating Marlon's empathy with expressions of concern for Elvis's well-being and his own initiative to get help for Elvis. In this one letter, then, Marlon confirmed in his statements many of the most salient traits that were revealed in his handwriting.

The responsibility loop in Marlon's handwriting shows up principally when he writes the name Elvis, suggesting that he has accepted some personal responsibility for his friend.

"Marlon's handwriting also shows him to be fiercely honest, with high standards for his work and for behavior that affects others. It appears that this may be due to a stubborn feeling of self-consciousness caused by a fear of being considered 'less than' others, or possibly by being ridiculed during his childhood."

Self-consciousness is displayed in Marlon's handwriting when the second hump in the letter "n" or the second instance of a double-letter "l" or "t" is taller than the first one.

I told Jane that Marlon's father was extremely rigid, according to his children, and was known for his emotional remoteness and frequent absences from the family. "While Marlon was going to the Lincoln School, his father never once showed up there, even on Parents' Day," I said. "That could make a child feel somewhat 'less than' the other kids around him, I would think."

"Issues occurring early in life," Jane said, "usually have less influence on personality than more current events. I see this in Marlon's handwriting. The self-consciousness caused by parental influence is outweighed in the writing by the strong will and confidence exhibited in his later writing. It appears from this first handwriting sample that he eventually worked through these parental issues and felt accepted by both his mother and father.

"It's true, however, that Marlon was devastated when his parents separated for a time. This shows up in Graphoanalysis when the capital 'I' shows a 'hole' between the upper loop, which indicates the mother figure, and the lower loop to the left, which indicates the father figure. Marlon may have been looking for a replacement mother figure in Jeni."

A "hole" between the upper loop of a capital "I," representing the
mother's influence, and the bottom loop, relating to the father figure,
indicates that Marlon's parents emotionally hurt him.

"What about that mysterious 'Jeni' letter in which Marlon seemed to channel the spirit of Elvis's dead girlfriend?" I asked.

Jane explained. "Graphoanalysis cannot identify writing under the influence of substances, writing as an 'alter' of a person with dissociative identity disorder, or writing channeled by the spirit of a deceased person. But handwriting analysis can identify writing by the same person, even when disguised, as well as mood shifts, trait changes and other transient revisions to the personality."

"If Jeni was in some way communicating through Marlon," I suggested, "or if he was unconsciously adopting another identity he named Jeni, I would expect the handwriting of the Jeni letter to be quite different from Marlon's normal script. Wouldn't you?"

"I would. And in fact, the letter in which he signed the name Jeni is so different from the first sample provided to me that I checked both samples again to make sure that they were both written by the same person. I'm satisfied that they were. The changes in personality represented in the Jeni letter are what would be expected if Marlon were channeling another spirit—Marlon's characteristic handwriting mixed with some profoundly different traits.

"In the Jeni letter, Marlon—who physically wrote the letter—adjusted the size of the script to reflect his emotional state at the time of writing. He wrote bigger. This occurs rarely in handwriting. It indicates high intellectual capabilities in the writer and possibly a heightened need for awareness of the surroundings. The smaller writing in the first letter shows a concentrated, focused, well-organized mind. Larger letters in handwriting show a need to see a bigger picture. Metaphorically, you could see this larger handwriting as striving for broader surveillance to help better protect the writer from more threats."

"Could he be a bit paranoid in the Jeni letter?" I asked.

"Paranoia is what we call an evaluated trait, which means that there is no single stroke that indicates paranoia. Instead, we must see several different strokes present to identify it. Paranoia is based on fear, but also requires a desire to 'hide out' physically or emotionally from others, something we call clannishness. You can think of it as being secretive. Elvis showed a degree of clannishness but surprisingly little fear. Marlon, on the other hand, showed no clannishness and little fear. The lack of these traits pretty much rules out paranoia in Marlon.

"I would say that a plausible explanation for the Jeni letters, with their larger writing, is that Marlon was looking for realistic reasons to be fearful so he could devise safety precautions. In other words, the Jeni letter shows a person on high alert. Since this is not Marlon's usual mode of behavior, when the alert mode was triggered, perhaps he switched into another mode.

"I should point out that the Jeni handwriting also shows some restlessness, or perhaps a confusion of interests. It also shows that the writer has been influenced by the death of one or more persons. Since Jeni had presumably passed away, it might be possible that she was the influence referred to in the handwriting. This influence is shown by an 'X,' which occurs frequently in the Jeni sample but not in the MB1 sample. Your speculation of what this means is probably as good as mine, but it certainly is fascinating.

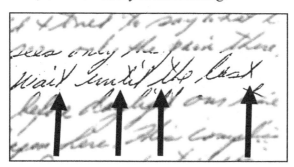

Notice how the "t's" in this "Jeni" letter form "X's," indicating that the writer has been influenced by the death of someone.

95

"If you believe in such things as energy fields, which is the underpinning of energy healing techniques such as Reiki and Qigong, another explanation for the Jeni ghost image that Marlon saw and his 'spirit writing' is that it may be possible for energy to be transferred from one personality to another. In this case, perhaps there was some type of energy transfer between Elvis, Marlon and Jeni. Could it be that when a problem reaches a certain size some of the energy left behind by a deceased party can materialize or communicate, possibly to provide hope to those remaining? Maybe this is just an explanation for how 'channeling' might work. It's certainly not something that Graphoanalysis or psychology can comment on directly."

"The letters portray Elvis and Marlon as close friends who looked out for each other," I said. "Do you see signs of compatibility in the handwriting of these two men?"

Jane replied, "In Graphoanalysis, compatibility is defined by the degree of similarity of personalities. In my experience it would be hard to find two personalities, each of which have such pronounced willfulness and need to control their own lives, that are so alike as Elvis's and Marlon's. When they were listening to each other, I can imagine they had a tremendous trust and bond working for them. But when they were both in a controlling mode, I can imagine the sparks flying and frustration roiling."

Jane pulled out the letters written by Tom Jones that I had given her for analysis. "Based on the principles of Graphoanalysis, the extraordinary handwriting of Tom Jones shows a man of immense emotional and physical energy and a compassionate nature, though he exhibits a bit less interest in caring for others than Elvis, Marlon and Harry."

I mentioned that Tom's exuberant handwriting had brought up an interesting issue. My publisher, who was born and raised in the UK, had joked that Jones would have had the tar beaten out of him at school for writing like that, and worried that the way Tom formed some of his letters made him skeptical as to whether or not the writer had been taught handwriting in a British school.

From my mother I had learned that the handwriting method by which one learns to write is almost immediately personalized by the writer's personality, otherwise everyone's writing would look exactly like the letter forms that are taught. Over time, a person's writing departs even more from the learned method of writing, due to cultural and other influences. Commenting on BBC Radio Oxford, graphologist Gill Beale said, "The words that are written on the page are irrelevant to the analysis and the graphologist cannot tell age, gender, nationality, or occupation of the writer." He could have added that handwriting also cannot reveal weight, sex, handedness or future events.

In responding to my publisher's concern, Jane said, "Handwriting analysis actually shows how we deviate from the way we're taught to write. This is why a person who has perfect script—in other words, handwriting that is very close to the taught appearance of letters—can be a bit dull. Such writing is often found in persons on the low side of the intelligence scale.

"Graphoanalysis takes into account the more 'gestalt' or holistic traits apparent in the writing, and this analysis shows that Tom is in some ways very much unlike his countrymen. Culturally, many people in the UK tend to be more restrained, 'held back' in their emotions, less likely to be demonstrative. Tom is not like this at all, which may be why he enjoyed living in the US.

"I would guess that he was incredibly impressed by Elvis's success and theatrical performances, which may have spurred Tom on to even greater theatricality in his own shows. Tom's writing exposes a willingness to do whatever is necessary to be close to successful people like Elvis with the purpose of emulating behavior and personality. He has a bit of 'I'll copy someone to make myself look better' in him. It doesn't surprise me that his handwriting shows a departure from British influence and a degree of Americanization in a cultural sense. His writing certainly is eccentric to an extreme.

"But there is more to him than this. Tom sets high goals for himself and has great persistence, refusing to give up even when most people would and resenting anyone who gets in his way. He doesn't forget or forgive easily.

Resentment is displayed in Tom's handwriting by a straight stroke that precedes a letter that does not need one, as in these two "w's."

"He often looks at what had worked in the past for guidance and shows an ability to learn from previous mistakes. The abnormally long t-bars in his writing vigorously display contagious enthusiasm. Coupled with his high confidence and self-reliance, he could be practically unstoppable in accomplishing whatever he set his mind on.

Tom's exuberant, contagious enthusiasm is visible in the long t-bars that sometimes connect several t-stems, even multiple words.

"Too often, perhaps, Tom rationalizes what he does. This means that he contrives arguments to mislead himself about certain actions so that he can feel good about how he operates in life.

Rationalization is displayed in Tom's writing by letters that begin with an opening loop.

"Tom is generally open to listening to others and has a desire to learn more about philosophy, spirituality and other more abstract concepts, but not as much as his friends Elvis and Harry. He loves the challenge of a good debate but doesn't have the quick perception or keen comprehension of a fast-paced thinker like Harry Belafonte. When confronted with serious issues, he usually thinks about them deeply.

"His handwriting shows some generosity, but in Tom's case generosity may be a means of gaining positive attention for himself.

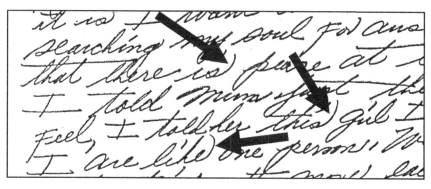

Long ending strokes show a generous nature. When ending strokes are overdone, like the ones in Tom's handwriting, it means that the writer wants to be seen by others as generous, in Tom's case perhaps to appear generous like Elvis.

"Tom sometimes takes on responsibilities other than the usual demands of his career, but usually doesn't like doing it and can develop resentment about it. At the time he wrote the letters I analyzed, Tom's handwriting showed that he felt some responsibility for his mother, Freda, who raised him and his sister. As long as Freda continued to encourage her son, he would probably feel fine about this responsibility, otherwise it is likely he'd resent her and feel worn down by it.

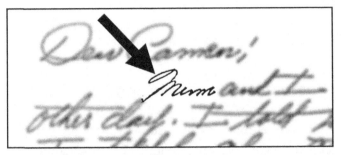

The opening loop in the word "Mum" is called a responsibility loop. As it mainly shows up in references to his mother, it shows he feels some responsibility for her.

"Interestingly, Tom's handwriting shows that he has grown beyond parental influence. Graphoanalysis maintains that when the usual loops in the capital "I," which represent imagination, are replaced by straight strokes, it means the writer has made peace with the influence of his parents. This may be due to the writer's rejection of poor parenting or a decision to go a different direction in life, usually with parental encouragement.

The stick-figure personal pronoun "I," which is devoid of any loops, displays a nearly total lack of parental influence in Tom.

"I can imagine that Tom very much wanted to be in this group of high-achievers, especially when he was getting started. He contributed a generally upbeat nature to a circle of friends that had plenty of downbeat moments."

Carmen Montez

We have only one letter by Carmen Montez. She wrote it to Carmen Rayburn in March 1980. I gave it to Jane Hollis and asked her what she could tell me about Montez.

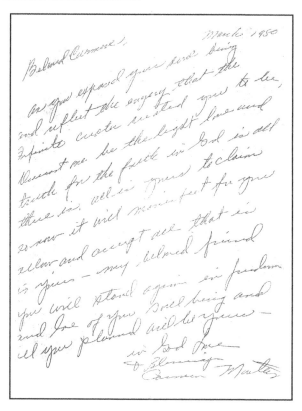

In 1980, during their attempt to collaborate on a book, Carmen Montez wrote this letter of encouragement to her best friend, Carmen Rayburn.

"In this letter," Hollis said, "we see a radical, upward slope to the lines of writing, which usually shows an abundance of optimism, a useful trait in her line of work. In this case, because of the extreme slope of Carmen's writing, I immediately suspected that this high degree of optimism might be more of a forced frame of mind that she has mentally built up as a coping mechanism to help her deal with life and difficult interactions with others. Using Graphoanalysis

I was able to investigate how other discoverable traits may have influenced her optimism.

"I immediately noticed a peculiar pattern of marks that indicated Carmen may have been troubled by a physical defect or injury in a lower leg, probably the right one, resulting in a limp. This is suggested by a number of tiny blobs in her lower loops—too many of them identically placed to be coincidental or merely a flaw of her pen or the ink.

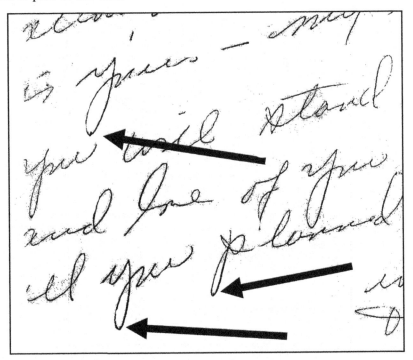

Tiny blobs at the bottom of lower loops, which are more apparent
when using a magnifying glass, can indicate a leg defect or injury,
or a close connection to someone who has such a condition, when
other supportive strokes are also found in the writing sample, such as
in the example below.

Further evidence of a lower leg defect can be seen in the unusual
space made by the pen "skipping" on the upstroke of the lower loops
as highlighted by the arrows.

"Research into the relationship between certain handwriting strokes and medical conditions is limited but ongoing, chiefly by neurologists, so it's also possible that Carmen herself did not have such a condition but empathized so deeply with someone who did—perhaps a close friend or relative—that she took on the psychological characteristics that person had acquired due to the medical condition.

When the second hump in an "m" is higher than the first, it reveals
self-consciousness.

"Surprisingly, Carmen shows quite a lot of self-consciousness, perhaps because of that leg problem. Self-consciousness can stick with a person long after a physical ailment is fixed. This makes her overly sensitive to personal criticism.

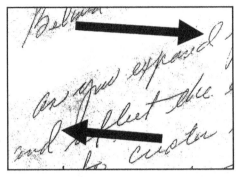

Wide loops on the d-stems indicate sensitivity to personal criticism.

"Self-consciousness could be a cause of Carmen's resentment about something or someone in her past. I wonder if someone teased her or bullied her over her leg defect. The effects of that kind of thing can linger for years, even for a lifetime. Oddly, she seems to resent more the way she has been forced to present an artificial self to others than any real emotional damage she may have suffered from teasing or bullying.

Resentment is shown by an inflexible, straight initial stroke that rises from the baseline as shown in this "y."

"Carmen shows an argumentative nature—she loves a good debate, and this undoubtedly has contributed to a strong competitive spirit. Carmen persistently compares herself to others and works to best them. She certainly could hold her own in any debate with Elvis, Harry, Tom or Marlon.

The stroke that completes the upper loop of the "p" and then turns back to the right to connect with the "l" is the "debating" stroke that identifies an argumentative nature.

"Carmen's strongly developed persistence adds strength to her arguments and competitiveness. At times she can be unrelenting in pressing her point of view.

The triangular "tie" stroke in this "s" (looks like a figure 8) indicates the persistence trait.

"Tempering her competitiveness, however, Carmen also reveals a great deal of self-castigation. This causes her to feel unworthy of happiness or success.

A t-bar that appears as a "stabbing" arrow pointing to the left demonstrates self-castigation.

"On one hand, self-castigation can be a bid for attention. On the other hand, it can cause self-destructive behaviors. It's a coin with two sides—self-blame and self-punishment. With Carmen, the reason for this is unclear. It could be that she believes she is often doing something intentionally wrong. Or it could be that others close to her, even in her childhood, have caused her to believe she didn't 'belong' or was 'bad' in some way."

"Since this letter to Carmen Rayburn was written in 1980," I interjected, "and at that time she was working with her friend on a project to publicize Elvis's personal letters to her, maybe she was feeling some remorse at betraying that confidence. This would be fresh in her mind."

"That's a great point. Through her handwriting Carmen tries to put up an argument for her 'goodness' and her optimism in the future of herself and humanity. This could be a defense against doing something that seemed 'bad.' It may have been inevitable that she turned to religion as a support.

"Her religious training and spiritual instincts may have contributed to her generous nature. She would do almost anything to help someone in need.

The overlong final strokes in "yours" and "you," both of which end above the preceding letters, reveal Carmen's generosity.

"Her outward persona is one of a spiritual person who is open and accepting. This is reinforced by a highly empathic nature. She can immediately sense a person's emotions and provide just the right support. But rather than ministering with a carefully planned and rational approach, Carmen often responds out of desperation with uncalculated acts of coaxing optimism from despair or implanting hopeful thoughts. Such tactics may not provide long-term solutions but can provide important first aid to a hopeless soul.

"Carmen sincerely believed that everything would eventually turn out well even when there were no objective reasons. No wonder Elvis and the others bared their souls to her and sought answers to their difficult questions. Perhaps Carmen learned to use the coping skills she developed at an early age as a 'lifesaver' for others such as Elvis, who credited her with saving his life when he was contemplating suicide."

Girls! Girls! Girls!

Much has been written about Elvis's relationships with women—his flirtations, his affairs, his loves. Certainly, his mother Gladys was the love of his life, and as Elvis told Carmen many times, he never met a woman who measured up to his mother, with one exception.

On one hot summer day, my tabloid sensibilities got the best of me. During a long interview with Carmen Rayburn, I asked if her best friend, Carmen Montez, had mentioned two of Elvis's most famous affairs.

"For Elvis, Nancy Sinatra was a pest with a big stinger, like a bee at a picnic," Carmen told me. "And Ann-Margret was one of his biggest disappointments because she had touched him very deeply—and then double-crossed him, at least in his eyes. He spent a lot of time talking to Carmen [Montez] about those two."

This chapter includes information revealed by Carmen Montez that is corroborated by interviews with Rayburn and letters authored by Elvis, Marlon Brando and Tom Jones. In some cases, these male friends shared stories with Montez that Elvis had told them but had not told Montez for reasons I don't always understand. Elvis had sensitivities that are hard to fathom at times. Some information may have been too sensitive for him to share with his female confidante until after he'd processed it by sharing with his closest male buddies. In one case he failed to communicate deeply personal information to Carmen for six months after an emotional event. Was he trying to protect his image with Carmen? I don't think so; he confessed to her some extremely unflattering things about himself. Did his issues with women throttle or distort his relationship with Carmen in ways that are hard to detect? Possibly, but his letters show an earnestness to share feelings—*most* feelings, anyway—with his spiritual advisor. There were always a few things, though, that he kept locked up, and even his confessional letters may not give us the full story.

* * *

In a retelling of commonly known history, Nancy Sinatra was born in 1940, the daughter of a teen idol from a previous generation. A teenager herself, she had avidly followed the career of Elvis. As a celebrity offspring, she had maneuvered herself into a relationship with him before he was drafted on March 24, 1958. When he was sent to Germany, she waited impatiently for his return.

Unfortunately for Nancy, soon after arriving in Germany Elvis met a pretty American girl named Priscilla Beaulieu at a party. Priscilla, who was fourteen years old, was the adopted daughter of Joseph Beaulieu, a US Air Force captain stationed in Germany. As Elvis's relationship with Priscilla deepened, Priscilla started reading about her suitor's romantic entanglement with Nancy Sinatra in the United States. Back home, Nancy Sinatra was reading with dismay about Elvis's crush on a little girl in Germany.

Two years later, Elvis's tour of duty ended. At eight a.m. on March 3, 1960, Elvis and seventy-four other returning GIs landed in a snowstorm at McGuire Air Force Base in New Jersey. Among the soldiers disembarking from the MATS C-118 transport aircraft were Elvis, Alex Moore, and Rex Mansfield, who all had been drafted together. As Elvis stepped off the plane he was still trying to shake off the grogginess induced by sleeping pills he had taken to relieve his fear of flying.

At nearby Fort Dix, Elvis received $147 in mustering out pay and then dashed for a limousine chased by a half-dozen teenage girls. His soldier buddies yelled and hooted as he tried to escape the clutches of these aggressive females. His next stop was a two-hour press conference where he would face dozens of reporters and photographers. He did not yet know it, but he would also face one of the most aggressive women he would ever know, his old girlfriend Nancy Sinatra.

Priscilla had captured Elvis's heart, but for years to come Nancy would fight for it.

The press conference at Fort Dix had its share of celebrity greeters. Actress Tina Louise represented a New York radio station. Nancy Sinatra gave Elvis two lace-front shirts, telling him, "These are from my father." But Nancy was there for a greater purpose than to be Frank Sinatra's emissary. She wanted Elvis, and for a few weeks she believed she was winning him away from Priscilla.

Elvis and Nancy saw a lot of each other as Elvis prepared for his appearance on the Frank Sinatra-Timex Special *Welcome Home Elvis,* which was taped at the Fontainebleau Hotel in Miami on March 26 for airing six weeks later on ABC. The newspapers and tabloids went gaga over the famous couple.

In her book, *Elvis and Me*, Priscilla recalled the press coverage of her sweetheart and Nancy Sinatra. "Days passed into weeks," she wrote, "and I became more and more resigned to the fact that Elvis was now dating Nancy Sinatra and had completely forgotten me."

In the end, Nancy didn't get Elvis. Instead, Elvis invited Priscilla to spend Christmas with him at Graceland that year. In 1962, he persuaded Captain Beaulieu to let Priscilla come to America to live with him and his family in what is certainly one of the most bizarre courtships ever (with the possible exception of Elvis's daughter, Lisa Marie, and Michael Jackson). In 1963, Priscilla graduated from Memphis High School.

During her early days at Graceland, Priscilla continued to be troubled by rumors about Elvis and Nancy. Elvis truthfully explained to her that, as far as he was concerned, he and Nancy were just good friends. He was certainly not speaking for Nancy.

After Priscilla and Elvis were married in 1967, Frank Sinatra loaned his private Lear Jet to bring the couple from Las Vegas to

Palm Springs for their honeymoon. Priscilla immediately became pregnant with Lisa Marie. Then, as Elvis and Nancy began shooting the movie *Speedway* in June, rumors about Elvis and Nancy resumed in the papers. Many writers have now said that the romance between Elvis and Nancy had cooled by this time, and the two had merely become friends, which may have been true for Elvis, but not for Nancy.

Elvis and Priscilla Presley on their wedding day May 1,1967.

Elvis, however, was increasingly fearful of the heavy-handed tactics of Frank Sinatra and his mob connections. In a letter, he told Montez that he didn't want any dalliance with Nancy because toying with Frank's daughter seemed like playing with fire.

For Nancy, however, Elvis's marriage seemed to rekindle her passion and kick it into high gear. Elvis must have suspected that as a married man he was an even juicier target.

After failing to land Elvis years earlier, Nancy had settled for an Elvis clone. She married Tommy Sands, a singer who had been managed during his teen years by Colonel Parker, Elvis's manager. Sands and Elvis had performed together on New Year's Day, 1955 in

Houston and then had toured together on the "Louisiana Hayride." In 1957, Sands played a character loosely based on Elvis in *The Singing Idol*. The program aired on NBC as a Kraft Television Theatre special on January 30, 1957. For a time, Tommy Sands must have seemed to be the closest thing to Elvis that Nancy would ever have. But the marriage didn't last, and the two were divorced before *Speedway* began filming.

Newly single, Nancy seemed particularly vulnerable to the charms of her leading man during production. Elvis biographer Albert Goldman chronicled how Elvis and Nancy would "play games" in her dressing trailer. Some of these games were innocent pranks. For example, Elvis would mess up Nancy's hair and clothes to make it appear they'd been "intimate" when they left the trailer. Sometimes, though, Goldman claimed the gameplaying went further with the couple "dry humping" and verbally teasing each other. Near the end of shooting, Nancy recalled one occasion when she was standing in her dressing trailer in jeans and bra when Elvis suddenly burst out of the closet to surprise her. Nancy told Goldman that Elvis grabbed her and held her close. According to her account in *Elvis*:

> He just held me. He held me very quietly, very closely to him, and he lifted up my face and he kissed me and I started to melt. I really thought I was going to die. Then he pulled away and looked at me and said: "I'm sorry... I'm sorry." And he went out.

Elvis would come to regret his teasing and gameplaying. Nancy would find it hard to forget. While she would later tell Goldman that she didn't want to succumb to Elvis's temptations so long as he was married, Elvis and Marlon Brando painted quite a different picture for Carmen Montez.

Six months into Priscilla's pregnancy, after the filming of *Speedway*, Nancy inexplicably called Priscilla and offered to throw a baby shower. Priscilla was bewildered. Elvis took Nancy's gesture as a hopeful sign that she was willing to call a truce. Judging from

Nancy's later actions, it is more likely that she simply wanted a close-up look at the competition. In her account of Nancy's offer, Priscilla wrote:

> I didn't know her that well and thought it was a little strange that she was so accommodating. But Elvis assured me that she was very nice and that I should get to know her.

In truth, Elvis hoped that if a friendship developed between Nancy and Priscilla, it might cool Nancy's increasingly obsessive behavior toward him. Priscilla eventually agreed to the shower. In her book she wrote:

> It turned out quite nicely. Nancy was very friendly and very supportive. I found that I liked her and I decided to ignore the rumors.

The shower went well, and Priscilla eventually gave birth to Lisa Marie. Nancy, however didn't cool off—she became even more aggressive toward Elvis. As he explained to Carmen in a letter uncorroborated by other sources, he wasn't in love with Nancy, not even particularly attracted to her. She was too skinny for his tastes, too flip and aggressive; suitable as a playmate, apparently, but not one to be serious about.

Shortly after Lisa Marie was born, Elvis wrote to Carmen that he believed Priscilla had been unfaithful. Elvis never told Carmen who the suspected male partner was, but Elvis explained that he had grown extremely disillusioned with his young wife. He communicated in writing his feeling of torment and complained that Nancy Sinatra was "all over me."

In one of her conversations with Rayburn, Carmen Montez shared that she had written back to Elvis about this matter advising him to handle Nancy diplomatically. Clearly, Carmen understood Frank's reputation for protecting what he considered *his*. Carmen was also concerned that Elvis would use Priscilla's infidelity as an excuse to be unfaithful himself, so she set up a telephone call with Elvis, which she described as best she could to Rayburn. In the call,

Elvis tried to explain that no one could handle Nancy Sinatra and be diplomatic at the same time. Carmen asked if knowing that his wife had been untrue justified his having an affair. Elvis said that he was personally at odds with current moral standards and couldn't agree with some of his buddies that Priscilla's wrong could make it all right for him to do the same thing. The following dialogue is taken from Rayburn's recollection and supported by an Elvis letter which also describes Carmen's phone call in great detail.

"Nancy and I have been friends for a long time," he told Carmen. "I want her off my back, but I don't want to hurt her feelings."

"Maybe you have to remind her you're married and that means something to you," Carmen explained.

"She just says I'm too old-fashioned."

"What are you going to do?"

"I've thought about telling her that I'm homosexual. But knowing Nancy, she'd probably just tell me that she knows how to 'straighten me out.' About all I can think to do is to inconvenience her."

From the same Elvis letter I learned that he regretted his choice of playmates. He'd come to believe that Nancy was particularly dangerous—and not just because of her aggressiveness. He was clearly afraid of making enemies, "especially ones in the Mafia," he wrote, obviously reflecting on Frank Sinatra's mob ties. On one occasion, Elvis tried inconveniencing Nancy by hiding out at Marlon Brando's house.

As Marlon remarked in a letter to Carmen, he believed Nancy had missed her calling. She had the skills of a private eye. Nancy had tracked Elvis down and barged into Marlon's home, cornering her man while he was reading in bed. Marlon left the couple alone, but a few minutes later, Marlon heard a commotion and checked Elvis's room to make sure his friend was all right. He was amazed at what he saw. Nancy had gotten Elvis's pajamas off and had backed him into the shower, water and steam everywhere. Elvis was yelling to get out because the water was too hot, so Nancy turned on the cold water. Elvis kept yelling. Nancy was soaked and laughing.

114

Then the doorbell rang. It was one of Frank Sinatra's cronies who had been ordered to find Nancy. He had spotted her car outside Brando's house. Was she there?

A 1971 publicity photo of Nancy Sinatra.

Marlon invited the man in and went back to the room where Elvis and Nancy were out of the shower. Nancy became frightened when Marlon explained who was looking for her.

"You've got to get me out of here or my dad will kill me," she said, knowing that Frank was adamantly opposed to her having a relationship with Elvis.

"You're lucky *I* won't kill you," Marlon told her.

Nancy frantically dressed and went out the back door, her hair still dripping wet. Elvis blushed as Marlon gazed at him, then simply said, "After this I can face anything."

Nancy survived the incident without Marlon killing her.

For all his complaining about Nancy, Elvis would turn to her during one of his most difficult times.

* * *

In 1969, Elvis was again on the charts after years of mediocre songs and record sales. Colonel Parker, who had been flushing Elvis's career into the sewer with a succession of truly awful movies, penned a contract that had the entertainment business buzzing again. Elvis was going to headline a month of concerts at the soon-to-be-completed International Hotel in Las Vegas for a salary of a half million dollars. Parker somehow had convinced hotel management that the market for an Elvis comeback was immense, and the star's long absence from Vegas could only have stoked the public's appetite for an Elvis extravaganza.

Elvis was both thrilled and terrified. He felt anxious about performing again before an audience—he had not sung live anywhere in nine years. Las Vegas was the only city where he had bombed. That disaster was in 1956, thirteen years earlier, but the fear of that fiasco still haunted him.

The pressures were severe. The expectations for his show were proportionate to the unprecedented fee that he had commanded. In correspondence with his "Dear Sis," it was clear that he was doubtful his voice would undergo the strain of a long, uninterrupted concert every night. He was agonizingly apprehensive about whether or not he could still draw a crowd. He worried about everything, from his hair and costumes to the songs and choreography.

Deciding to take no chances, he handpicked the top sidemen in the music business and brought on board his favorite gospel group, the Imperial Quartet. Still, the personal strain was intense. During rehearsals he would sometimes explode, lashing out at everyone within earshot.

In Las Vegas, the 1969 Elvis show was becoming summer's big event. The city buzzed with excitement. Everywhere there were billboards, signs, news articles. The lobby of the International Hotel was taken over by Elvis paraphernalia—posters, T-shirts, records, balloons.

At last opening night came. The show was a knock-out success, and thousands of people were turned away night after night. In short, Elvis had conquered Las Vegas. The next day, an ecstatic International Hotel signed a five-year contract for Elvis to perform twice each year for one million dollars per year. A contract of that magnitude was unparalleled in 1969.

Elvis invited Carmen Montez to attend one of the concerts in secret, fearing that if Priscilla found out about Carmen she would misunderstand and fly into a jealous rage. I have not discovered the specific show Carmen attended, but that year she finally saw Elvis perform live for the first time.

Despite his success, Elvis continued to feel immense stress, and Montez grew very concerned for him. To many he seemed more confident and fit than ever. Inwardly, however, as revealed by his letters to Carmen, he continued to bottle up the frustration of his personal life, his disillusionment with Priscilla and the impossible strain of worrying about how he would sustain his momentum. A peculiar and cancerous insecurity began to overtake him. At times he felt like a fraud who would soon be found out. In his letters, he frequently asked Carmen for honest criticism of his songs and his movies. She obliged. Few around him knew the toll that these concerts were taking on him. The harder he tried to appear confident and in control, the weaker he felt.

Elvis barely made it through the last triumphant performance of the summer series on August 28, 1969. A few days later he collapsed and was placed in the hospital under a pseudonym, disappearing for several days. These facts were covered up, of course, which was not difficult since the month of shows had ended, and everyone expected Elvis to disappear for a while.

In early September, Elvis finally wrote Carmen a letter containing a remarkable tale of what had happened during those days after his collapse. According to Elvis, he remembered almost nothing after receiving a message from Carmen that she would be attending one of the shows during the last week of concerts. The rest was a blur. He remembered waking up at last in a hospital with a mass of people in white coats around him. Every few minutes, it seemed, a nurse would approach to insert a long needle into a muscle. The colonel was present in the room and explained to Elvis that he had been refusing to eat, and the medical team was trying to provide nourishment intravenously. He said Elvis had been fighting the needle and ripping it out, so they had finally restrained him. To his muddled way of thinking, Elvis believed he'd been put into a straitjacket.

Somehow, Elvis fled the hospital—he could not remember how—and went to Nancy Sinatra's room in the International Hotel where she was performing. He woke her up at five in the morning begging her to hide him. Three days later he woke up while she was shaving his beard. He had no recollection of how he had gotten there.

The hazy memories of needles and straitjackets had thrust Elvis into a state of paranoia. He just wanted to hide until he could piece things together, so he coerced Nancy into driving him to her home in Los Angeles on Friday night after her last show. He stayed there while she returned to Las Vegas, promising to check on him Sunday.

After Nancy left, Elvis reconsidered waiting for her to return. She had teased him unmercifully about being unusually amorous during his three days with her at the International Hotel. She painted vivid pictures of their exploits, but he remembered none of them. Waiting for her return seemed suddenly unwise.

Through means he could not recall, Elvis made it to Marlon's home. Marlon had guests, so Elvis hid for a time in the garage. Later, Marlon and his guests departed. The house was locked, but Elvis found an unlocked window and climbed through, making it to a bed. He knew that Marlon would take care of him.

This story as related to Carmen by Elvis and partially corroborated by a letter from Marlon seems far-fetched. After reading it the first time, I thought parts of it must be a delusion. There was so much blacking out and memory loss and weird imagery. Marlon confirmed that his friend had collapsed after his last show—the rest is Elvis's disjointed recollections of these missing days. Knowing that he was confused and disconnected from reality at least for parts of this episode, I can't believe that every detail of his story is accurate. But Elvis certainly went through an unpublicized collapse and was assisted in some way by his old friend Nancy Sinatra. We know from Marlon's letters that he showed up suddenly at Marlon's house and was taken in. The rest may be the roiling fog of his breakdown. But even if reduced to a series of hallucinations, it demonstrates the disturbed and paranoid state of his mind following the exhausting summer concerts of 1969.

* * *

Ann-Margret was the flip side of Nancy Sinatra. For a time, Elvis was genuinely crazy about her.

Discovered by comedian George Burns, Ann-Margret Olsson had made her movie debut in the 1961 movie *Pocketful of Miracles*. She was a classy lady full of talent and personality. She could sing and dance and act. She was sexy, sultry, charming and flirtatious. Before long she was dubbed "the female Elvis Presley."

In 1963, she performed in the movie *Bye Bye Birdie*, the tale of a singer loosely based on Elvis. Then she scored the real thing, a co-starring role opposite The King himself in the 1964 film *Viva Las Vegas*. To watch Ann-Margret and Elvis acting together in this film is to see real chemistry at work. Ann-Margret became the only true romance of Elvis's many dating relationships with movie stars.

At this time, of course, Priscilla was still growing up in the Presley household. This made Elvis's fascination with his co-star awkward, but he was too smitten with Ann-Margret to be smart. He would disappear for a day or two to be with her. It soon became clear to everyone that the relationship between those two was more than a tiny affair. In truth, Ann-Margret was a confident, sweet, genuine person who drew out Elvis's best attributes. But Elvis was also frightened by her independence, her dedication to her career, and his own vulnerability. His feelings for her became a wrestling match. Inevitably, Ann-Margret stepped over the line by telling the press that she and Elvis were going steady, and that he had given her a round pink bed as a gift. This public bragging was more than Elvis could bear, even though the articles had the imprint of studio publicity all over them. His insecurity caused him to opt for the little girl he believed he could control, Priscilla.

1968 promotional photo of Ann-Margret.

Elvis suddenly broke off the relationship. Ann-Margret was stunned and hurt. Later, Elvis told Carmen that making *Viva Las Vegas* was a bewildering time and that he intensely disliked everything to do with Ann-Margret. He said that Ann-Margret had treated him shabbily, and he could never understand why he had developed such an attraction to her.

As Carmen Montez told Carmen Rayburn, however, "Elvis never convinced me that he despised Ann-Margret. I think he knew he had made his choice, and there was no going back."

* * *

Elvis dated a lot of women, many of them stars or starlets. Most of them he only saw a few times. It's interesting to know which of these "relationships" he remembered most fondly. Certainly Ann-Margret had a left her mark on him, and Nancy Sinatra had scratched in her share of Elvis's memories, but it was a young actress named Annette Day whom Elvis would remember with genuine affection.

Annette Day debuted as a film actress in the co-starring role of Jillian Conway in the Elvis movie *Double Trouble*. Incidentally, many celebrities made their acting debut in Elvis movies, including Raquel Welch in *Roustabout* and Ed Asner in *Kid Galahad*. Producer Judd Bernard had discovered Annette in a London antique shop on Portobello Road where she worked for her father who owned the store. Annette had never acted before, not even in school stage productions. Bernard was first struck by her red-haired, blue-eyed good looks and charming manner. As it turned out, her sweetness was genuine.

In late September 1968, Elvis noticed that *Double Trouble* was going to be on TV. The movie brought back pleasant memories because of his co-star, Annette Day. In a letter he urged Carmen to watch the movie, then revealed his feelings for Annette.

Elvis explained that while shooting the movie, Annette and he had spent most of their off-time together and had grown very fond of each other. As Elvis explained to Carmen, "Not love, but a loving friendship." He admitted that Annette was not the most beautiful girl or the most talented, but he was touched by her genuinely sweet nature and thoughtfulness. She would do nice little things for him. Once she knit him socks, which touched him deeply. Another time she baked him a birthday cake that turned out lopsided and needed stilts to hold up one side, but Elvis thought it was amazing that she had personally baked the cake. He confessed that most of the girls he had known would never have bothered to do the little things that were so important to him. Annette, he told Carmen, really understood him, and this made her the kind of woman that he had searched for most of his life—an *understanding* woman.

* * *

Not all women he confronted were so gentle. In one humorous incident, Elvis was recovering from a particularly traumatic incident at Marlon Brando's home. Marlon's wife, Movita, brought home an acquaintance named Tondelayo, a striking chorus dancer who was half Spanish and half Russian, had been born and raised in Tahiti, and spoke French with a little Spanish stirred in. Because she looked like a Native American, Tondelayo had been a dancer in the Elvis western *Stay Away Joe*. When Tondelayo came into the living room and saw Elvis sleeping on Marlon's sofa, her eyes grew as big as softballs. She ran to the sofa and began kissing him with Tahitian enthusiasm. Elvis woke with a start, then laughed.

Movita called for Marlon, who was making tea in the kitchen, to come and break things up. When he entered the living room, Tondelayo was sitting on top of Elvis with her hands latching his hair. She wouldn't let go. She had managed to get his shirt unbuttoned to his waist. Elvis was yelling, "How do you turn her off?"

Marlon replied, "Try French!"

Elvis didn't know any.

"Try Spanish!" Marlon suggested. The only Spanish Elvis knew was *Sí, sí*, which didn't help.

"That gal didn't care where she was or who was there," Marlon told Carmen in a letter. He finally got her detached from Elvis, who had probably decided he should learn a second language.

* * *

During the 1968 filming of the movie *Charro!*, Elvis's co-star Lynn Kellogg often made him uncomfortable by rubbing provocatively against him and whispering obscene suggestions in his ear during love scenes. She was beautiful, but too much of a flirt—not Elvis's type at all. Besides playing up to Elvis, she openly toyed with the guys attending him too.

Marlon was on the set during the shooting of the *Charro!* dance hall scene and reported to Carmen that during a break, the "Kellogg girl" took off her red scarf, hung it around the neck of Joe Esposito, Elvis's good friend and secretary, and "just played up to Joe." Both Elvis and Joe were embarrassed.

On another day, according to Marlon, he met Elvis for lunch at the MGM Culver City studio where interiors for *Charro!* were being filmed. Elvis suggested they make sandwiches in his dressing room, a private trailer on the studio lot parked with its back window lined up almost perfectly with Lynn Kellogg's dressing room window. While Elvis made sandwiches, Marlon looked through the trailer's back window into Kellogg's dressing room. "Elvis," he said, "did you know that Kellogg girl is running around in her room stark naked?"

Elvis didn't look up, just kept making the sandwiches. "Yep, does that a lot." He finished making lunch and offered a sandwich to Marlon, then grabbed one and sat down with his back to the window. "Trouble is," he said, "my Venetian blind is stuck."

That afternoon, Marlon watched the filming of a scene in which Elvis had to lie close to Kellogg while she tenderly ran her fingers through his hair. Elvis had some simple dialogue to deliver, but he kept muffing his lines and flushing with embarrassment. Marlon assumed Elvis was trying too hard to impress his world-class actor friend. After nine takes, Elvis got through his lines. The director yelled, "Cut—and print!" Despite this eventual success, Elvis looked disappointed. When Marlon asked what was wrong, Elvis said, "Lynn is one of my leading ladies, so I have to be a gentleman with her. But it's tough to focus on your lines when someone is running their fingers up and down your spine."

* * *

123

The true love of Elvis's life—aside from his mother—was not Priscilla, Ann-Margret, Annette Day or any other starlet that he dated. There was one young woman who haunted Elvis throughout much of his life but to this day remains a mysterious figure. We can know her only by fleeting comments about her that Elvis wrote to Carmen. As far as I know, his feelings about her were so deep and personal he never mentioned this mystery woman to anyone but Carmen and Marlon.

Her name was Jeni Pearson. Here is everything we know about her, all of it revealed in letters by Elvis and Marlon.

Elvis first mentioned Jeni to Carmen after he had come across a magazine photo of them together. Eventually, Elvis sent the magazine to Carmen so she could see what Jeni looked like. Carmen Montez explained to Rayburn that Elvis had allowed her to keep the magazine, though it was not among the items Rayburn purchased from Carmen's estate. The accompanying article was one of those "happy couples in love" pieces about Elvis and Priscilla. Ironically, the magazine had mistakenly included the photo of Jeni Pearson, calling her "Priscilla" in the caption. Apparently, the magazine had obtained the photograph from a Memphis source and attached the caption without any fact-checking, which was a big mistake because Jeni and Priscilla did not look anything alike.

Elvis also gave Carmen a shampoo ad that featured Jeni. We don't know if Jeni was from Mississippi or somewhere else, but Elvis had brought her to Hollywood to start a modeling career, which she eventually abandoned. Unfortunately, the shampoo ad was not in the suitcase Rayburn bought either. Elvis's last written words to Carmen about the image of Jeni in the ad were, "Take good care of her for me."

Jeni was the only woman whom Elvis ever referred to in the same breath as his cherished mother, Gladys. He told Carmen that these two were the only women who really understood him completely. In a letter to Carmen, Elvis said that during many of his haunted, sleepless nights, he would be comforted by memories of Jeni and his mother, sometimes sensing that they had actually "visited" him, even though Gladys had died, and Jeni had disappeared.

Elvis often grew melancholy as he spoke to Carmen about his happy times with Jeni. He vowed to find her again and possibly live with her. He called Jeni his "Dresden doll" and lamented about how he had not kept her on a pedestal where she deserved to be. As far as I know, he never revealed to Carmen the circumstances of his separation from Jeni or how she had vanished, but he told Carmen she was the one woman he believed he could have had a lasting relationship with. Unfortunately, he had let her get away.

Elvis told Carmen that he had helped Don Robertson and Hal Keller Blair write the song "No More" as a message to Jeni early in their separation. The song was used in the movie *Blue Hawaii.* I don't know if Jeni ever got the message. He also claimed that he had helped write "Sylvia," a song he recorded on June 8, 1970, which is credited to composers Geoff Stephens and Barry Mason. The purpose in tweaking the "Sylvia" lyrics, according to Elvis, was to help flush out Jeni who had disappeared from his life. He hoped that she would respond to the title of the song, which was the name of a mutual friend. He expressed fear that if Jeni did not respond it might mean that she had died. For Elvis, the memory of Jeni grew even more vivid as time passed.

Elvis's comparisons of Priscilla to Jeni never flattered Priscilla. On one warm July evening in 1970, Elvis told Carmen that he feared his life was growing short. He wondered aloud why he and Carmen had continued to grow so close when his relationships with other women were increasingly distant. He questioned why he had felt a special closeness to "Mama and Jeni" in previous weeks. Maybe, he thought, the three understanding women in his life—Gladys, Jeni and Carmen—were spiritually gathering around him to protect and guide him in his final days. He feared that Jeni had joined his mother in death and told Carmen he was overcome with peace when he realized that he might be with them in the near future.

For Elvis's friend, Marlon Brando, the specter of Jeni became manifest during a joint Christmas and going-away party in Elvis's new two-story Bel Air home. The event had been hastily organized for Priscilla's benefit—she was just weeks away from giving birth to Lisa Marie. The Presleys were going to Memphis for a few days because he had rented the Manhattan Club near Graceland to throw a New Year's Eve party for five hundred guests.

In a letter, Marlon explained to Carmen that Elvis was looking extremely tired and haggard that evening, "ready to crack up." Priscilla, who had taken to taunting Elvis with nasty names, had begun again early that night. For a while, Elvis simply took it, though Marlon suspected he was embarrassed by her antics. Finally reaching his limit of toleration, Elvis leaped on top of the piano and began performing a maneuver Brando called his "famous bedroom wiggle." In this obscenely defiant act, Elvis stood perfectly still yet seemed to tremble all over. A mocking smile drove the message home to Priscilla, Marlon wrote, and some of the women who watched seemed to be quivering even more than Elvis. Priscilla stormed out of the room. A few minutes later Marlon went into the den, where the coffee was located, to make a phone call. The room was empty, so he closed the door behind him. The line was busy, and he sat down in a large chair on the far end of the room to relax for a minute.

Behind him, the door opened. Two beautiful twin sisters entered without noticing him. Thinking the room was empty, they began chattering to themselves about their desire to "score big" with Elvis. Marlon remained out of view. As the sisters prattled away, Elvis entered, smiled benignly at the twins and poured two cups of coffee. As he picked up the steaming cups, the twins descended on him. One of them threw her arms around his neck. The other one unbuttoned his shirt and managed to get his fly unzipped as Elvis tried desperately not to scald them with hot coffee. "Cut it out now," he told them. "Act like ladies."

Suddenly Priscilla marched in, catching the women hanging on her husband. She launched a few well-aimed profanities, then spun and left the room. The twins fled. Elvis set down the cups and sank into a leather chair near the coffee table, head in hands. Marlon was tempted to speak up, to comfort Elvis somehow, but held back. As he watched his friend begin to cry, Marlon claims that an image of a woman appeared standing over Elvis, a woman in a blue dress.

At first Marlon was confused because he had not seen this woman enter—had not seen her at the party, in fact. Her head was bent very close to Elvis, and she looked as if she wanted to reach out and put her arms around him. But just then she looked up and saw Marlon watching her. As if telling him to stay hidden, she shook her head slowly, and after a few moments she disappeared.

Marlon knew instantly that the woman in the blue dress was Jeni. It was his first encounter with her, but not his last.

Jeni had apparently found an ally in Marlon. As he explained to Carmen, a short time after this incident Jeni began taking temporary possession of him. When writing to Carmen, Marlon occasionally would go into a trance after which he could remember nothing. But new words would have appeared. On reading the new passage written on the note paper in front of him, he would discover a message to Carmen, written in a different hand than his own and signed "Jeni."

Jeni's "spirit" passages always reflected keen insights into the problems and temperaments of the three musketeers—Elvis, Marlon, and Tom Jones. Jeni often gave advice, predicted future events, and expressed her love and concern. Marlon found these writing sessions very draining and sometimes alarming. The events mentioned in the letters often proved startlingly accurate. Just as Elvis had tried in his own secretive ways to communicate with Jeni, Marlon surmised that she may have found a way to respond.

I have closely examined the Brando letters containing these "spirit" passages, and I can't explain them. I also have no explanation for the eerie image of a woman in a blue dress that Marlon reports so vividly. Making sense of these images and messages from Jeni— the "spirit" passages objectively exist, and the handwriting has been analyzed—is a personal decision. Maybe Marlon and Elvis were delusional. Perhaps Marlon suffered from a psychotic break or a split personality. Possibly he was drunk the night of the Christmas party and dreamed of a ghost. Or maybe Jeni's spirit visited Elvis at the party and used Marlon as a channel for communicating to a circle of friends.

I can offer nothing more than the unusual testimony of Marlon to his confidante.

I do not know for sure, but I believe that Elvis was thinking about his mother on the day he died. He thought of her often. I strongly suspect that he was thinking of Jeni, too, because he told Carmen that not a day went by without the memory of Jeni haunting him. I wish I knew more about Jeni Pearson, a mysterious woman who must have loved very deeply to have had such a powerful and mesmerizing effect on Elvis and to have possessed another man whom she had never met.

Then again, maybe her story will surface now that we know her name.

Legal Quicksand

There is a reason why there are so few verbatim extracts from the Elvis letters in this book. The blame can be placed directly on Queen Anne. In 1710, the British Parliament passed the first statute that regulated copyright by the government and courts instead of by private parties, a watershed event in Anglo-American copyright history.

The long title of the statute is worthy of its own copyright: "An Act for the Encouragement of Learning, by Vesting the Copies of Printed Books in the Authors or Purchasers of such Copies, during the Times therein mentioned."

Since its passage, the statute many times has been replaced, amended, expanded and made more complicated, each time tightening the restrictions on the use of material from unpublished works. Today it is all but impossible to directly quote from personal letters that have not been published.

Let me share my frustration.

The preferred scenario for Carmen Rayburn and our team to make the content of these letters available to the public was simply to publish the letters, perhaps with an introduction and some explanatory context to help readers understand what they were reading. Fortunately, I made the decision to consult an intellectual property attorney. The attorney flatly said that such an act couldn't be legally done. In fact, that attorney and all the other attorneys consulted later, said that it was probably illegal to publish even a small extract from the letters.

Rayburn had originally believed that her ownership of the physical documents gave her the right to do whatever she wanted with that property, including publishing the content. But this belief was entirely wrong. It turns out that the owner of a physical document has the right to read it, display it, sell it to someone else, hide it, or even destroy it. But that owner cannot publish the words that comprise the content of that document.

This was succinctly stated in an opinion letter to Bill Mack from attorney Cherylyn D. Carr of the law firm Loeb and Loeb. Carr wrote:

> ...the author of a letter is the owner of the copyrighted material contained with the letter. Included in the exclusive rights under copyright is the right of first publication and, conversely, the right not to publish.

This legal fact brought our project to a sudden stop. Under the law, the author of any content that is written down by someone is automatically granted a copyright to that content. In other words, as Judge Pierre N. Leval, who ruled in a famous copyright case but was overruled on appeal, pointed out in his commentary "Toward a Fair Use Standard" published in *Harvard Law Review*:

> Copyright protection is available to very disparate categories of writings. If it be of original authorship, i.e., not copied from someone else, and recorded in a fixed medium, it is protected by the copyright. Thus, the great American novel, a report prepared as a duty of employment, a shopping list, or a loan shark's note on a debtor's door saying "Pay me by Friday or I'll break your goddamn arms" are all protected by the copyright.

Soon after the copyright was established by the Statute of Anne of 1710, courts began to agree that certain instances of unauthorized copying or "quoting" from copyrighted material—today called "fair use"—would not infringe authors' rights. The Copyright Act of 1976 states that "the fair use of a copyrighted work… is not an infringement of copyright."

Unfortunately, as Benjamin Moskowitz wrote in the *Intellectual Property, Media and Entertainment Law Journal* (yes, there is such a publication):

> The fair use doctrine is one of the most divisive issues in copyright law today. As Professor Neil Weinstock Netanel wrote, "Numerous commentators have lambasted the fair use doctrine as hopelessly unpredictable and indeterminate."

This makes any "fair use" of copyrighted material, such as quoting brief passages from the Elvis or Brando letters, a precarious decision for authors and publishers. As Judge Leval pointedly complained:

> Judges do not share a consensus on the meaning of fair use. Earlier decisions provide little basis for predicting later ones. Reversals and divided courts are commonplace. The opinions reflect widely differing notions of the meaning of fair use. Decisions are not governed by consistent principles but seem rather to result from intuitive reactions to individual fact patterns.

In other words, authors and publishers must use their best judgment about which quoted passages a future court will decide are legally copied under the amorphous "fair use" doctrine and then wait until they are sued to find out if they broke the law. Guessing wrong can be very expensive.

Bill Mack spent tens of thousands of dollars on legal opinions to guide us in legally using small portions of the Elvis letters in a book. He was repeatedly told that this area of law was undeveloped, unsettled, murky, and fraught with peril. Attorney Cherylyn Carr's advice in her opinion letter capsulizes the futility of getting meaningful legal advice in this divisive and rapidly evolving area. She wrote:

> For the time being, the guidance that can be given
> continues to be limited. One suggestion may be to
> remove any quotation of the letters whatsoever from
> the book.

Yes, that certainly would reduce the risk.

After careful study of the law, we also learned that "fair use" reproduction of small passages of copyrighted content was even more restricted for *unpublished* material, such as letters, than for *published* works, such as books, newspapers and magazines. In other words, it would be easier to justify quoting from *The Da Vinci Code* than from President Reagan's letter to Santa. This is because the copyright holder maintains the right to publish or not publish the copyrighted content.

If your book about Reagan quoted significantly from his letter to Santa, the value of subsequent publishing of the Reagan letter itself could be diminished, and you may be ordered to pay damages or pull your book from distribution if it had been published.

Since directly quoting portions of the letters seemed so perilous, I immediately thought we might be able to paraphrase passages and still communicate the facts and meaning. But even this seemed dangerous. In Wright v. Warner, a famous copyright case involving fair use of text quoted from letters by author Richard Wright, courts found some examples of paraphrased content justified as fair use, but other examples were declared as crossing the line. The following examples are confusing and fail to provide any meaningful guidance in understanding the difference.

These two comparisons between Wright's letter and a biographer's paraphrase were highlighted by the court as examples of acceptable fair use:

Example 1: Wright's letter

> I have had no word from the publisher, but I hope to
> before the week is out.

Biographer's acceptable paraphrase

In another letter Wright tells of the progression of his novel Native Son, saying he looked forward to hearing from the publisher within a week.

Example 2: Wright's letter

...fight for your rights as a creative writer or get out and function as best you can.

Biographer's acceptable paraphrase

...he told me to fight for my rights as a creative writer.

On the other hand, the following example cited by the appellate court was called unjustified under fair use:

Example 3: Wright's letter

Spoke with a Negro poet named Owen Dodson over the phone; he said that he had talked with two or three people who had read the galleys of BLACK BOY; he said that Dr. Locke said that he did not know why Wright dug up all that old stuff; that I had tossed away good writing... and that the book made him shiver a little. Well, he needs to shiver a little, life is cold.

Biographer's infringing paraphrase

In 1945, Wright talked with Owen Dodson about Black Boy. Dodson told Wright that Alain Locke said that Wright had thrown away good writing and could not see why Wright wouldn't just let things stay buried. According to Dodson, Locke said the book made him shiver. Wright's response was that life was cold.

It is difficult to see the difference between the two "acceptable" paraphrases and the one cited as infringing on copyright. One of our attorneys pointed out that the illegal example appeared to

133

focus more on the author's personal thoughts, ideas and manner of relating them while the two acceptable examples seemed mainly to report facts or events. Perhaps that was the difference. But other attorneys disagreed. The only thing clear is that the judge's rationale was unclear.

The courts have generally agreed that pure facts are not subject to copyright. An author is free to use historical facts referred to in a protected work without violating the copyright laws or relying on a fair use defense, but it is not always fathomable when an author has just used "facts." In some cases, the courts have muddied the waters even in this seemingly simple determination by declaring that some use of "facts" in a copyrighted work may merge with an author's unique expression of those facts to produce something called "borderline expression" that only a court can define as legal or illegal.

The Supreme Court stated in Harper & Row Publishers, Inc. v. Nation Enterprises that "the law is currently unsettled regarding the ways in which uncopyrightable elements combine with the author's original contributions to form protected expression."

It appears, then, that the courts have agreed on only one thing: there is no bright-line test for distinguishing between factual and non-factual elements in unpublished works. This means the existence of copyright infringement will continue to be decided on a case-by-case basis by judges who do not always agree with previous cases and often disagree with each other.

As attorney Cherylyn Carr advised Bill Mack, "The majority of cases in this area mandate that you cannot rely on the fair use defense without putting yourself in a risky position."

How nice it would be if copyright infringement of unpublished letters were the only thorny legal issue confronting the Elvis letters project. As our attorneys often reminded us, we also needed to be mindful of issues concerning rights of privacy and publicity of other persons to whom we refer, as well as unfair competition claims.

The many legal obstacles shut down publication of this book for thirty years.

As an author, it is frustrating to have access to so many authentic, emotional and colorful statements and then be prohibited from sharing them directly with the public. I would much rather weave this book around the actual testimony of the participants. Since that is not possible, I have instead used every legal means of writing this book to communicate the essence of the remarkable story revealed by the letters.

Priscilla and Me

In her memoir, *Elvis and Me*, Priscilla Presley reported to co-author Sandra Harmon the story of her years with Elvis. Most of the book recounts her experiences with Elvis prior to their wedding. The last third covers the period during which Elvis and his friends corresponded with Carmen Montez but never mentions the friendships between Elvis and the close friends depicted in the letters.

Since Priscilla's memoir is by definition a one-sided reporting of events remembered a decade or more later, it seems fair that Elvis, through his letters, be allowed to give his side. Fortunately, we have his personal account in handwritten letters—"contemporaneous notes" as made famous by FBI director James Comey during the special investigator's inquiry into his firing by US President Donald Trump. Elvis's letters were written just hours or days after important events occurred and usually while he was still experiencing the emotions they stirred up.

A memoir such as Priscilla's also provokes suspicions that the author's reporting may be biased, consciously or subconsciously, to counter known criticisms or buff the author's reputation. An author's memories are malleable—they can be reshaped and reconfigured, sometimes by collaborators, to provide a better, more marketable story. I'm not saying that *Elvis and Me* is a dishonest attempt to reconstruct the relationship between Priscilla and Elvis, but in my mind it can't fairly represent Elvis's point-of-view, which in some cases contradicts Priscilla's.

Both Elvis and Priscilla wanted to have children, but Elvis wanted to have them with Priscilla, and Priscilla seems to have been less committed to that goal.

In *Elvis and Me*, Priscilla wrote:

> Elvis and I often talked of having children, but we certainly weren't planning on having them right away. Then one day... I lay in bed and felt a strange sensation in my stomach, a sensation I'd never felt before.

Priscilla's book is short on specific dates, but her daughter, Lisa Marie, was born February 1, 1968, exactly nine months after Priscilla married Elvis, so the event depicted in the book occurred in the latter half of 1967. Priscilla was probably telling the truth, so far as her memory allowed, about conversations with Elvis reported in *Elvis and Me*.

In a letter to Carmen written a few days before his daughter was born, Elvis confessed how he had longed for a very long time to have a "bunch of kids." He explained that his conscience, along with the loneliness he had felt growing up with no brothers or sisters, had led him to conclude it would be a mistake to rear a child without siblings.

Elvis and Priscilla show their infant daughter Lisa Marie to adoring fans.

137

In June, shortly after watching his new movie *Speedway* for the first time, Elvis wrote that he and Priscilla had agreed to have eight children. But he told Carmen that he didn't think he could continue being with Priscilla, which meant his family plans had gone up in smoke. On his next trip home to Memphis, he planned to seek counseling, just to see if things could be patched up. Obviously torn, he then wrote that if he stayed with Priscilla, it would only be because of Lisa Marie.

It was unfortunate, then, that just before writing this letter Priscilla had revealed to Elvis that she might be pregnant again. He wasn't sure whether to believe her or not. He suspected that she was lying about her pregnancy to turn around their deteriorating relationship—or maybe to exact revenge for any of his numerous offenses, which she could easily name.

Within a month her pregnancy was confirmed. Elvis and Priscilla talked about whether to announce the news, but Elvis vetoed any publicity. Priscilla was confused about why her husband, who normally craved publicity, would be against announcing her pregnancy. Elvis explained his reasoning to Carmen—having a baby would complicate his option of separating from Priscilla. His decision to keep the pregnancy secret worked. The historical record makes no mention of a second pregnancy—we know about it only because of Elvis's letter to Carmen in which he was either honestly sharing details as he recalled them, lying or exaggerating for some unknown reason, or betraying worrisome delusions. These are the same considerations, by the way, for judging the veracity of all written correspondence that informs the search for truth.

In early August, tragedy struck. Elvis had just finished the movie *Charro!* and was back at home in Los Angeles. After waking up one morning, he went into the nursery to see his nearly seven-month-old daughter and accidentally woke her up. Lisa Marie's crying summoned an angry Priscilla to the room, who scolded Elvis for waking up their child. As Elvis described the scene to Carmen, the scolding escalated into a venomous shouting match. Fiercely angry, Elvis stormed out of the nursery toward the garage. He had planned to drive up to Palm Springs that morning to check on some contractor work on his house there. The fight with Priscilla convinced him to leave immediately.

Elvis told Carmen how Priscilla followed him to the car, continuing her tirade "until my nerves were raw," he wrote. His hope of a peaceful drive evaporated when Priscilla jumped into the seat next to him demanding that she be allowed to ride along.

In his telling, he started to back out of the driveway, slammed on the brakes and told her to get out—he didn't want her riding along to Palm Springs. He needed some peace and quiet, and he couldn't get that while she was relentlessly tormenting him. Priscilla objected but finally got out of the car. I can imagine her slamming the door. Elvis shouted for her to close the driveway gate after he had gone. Shaking with emotion, he continued backing up without checking the mirror. He claimed that a tap on the rear end made him stomp on the brake. Angered by all the interruptions, he flung open the door and leaped out to see what had happened. Horrified, he saw Priscilla lying face down behind the car. He had backed right into her.

Elvis must have yelled because his buddy Alan Fortas, his cousin Patsy, who was working as his secretary, and a couple of others ran out of the house. They picked up Priscilla and put her into another vehicle. As they prepared to leave for a nearby hospital, Patsy clung to Elvis's arm, keeping him from getting into the vehicle with his wife. She explained that his presence would be a magnet for the news media. The team, she said, would get Priscilla admitted under a false name, as usual.

Elvis told Carmen that he prayed for Priscilla for many hours. Around six that evening he received a call from the hospital. The baby had died, but Priscilla would make it. He sobbed for a long time, and then Patsy managed to get him to eat some soup while his staff tried to reach Priscilla's personal doctor.

About nine o'clock, the doctor called Elvis. "She has some injuries that mean she should probably not have any more children," the doctor explained. "Having one baby, and now two miscarriages within six months—that's just too much."

It took a few minutes after hanging up for Elvis to recall the doctor's statement that Priscilla had suffered *two* miscarriages in the past six months. He called the doctor back and was told the records were clear on this matter. She'd had a previous miscarriage in May. At that time the baby had been two-and-a-half months along.

Elvis could do the math, and he laid it out for Carmen. His wife had gotten pregnant about four to six weeks after giving birth to Lisa Marie. Elvis and Priscilla had been estranged during that period, and he was sure they had not had sex. But as he wrote in a letter to Carmen, he remained concerned about Priscilla's health.

According to Elvis's calculations, about two weeks after that first miscarriage Priscilla got pregnant again, and Elvis could remember that occasion, a fleeting moment of intimacy. He was certain that the baby he had just killed was his own. But if this tragedy had not occurred, he never would have learned of the other pregnancy and miscarriage.

In a written outpouring of emotion to Carmen, Elvis wrestled with conflicting sentiments. He was at fault for the accident and Priscilla's injuries. He felt bad about letting his feelings cloud his judgment while he was behind the wheel. He knew that he should apologize for his actions and set aside the feud with Priscilla for the sake of the beautiful baby girl they were raising. But he admitted that his pride would not let him forgive his wife's infidelity and deceit.

Elvis must have confided to Marlon Brando about the miscarriages because, in a letter to Carmen, Brando confessed, "It's almost masochistic, like he's asking to be hurt. I don't think I could sleep with a wife pregnant with somebody else's child while I was her husband."

After a short recovery in the hospital, Priscilla apparently went back to Memphis for a while, and Elvis finally made his trip to Palm Springs.

The depth of detail conveyed by Elvis in this confessional tale makes it hard to dismiss as a hallucinogenic episode or a made-up story created to sully Carmen's view of Priscilla for some unknown reason. The language he uses to describe his torment is convincingly emotional and sincere, and the threads of the story are strange but remarkably coherent. I suspect that some of the facts he presents are misremembered or distorted by the surge of emotions he was experiencing, and yet it is entirely plausible.

Even so, for a long time I kept wondering if this dramatic driveway mishap had occurred. It's possible, I think, that some of the facts of this event leaked out, and the grapevine twisted them into a popular rumor that circulated widely around this time. According to the rumor, Elvis had killed someone in a hit-and-run accident. Elvis's manager, Colonel Tom Parker, had hushed it up but was using it as blackmail to keep Elvis compliant. In Elvis's world, neither the reported event nor the rumor stretches credibility in my mind.

I have not been able to confirm Priscilla's pregnancy or admission to the hospital, but then I did not expect to. For the Presleys, the use of assumed names and cover-ups was a way of life, and the Colonel was a master of keeping unsavory details under wraps.

The Elvis-Priscilla feud unfortunately did not end, and neither side seemed capable of terminating their up-and-down relationship. Both sides in this marital standoff found numerous creative ways to behave badly, provoking each other.

* * *

A major incident, revealed for the first time in a single letter from Marlon Brando, occurred about two weeks before Christmas, in 1968. Marlon had shown up at Elvis's home about nine o'clock that evening to continue a series of informal acting lessons. Elvis appreciated these lessons because they were private—no one else knew he was being tutored, and he could trust Marlon to keep the secret. Marlon was a tough teacher and even assigned homework to his famous student. Elvis had been studying a book on acting theory that Marlon had lent him.

Marlon arrived at Elvis's Monovale house and walked past the bedroom windows to the back door, noticing that Elvis's light was on. He was about to knock on the back door when he realized that Priscilla was home. He knew Elvis and Priscilla had been spending most of their time apart because of marital strains. He didn't want to get in the middle of that messiness, so he walked back to the front door and knocked. Patsy Presley Gambill, Elvis's secretary, let him in.

Patsy was Elvis's double cousin. She was the daughter of Elvis's Uncle Vester, his father's brother. But because Vester was married to Clettes, the sister of Elvis's mother, Patsy was Elvis's cousin on both the paternal and maternal side. In 1967, Patsy had married Elvis's valet and chauffeur, Marvin "Gee Gee" Gambill, Jr. Marrying into the Presley clan had given Gee Gee a favored position in the Memphis Mafia.

Patsy led Marlon to the closed door of Elvis's bedroom and knocked. Elvis came out of his room, and the two men went into the study where Marlon placed his car keys and wallet on a table to allow greater freedom of movement during the lesson.

"I see Priscilla is staying in the house," Marlon said. "I was a little surprised to see her here."

Elvis looked down at his feet and said, "Well… you know my feelings about her right now, but it's Christmas and all. You know how it is."

For months, Marlon had been encouraging Elvis to ditch Priscilla. He was itching to chastise his friend who had often said he was fed up and wanted to end the marriage. But thinking back on all the stress Elvis had endured, Marlon dropped the issue, deciding it might be best for Elvis to have a woman around for a while. He changed the subject, and the two men chatted for a few minutes before getting down to business.

About ninety minutes later, they finished the acting lesson and wandered into the kitchen for some milk, Elvis's preferred nighttime beverage. Patsy was in the kitchen waiting for them to finish. She said they must have worked hard because they looked hungry. Then she made some sandwiches, which she shared with them.

Around eleven o'clock, Marlon said goodbye and left through the back door, noticing that Elvis's room was dark. The lights were on in the guest house where Patsy and her husband Gee Gee Gambill lived. As Marlon passed close to one of the guest house windows, he saw Priscilla and Gee Gee inside, "and they weren't playing checkers," he told Carmen. "I said a little prayer that Elvis wouldn't know."

Back at his car, Marlon discovered he had left his keys in Elvis's study, so he returned to the house, and Patsy let him in again. He found his way to the study and grabbed his keys. As he turned to leave the room, Elvis entered.

"I'm glad you came back," Elvis said. "I was meaning to give back that book you gave me—it's in my room. I'm sure Priscilla will have drunk herself into a coma by now."

Marlon followed Elvis to his large bedroom and watched him open the door. The hallway light illuminated the still-made bed.

Elvis stated the obvious: "She's not here." He switched on the overhead light and picked up the acting theory book from a nightstand. "Where the hell is that woman?" he shouted at Patsy, who stood passively in the open doorway. Marlon nervously followed Elvis and Patsy around the house as they called out for Priscilla. With every step, Elvis was getting angrier. After searching the house, Elvis exploded through the front door and marched to the guest house, one of the last places his wife could be. Marlon noticed that the lights were out. He hoped Priscilla had gone.

Elvis pounded on the guest house door as if he knew Priscilla was inside. He shouted for her to open the door. When there was no response, he kicked open the door and found Priscilla still in bed with Gee Gee, who was wearing Elvis's robe. The confrontation was potentially dangerous—Gee Gee served as Elvis's part-time bodyguard and was licensed to carry a gun.

"I'm telling you, Carmen, I thought Elvis would kill them both," Marlon wrote.

In a fury, Elvis pulled out Gee Gee's dresser drawers and threw the contents outside, then ferociously emptied out the closets. He grabbed the stunned Gee Gee and flung him onto a pile of clothes, then stood him up and "half killed him," according to Marlon. Finally, he grabbed Patsy and started dragging her into the house.

"Two more can play this game!" he shouted.

Marlon followed as Elvis pulled Patsy into his bedroom and locked the door. Fearing that Elvis would vent his frustration on her, Marlon banged on the door, demanding that Elvis open it. Moments later, Patsy unlocked the door. Her mascara was running, but she was unharmed. Marlon could see Elvis sitting on the bed, shaking and crying.

"Are you OK?" Marlon asked Patsy.

She nodded her head. "The only thing that kept me from falling apart was trying to keep Elvis in one piece."

In a letter to Carmen, Elvis explained how devastated he was that Gee Gee had betrayed him in his house, with his wife, and with Lisa Marie and his cousin—Gee Gee's own wife—right there. "I can never forgive him," he wrote.

But he did. Before long, Gee Gee and Priscilla were again part of Elvis's dysfunctional family. One of Elvis's greatest faults, perhaps, was the inability to quit on people, even the toxic ones.

This never kept him from seeking revenge, though. According to another Marlon letter to Carmen, a few days after the Gee Gee incident Elvis called actress and singer Connie Stevens, whom he had dated briefly in 1961, and asked her to go to the fights with him. Marlon told Carmen that Elvis had done this "on purpose" to hurt Priscilla, and that after a public date all of Hollywood would be buzzing about it. Stevens, though separated, was still married to singer Eddie Fisher, a very powerful man in the entertainment industry. Marlon begged Carmen to bring Elvis to his senses.

"That gal's nothing but a tramp…" Marlon wrote. "It isn't worth destroying his name over Priscilla. All Elvis needs is Eddie Fisher on his neck."

Elvis called off the date.

Loyalties and affections in the Elvis household continued to evolve and devolve rapidly. Just before Easter, in 1969, Patsy surprised Elvis by suddenly packing up and returning to Graceland. Elvis sought an explanation from another family member, cousin Gene Smith, who was the son of Gladys's sister Levalle. Gene was now Elvis's sole chauffeur and valet in the absence of Gee Gee, who had not yet been invited back into the family.

"'Cilla accused Patsy of sleeping with you," Gene said. "And she was really mad that Patsy was sort of hogging your time just about every night since Gee Gee left. Patsy left so there wouldn't be more trouble."

In a note to Carmen, Elvis said that Gene's explanation revealed a big misunderstanding because he'd never slept with his cousin Patsy. He recalled that a few weeks after he'd thrown out Gee Gee, he'd become quite ill and stayed at Marlon's. Patsy had gone there to check up on him and ended up sleeping on Elvis's bed for a couple of nights. Elvis was mostly unconscious but told Carmen he had felt less lonely with Patsy there, even in his delirium. As for the notion that Patsy had been monopolizing him, he guessed that a stronger bond had developed between him and Patsy since both had been betrayed by their spouses.

He told Carmen that Priscilla had called him to say she wanted him back, and as much as he had tried to hate her, he kept recalling that little girl he had once loved so deeply. He had to forgive her for the pain she had caused him. But he was adamant that before taking her back, he'd have to be convinced she was ready to settle down and be his wife. He just didn't know how such a thing could ever be guaranteed. He expected more from Priscilla than she seemed ready to give.

They got back together, but their marriage had become an uneasy truce.

* * *

Hotels were often war zones for the Presleys. For Elvis, the conflicts may have been due to the stress and exhaustion of his endless performances and Priscilla's submissiveness to the lures of adventure and attention. On July 31, 1969, four months after Patsy had left Los Angeles and then returned, Elvis stood backstage at the International Hotel in Las Vegas listening to the

145

Sweet Inspirations perform the first segment of the invitation-only opening night of a four-week engagement. Eventually, a record-breaking 101,500 people would attend these shows. Vegas top-draw Dean Martin, by comparison, had drawn 50,000 to the Riviera over three weeks that summer. Scores of celebrities attended Elvis's show, including Phil Ochs, Cary Grant, Fats Domino, Pat Boone, and Carol Channing.

The opening-night event was planned to be Elvis's triumphant return to Las Vegas—his first live performance in nine years—and he was very nervous. The stakes had never been so high. He was coming out of a musical dark age and about to leave behind an uninspired movie career. For weeks he had dieted until he looked as fit and trim as an athlete.

Suddenly, his heart started racing, and sweat poured down his face. He grew dizzy. A panic attack gripped him and didn't release him until 10:15 p.m., after comedian Sammy Shore's routine, when he went on stage with almost no fanfare, hesitated for a few seconds and then brought down the house with an all-out version of "Blue Suede Shoes."

The panic attack was gone for the evening.

He had never performed hour-long sets, but tonight, and for the next fifty-six performances, he would pour himself into the taxing, longer format. Slick with sweat, with glistening rings and a chic black tunic, he pummeled and seduced and dazzled the spectators who released every bottled-up ounce of energy. Elvis was magnetic and spirited. He punched and kicked the air, slid across the floor on his knees, somersaulted, prowled like a panther, coaxed out cheers, roars and squeals. The audience response was cataclysmic, and reviewers universally raved.

In a detailed letter written to Carmen, Elvis described an event that took place the next evening. Priscilla had arrived in Vegas just in time to watch the July 27th rehearsal, which oddly was the first time she had ever seen Elvis perform live. Since arriving, she had been staying in her own suite a floor below Elvis, allowing him to focus entirely on perfecting the upcoming show.

According to Elvis, just after the 8:15 show—which was the first concert for the general public—Priscilla found her husband backstage fending off adulations. Just then Tom Jones approached Elvis to deliver some praise. Before he could speak, Priscilla got Elvis's attention by flashing a key and a broad grin that Elvis could not ignore.

"How did you get my room key?" Elvis asked.

"From the front desk. Spousal rights," Priscilla said. "I'm all yours after the late show." She smugly marched off.

Apparently, though, she was not on Elvis's menu for the evening. Based on facts contained in a letter to Carmen, Elvis pulled Tom closer and said, "I need a favor."

The desperation in Elvis's voice caught Tom off guard. "Sure—anything," Tom replied.

"I need you to stay with me in my room. After the late show, Pris is planning to sleep with me, and I just can't handle that tonight. I really can't. If you're there, she'll go back to her room."

Tom agreed with a shrug to sleep in Elvis's suite that night, even though all his things were in his room at the Flamingo.

* * *

Tom and Elvis had first met in 1965 while Tom was on his first American tour. Tom was making it big with three hit records and a top-selling album. Elvis had become a fan and invited Tom over to the Paramount movie set where he was shooting *Paradise, Hawaiian Style.* As he watched the King shoot a scene in a fake helicopter, Tom thought, *Oh, my God! Surely Elvis Presley doesn't know who I am.* After finishing the scene, Elvis smiled and walked toward Tom singing "With These Hands," a song Tom had made famous. He sang it all the way through.

"I know every track on your album," Elvis said. "How the hell do you sing the way you do?"

Tom shuffled his feet and replied, "Well, you're to blame, because I listened to all your records in the 1950s."

Mutual respect grew into a deep friendship. Several years later, dripping with sweat after a show at the Flamingo in Vegas, Tom strutted off stage to his dressing room. Elvis was eagerly waiting to tell him about a new song someone had pitched to him but seemed much better for Tom.

Putting his hands up, Tom said he needed to clean up first. He showered and with soap in his eyes heard Elvis singing. According to Tom's autobiography, "I thought, I'm going nuts; I've been in Vegas too long—I'm hearing Elvis Presley in the shower." After clearing the soap out of his eyes, he saw Elvis, standing near the sink, singing the new song to Tom through an open shower door.

When Tom finally climbed out of the shower to dry off, he saw that Elvis had just used the toilet and was standing there with his leather pants around his ankles. Red, one of Elvis's entourage, was helping raise up the trousers as Elvis kept babbling about the song.

At last, Elvis stepped into the dressing room where a gaggle of insiders had now gathered. As Tom tied his towel around his waist, he noticed that Elvis had left a loaded .45 automatic pistol on the toilet tank. "This was my first real glimpse of the paranoia that Elvis lived with as a matter of course," Tom wrote in his autobiography. He wrapped the gun in a towel and handed it to Elvis who said, "Thank you very much." Then in plain sight Elvis pulled out the gun and slipped it into a holster at the small of his back.

* * *

Flash forward to the International Hotel in 1969. In the story Elvis related to Carmen, he had just recruited Tom Jones to sleep in his room so Priscilla would be forced to go elsewhere. As usual, a post-performance party popped up after Elvis's last show. Elvis kept his eye on Priscilla who was buoyant because of the attention of many admirers. Around four-thirty in the morning, Tom and Elvis slipped out of the party unnoticed by Priscilla and went to Elvis's suite.

Elvis was exhausted, and Tom had a sore leg, so they immediately went into the bedroom, closed the door to the sitting room, stripped off their shoes and clothes, and flopped backward onto separate double beds. As they lay there muttering to each other incoherently, Priscilla's key rattled in the hallway door, and she burst into the sitting room. Elvis rolled his eyes and crawled under the covers, pretending to be asleep. Tom copied him, figuring that feigned sleep was a good way to avoid a scene.

Priscilla, clutching a small overnight bag, marched past them to the bathroom, emerging a few minutes later in a nightgown. Ignoring the lump in the second bed, she tucked herself under the covers next to Elvis.

Irritated, Elvis leaped out of the bed. "I have a friend here," he growled.

"Hush! He's sound asleep," she whispered. "Anyway, so what? He's got his own big bed."

Tom had his back to them, but he heard an angry, "It matters to me," and then sounds of dressing and feet stomping into the sitting room.

"What's the matter with you?" Priscilla asked, following her husband and then closing the bedroom door behind her.

In a letter to Carmen, Tom describes bounding out of bed and dressing quickly as the verbal sparring continued. Then the hallway door slammed. All went quiet. Tom peeked into the sitting room and found it empty, so he went out in search of Elvis.

The International Hotel was vast, and after wandering for about twenty minutes he ran into Carol Channing and her agent, who invited him to a game of blackjack. After a half-hour or so, he caught a glimpse of Priscilla and a man—definitely not Elvis— walking toward the street exit.

The sun had come up, and Tom's leg was still bothering him, so he excused himself from the game and went back to Elvis's suite. Exhausted now and moving like a drunk, he removed his clothes, shut the curtains and crawled under the sheet.

"I'd just gotten off to sleep when something woke me," Tom wrote to Carmen the next day. He thought Elvis had just come in, but then realized that he had been woken by fingers running through his hair. It was too dark, though, to make out who was moving those fingers.

He switched on the nightstand lamp just as Priscilla yanked the covering sheet completely off the bed, exposing him. Tom quickly rolled onto his stomach, angry and embarrassed, insisting that she give the sheet back. She did, finally, and he turned off the lamp but immediately snapped on the overhead light and started tickling him.

In horror, Tom heard Elvis's key open the outer door, so he did the obvious thing—he ran into the shower. "Man, this is it. He's never going to believe this!" he explained to Carmen later.

Elvis entered the bedroom and started yelling at Priscilla, then heard the shower running. He opened the bathroom door, and Tom did the only thing he could think of. He asked Elvis to throw him a robe, which Elvis did.

Tom may have been wondering about Elvis's .45 automatic when Priscilla said to her husband, "When I came back, I heard the shower and thought it was you."

Tom Jones told Carmen, "I was hoping Elvis would be naïve enough to swallow that bare-faced lie, because I knew had I been in his place I wouldn't have believed the truth. But I guess he's been up against this sort of thing before."

Elvis walked Tom downstairs to the cab stand, apologizing for his wife all the way. "I can't go back to the suite," Elvis said. "I've got a hideaway over at the Aladdin. Should've just gone there to begin with. I'll drop you at the Flamingo."

Tom silently nodded.

Then Elvis added, "You're about the only person I trust."

In his letter, Tom explained to Carmen, "Believe me, I have no interest whatsoever in Elvis's wife. She's a phony painted doll and brazen as the devil. She had me in a most uncomfortable and compromising position. I'll do anything I can for Elvis—except share a room with him while his wife's anywhere in the vicinity."

Ironically, during the drafting of this book, I discovered the following 2017 article on DailyMail.com:

Sir Tom Jones has reportedly struck up a romantic relationship with Priscilla Presley. The Welsh star, 76, is said to be 'courting' the 71-year-old actress, who was married to rock 'n' roll icon Elvis Presley, almost a year after his wife Linda died of cancer.

* * *

Six months after the Tom-and-Priscilla scene at the International Hotel, Elvis opened a four-week engagement there. In those shows, Elvis started incorporating karate moves into the choreography. Writing in *Elvis*, Albert Goldman observed that the show seemed to revolve around a series of dramatic poses—"Elvis as the Discus Hurler, Elvis as Sagittarius, Elvis as the Dying Gaul." For greater freedom of movement, Elvis for the first time appeared in one-piece jumpsuits, alternating from all-white to all-black. *The Los Angeles Herald-Examiner* summed up the mostly rave reviews by concluding, "The new decade will belong to him."

Two days later, Priscilla and Lisa Marie flew into Vegas unannounced and took a suite one floor below Elvis. Priscilla tried valiantly to entice Elvis to stay with her, but he ardently refused. On Sunday, February 1, Priscilla brought Lisa Marie to Elvis's dinner show to celebrate her second birthday, delighting her father.

According to Elvis, Priscilla got very drunk on Friday night and called Elvis after the late show to say she was going to jump out of the window. Elvis believed that was a ruse to get him to Priscilla's room. "She had no one to sleep with that night," he told Carmen. About an hour later, Priscilla called him again and said she had given Lisa Marie three sleeping pills—but not to worry because they wouldn't hurt her, just help her sleep soundly. After Priscilla's previous suicide bluff, Elvis suspected she had made up the story just to get him to her room where he'd likely stay until Lisa woke up.

When Priscilla called again and said something was wrong with Lisa, he couldn't take a chance it was a bluff. He rushed to Priscilla's suite and found Lisa Marie's face "turning blue." Priscilla had not been lying about the sleeping pills. Elvis immediately called the house doctor, who at first wanted to send Lisa Marie to the local hospital. Within several minutes, however, he determined the little girl was having an allergic reaction to the pills and was able to administer a remedy.

Elvis was livid that his wife would be so irresponsible and do "by far the lowest thing" she had ever done. He wrote that he would probably never be able to forgive her, but repeatedly, throughout his life, he did.

In Elvis's summary of the event, Priscilla not only showed no remorse but continued to behave childishly. After the late show on Friday the 13th, a representative from RCA, which had been recording the Vegas shows for the upcoming *On Stage* album, threw a party for Elvis in one of the hotel's rooftop restaurants. Priscilla crashed the party, got drunk, and then disappeared. Elvis and the RCA man were seated together and had just ordered steaks. Elvis was famished because he hadn't eaten since twelve thirty that afternoon, and it was now close to midnight. Just then a server told Elvis there was a call waiting for him. When he got to the telephone, expecting another call from Priscilla, no one was there.

Elvis claimed that while he was away his tablemate was also paged for a call, but no caller was present when he picked up. Both confused men returned to the table. Within a minute, the RCA chief and his wife joined the table on Elvis's left, and a Memphis-based reporter and her lady friend sat down on his right. The six of them exchanged small talk as a server brought Elvis and his original tablemate their steaks. Elvis dug into his meal with gusto but suddenly felt something "creeping up" his leg.

Elvis told Carmen he purposely dropped his fork so he could bend over and see what was going on beneath the table, which had a white tablecloth that reached the floor. He discovered that Priscilla had managed to crawl under the table while the two men were answering her fraudulent pages. By now Priscilla's hand had unzipped Elvis's pants. Embarrassed and furious, Elvis ground the heel of his shoe into Priscilla's other hand, which was on the floor.

At this point, Charlie Hodge, an army buddy of Elvis and trusted aide, approached the table and asked if anyone had seen Priscilla.

"I haven't," Elvis said loudly, "but I'm going to kill her if she doesn't put something back where she found it."

Priscilla must have received the message because a moment later Elvis was able to stand up, excuse himself and head straight to his room. Later that evening, Priscilla called Elvis's suite six times. Elvis never picked up—in fact, he told Carmen shortly after the incident that he never wanted to talk to Priscilla again.

These are rather bizarre stories that Elvis told about his wife. In reading them for the first time, I wondered to what purpose he would make up such stories. He was writing for an audience of one—Carmen Montez. He had no reason to suspect that anyone else would ever read his words. Was he so distressed by his marital relationship that he was driven to exaggerate Priscilla's immaturity and recklessness to the one person he trusted most in the world? There was nothing personally to be gained except the pleasure of venting his anger and frustration. In the end, I believe that Elvis would not have consciously lied to Carmen about these matters. The letters in which these events were described, which also included some humdrum reporting of miscellaneous prosaic matters, were written in a matter-of-fact manner and showed no indication that he was suffering from delusions or fantasies. Readers should interpret for themselves the veracity of the events described above.

The Big Pitch

A book doesn't get published by accident. In the case of books which might make some noise in the market, the process often starts when an author attracts a literary agent who's willing to commit significant time to pitch a book, or a book proposal, to publishers. If this happens (most books never find an agent) the author collaborates with the agent on a book proposal that includes everything a publisher needs to "green light" the project. Next, the agent ships or delivers the proposal to publishers with whom he or she has a relationship or that are in the best position to publish and promote the book. And finally, if everything goes exactly right, the agent helps negotiate a good financial deal for the author.

The Elvis project deviated from this plan in key ways. In step one, because he had bought out the original literary agent, Bill Mack was now legally a co-owner of the project and the agent representing the project. This turned the author-agent relationship upside down; in this case, the agent had found and signed the author—me.

Step two, creating a book proposal, was not a collaboration of experts but of amateurs. Bill Mack and I were smart, but neither of us had ever developed a book proposal before, so with confidence supported by ignorance we set out to craft a sure-fire proposal.

Step three really left us out in the cold. Neither Bill nor I knew any of the big New York publishers, and they certainly didn't know us. We couldn't work the phones because we didn't know who to call. Bill was not a recognized agent, and no publisher would accept a blind, unagented submission. All of which means that we had no way of getting all the way to step four, negotiating a publishing agreement, not to mention step two.

While we tried to break through to publishers, I was also working on the proposal. The project obviously had celebrity appeal, but we were concerned that if we directly stated what we had—Elvis's secret letters—the secret would be leaked, and enemies of the project would try to blow it up. The potential enemies were many: family members mentioned unflatteringly by Elvis; entertainers with career interests potentially undermined by the contents of the letters; Elvis Presley Enterprises, which was known to be highly litigious in guarding its rights to everything Elvis; or envious publishers that had not successfully bid for the publishing rights.

Our plan was to get a face-to-face meeting with a senior editor of a big publisher without disclosing the specific content of our book, then require the publisher to sign an NDA—a non-disclosure agreement—before sharing our formal book proposal.

That strategy was dead in the water. Submissions staffers with no authority to consider the project unless we disclosed the subject of our book, batted down our calls. When we tried by telephone to get a non-disclosure signed before a meeting, we were flatly rejected. "Publishers," we were told, "do not sign NDAs for book proposals."

Bill decided that since I had raised millions of dollars for an independent feature film and had negotiated a distribution deal with Paramount Pictures, I should assist in organizing and drafting the proposal. To start, I made a list of everything I thought a publisher would need to know and a few things that would grab their interest. The final proposal was 150 pages long—much longer than recommended by any of the book proposal how-to books I had consulted. But I believed the publishers would have many questions we should answer.

Here is the final outline for the proposal:

- **About Elvis Presley**—a short introduction to the impact he'd had on the world and how the scores of biographies and reminiscences about him are totally insufficient because none has the most secret thoughts and contemporaneous personal reporting of Elvis's life events.

- **The Presley Letters**—a concise description of Elvis's handwritten letters and those of his close friends to their common secret confidante.

- **The Authors**—brief biographies of Robert Slatzer and Carmen Rayburn.

- **Authors' Proposal**—a summary of the reasons a publisher should be interested in this unique and exclusive project, ending with these words: *This is Elvis's story—based on his own written words.*

- **The Material**—a short history of how the letters came to be legally owned by Carmen Rayburn.

- **Authentication**—Signed letters of handwriting authentication with a generous collection of the fragments of Elvis's letters provided to the expert handwriting analyst.

- **Book Outline**—a sample Table of Contents of the book as we currently envisioned it, with descriptions of each chapter. (I slaved over this outline, trying to reflect the impact that I knew the contents of the letters could deliver.)

- **Introduction**—a completed chapter illustrating how the premise of the book could be written to grab the reader right from the start.

- **Chapter Excerpts**—several pages from a few of the most compelling chapters to dramatize some of the astonishing stories revealed in the letters and demonstrate an approach to writing them.

- **Pertinent Law and Legal Opinions**—a legal summary and opinion by our lawyers related to copyright and fair use of quoting and paraphrasing content from unpublished letters, the main obstacle in publishing our book. We included many pages of court cases and opinions for the benefit of the publishers' attorneys.

Being an artist, Bill Mack took charge of designing the physical proposal. He chose 32 lb. cream paper stock with rounded corners collated into three-ring binders with stitched leather covers and gold protective corners. Very impressive. Our new plan was to disclose the Elvis project in general terms to get a meeting scheduled and, when face-to-face, pass out binders and walk through the proposal, pointing out all the details we were providing. We would explain that with an expression of interest and a signed NDA, we would allow representatives of the publishing firm to peruse the original letters in a secure room under our supervision.

Leather binders used for publisher presentations.

I called a friend of mine, Annemarie Osborne, who provided publicity services to publishers and authors. Annemarie compiled a call list of specific people within the most appropriate publishing companies. The strategy worked. When we revealed the exciting nature of our book project to the right people, we got invited to meetings in New York.

Our most interesting meeting was with a senior editor at Simon & Schuster. For close to two hours, Bill Mack and I made our case to the editor and two assistants, who seemed sincerely enthusiastic about the project. At the end of the meeting, we were invited to dinner at the editor's Manhattan home. Dinner was mostly social, with almost no business discussed. We felt like we were being courted, a potentially positive sign.

We had other positive meetings as well. In other words, no one threw us out. Most of the questions we answered were about publishing risks such as the well-known copyright issues and rights to privacy concerns. It became clear that a decision to publish most likely would be made by the legal section, not the editorial department.

After several weeks, we had not heard back from any of the publishers. This meant, of course, that either they were studying the issues deeply to justify saying yes, or they just didn't know how to break our hearts and say no. Bill Mack called the senior editor at Simon & Schuster multiple times, but he had disappeared under a cone of silence.

Finally, we got some written responses. Our dinner host at Simon & Schuster wrote: "The sample sections you showed us, while shocking, are startlingly implausible, as are a few of the other promised revelations (the kidnapping, for example). Please understand that we are not challenging your veracity, nor do we doubt the validity of the letters. Rather, we wonder if maybe in writing the letters our subject was fantasizing just a bit. Unfortunately, that doubt, coupled with all the other complications, has caused us to decide against pursuing."

We tried to reach the editor to explain that we had corroboration for those doubted events, but we could never reach him again.

Warner had decided that the copyright issues were too unsettled for them to base a book on the unpublished letters. The editor wrote:

"Because of the nature of these events and the fact that by law we could never acknowledge the existence of these letters in any way, mentioning the events would be extremely risky. Without mentioning them, there would not be enough here for a publishable book."

With that last sentence, both Bill and I firmly agreed. But our understanding of the various legal opinions we had received was quite different. The unsettled law, we believed, made it difficult to legally use the letters, but there was a path to doing so successfully.

Random House was more honest than the others about their cowardice, which we believed was the most common issue among the publishers. The editor wrote: "...it seems you have a real hot property here. The chapter about the break-in at Elvis's house was horrifying... Unfortunately, we had such a bad experience with the litigiousness of the Presley estate over [another Elvis book] that we don't really want to subject ourselves to that again. And although the book will probably ultimately be good, I believe the legal issues could be a real problem." Evidently, our book was *too* hot.

You get the idea. We had a "real hot property," but no one would touch it. We took some solace in the fact that no publisher had questioned the authenticity of the letters after studying our documentation. But in the end, accepting the letters as genuine didn't matter. For another ten years, we concocted various ways of approaching the book—none of them workable—and waited patiently for endless court appeals of the landmark copyright cases that had so unsettled the law.

* * *

In 1997, my friend Carmen Rayburn died of cervical cancer. I received the disturbing call from her niece, Raven. For a few years, Carmen had begged me to quickly find a path to getting the book published. "I'm not well, you know, and I may not have much time left to enjoy my island," she'd tell me. And I always thought she was just trying to motivate me.

By 2005, Bob Slatzer had also passed away after several long bouts of illness. Before he died, he repaid big-hearted Bill Mack for advances he'd been given by granting Bill the rights to his second manuscript about Marilyn Monroe. "It has everything I didn't dare reveal in my previous book, but now I can—incredible stuff," Bob claimed, making his big pitch right up to the end.

The Elvis project eventually faded from everyone's mind, becoming one of those "what if" stories that pops to the surface of a normal person's consciousness every couple of years. But I could never let go of it; like a howling dog, it has deprived me of sleep for decades.

The Girl with Many Names

Cathy

Of the many letters to Carmen Montez in our collection, the earliest one was written sometime in July 1966 by Harry Belafonte. There must have been earlier correspondence that did not survive, however, because this July letter jumps right into the middle of a drama that had begun earlier and would continue for several years.

This Belafonte letter begins by declaring the profound shame Harry felt because of his behavior. Unfortunately, it does not explain what behavior shamed him, but it does expound on the consequences of it. It seems that a young woman named Joi Sommers was so distressed by the mysterious behavior that she was refusing to speak to Harry, which caused him deep grief. When mutual friend Marlon Brando interceded with Joi at Harry's request, she hung up on the actor.

Naturally, I wondered what had transpired. I also wondered who this mysterious Joi Sommers was, how Harry and Marlon knew her and why her shunning of them had caused such despair. Over time I would learn that Joi Sommers was at the center of many of the letters by Belafonte, Brando and Jones, though Joi wasn't her real name, and that Elvis, too, would be caught in her magnetic pull in a most alarming way. She was also a close friend of Carmen Montez.

The information contained in this chapter about "Joi Sommers" and her interactions with Harry, Marlon and Tom comes exclusively from clues, facts and references scattered throughout their letters and remarks made by Carmen Montez to her best friend.

Carmen was more than a spiritual guide to people in the entertainment industry. She was also a "wannabe" movie producer. While ministering to the spiritually needy, like thousands of others in Hollywood she was also developing a "package" around a "property" that she controlled. In the movie business, a screenplay offered for sale commands greater consideration from the studios when it is "packaged" with known actors, directors, composers, executive producers and other experienced individuals who have committed to the project. The "property" in this case was a screenplay called *Let There Be Light*, written by a talented young Welsh woman named Cathy Kane (her last name is my best guess based on records research). In Welsh, Kane means beautiful, an apt description of Cathy.

In *Let There Be Light*, Carmen had found the perfect vehicle for advancing her movie career. Not only was the script brilliantly conceived and executed, but it was also deeply human and spiritual. The writing was mature beyond the age of its writer, who was in her early twenties. With this script, Carmen could perfectly blend her desire to nurture spirituality with her ambition to become a movie producer.

For several years, Carmen had been operating a fledgling talent agency that represented models, actors, stunt men and others. With Cathy, she had branched into movie packaging by acquiring the rights to the screenplay. Because this young writer was charismatic, beautiful and gifted, Carmen saw a mutually beneficial relationship; Carmen could help advance Cathy's career, and Cathy—with boundless sex appeal and charm—could help close deals.

From the beginning, however, Carmen had known secrets about Cathy that no one else knew. While Cathy could project great maturity and confidence the way an actress can portray a persona wholly different than herself, Cathy was insecure. While she was an immensely talented writer—and painter too—she thought of herself as a fraud, refusing to recognize her own gifts. These deficits made her vulnerable to anyone who could play on her weaknesses.

Unfortunately, one of those people was a young man of "mixed blood," as Harry Belafonte put it, with whom she was in love.

Jim Mathews worked in food service at the Century Plaza hotel, but like so many people in LA he was obsessed with establishing a movie career. He also had a gambling problem. He had been active in sports at UCLA but never graduated. Carmen frequently had observed Jim exhibiting the classic traits of manic depression, a condition from which Carmen's husband George Ramentol also suffered (the term "bipolar" wasn't used until 1980). Though Cathy loved Jim deeply, she feared his gambling habit and frequent mood swings.

A crisis had occurred when Cathy rejected Jim's offer to share her screenplay with a "friend in the business" in exchange for a percentage of profits and a producer credit if the project moved forward. Rebuffed, Jim had sunk into a deep depression when she gave the movie rights to Carmen, a woman she had known for several years and trusted completely.

Carmen sensed Jim's pain and worked out a plan to keep the peace. She offered Jim a small profit participation in the project and an associate producer credit if he introduced the project to his "friend," and as a result the project moved forward. All parties agreed to the truce. A draft of the screenplay was typed and given to Jim, who mailed it to his "friend," supposedly a Hollywood headliner. Combining an A-list star with an outstanding screenplay would provide a solid foundation for a package that could attract other talent.

In 1966, copies of scripts were typed by hand. There were no word processors, computers or copy machines, and carbon paper was used to make a smudged copy or two. No one would ever send a fuzzy carbon copy of a script to an actor or a studio, however. That was considered an insult. Unfortunately, producing "original" typed manuscripts was a tedious and expensive process.

The author's name on the script's freshly typed title page was Joi Sommers, a pen name Cathy used on her literary works for unknown reasons.

Joi

Jim's "friend in the business" turned out to be a famous singer and actor named Harry Belafonte. Ironically, as Harry made clear in a letter to Carmen, Jim Mathews and Harry Belafonte were more than "friends"—they were half-brothers who had only met once many years earlier. I have not found Jim Mathews mentioned in any Belafonte family trees or biographical information, but Harry confirmed this relationship in a letter to Carmen, and Jim verbally told Carmen that he and Harry were half-brothers.

When I first read Harry's claim that Jim Mathews was his half-brother, I thought the reference was an error, possibly evidence that the letter was the work of an inattentive forger. And then I came across another Belafonte letter in which the singer claimed he had just seen his ailing mother, Melvine, who thought she was dying and confessed that Jim was in fact Harry's full brother. In *Belafonte, An Unauthorized Biography*, author Arnold Shaw explained that in 1933, when Harry was six years old, his father, Harold Sr., left his mother for a white woman. Twelve years later, Harold Sr. and Melvine temporarily got together and produced another offspring. In a rare meeting, Harry told Carmen that Jim Mathews was raised by one of Melvine's sisters and during his early years thought his aunt was really his mother.

Harry Belafonte at a civil rights march in 1963.

Harry Belafonte, a deeply spiritual man, loved the screenplay *Then There Was Light*. Having been betrayed in business numerous times, he was not one to easily trust a new acquaintance, but in Carmen he instantly discovered a soulmate with whom he could confidently share his problems and most secret thoughts.

Carmen Montez told Rayburn that Harry wanted to meet the screenwriter to discuss some ideas about the work, so she gathered up the little money she had and arranged a lunch meeting at the Beverly Wilshire. Predictably, Harry was smitten with Joi Sommers. He couldn't keep from staring at the young writer, who exuded a dazzling and mysterious magnetism. She did not flirt; she tantalized. She did not supplicate; she seduced.

"Is it your real name—Joi Sommers?" Harry finally asked.

"Yes," Cathy lied. Why she misled Harry about her name we will never know. Maybe she felt she could project more confidence when playing the imaginary part of the screenwriter.

Harry's interest in Joi was multi-faceted. Verbally and through his letters, he confessed many times to Carmen that he had fallen in love with Joi but believed the age gap was too much of a barrier. Yet he longed for her when she was gone and worried about her almost all the time. Ongoing marital problems made Harry vulnerable to Joi's charms, but being married made a sexual relationship with Joi inconsistent with his sense of morality. The unrequited nature of his desire fueled a wish to please her in other ways, such as providing career advice and influence.

Carmen's relationship with Harry, as with all her spiritual "students," became centered around the exchange of letters. Even business dealings were conducted by correspondence. Carmen believed that the act of writing focused a person's feelings and helped organize their thoughts. The result often provided a more accurate rendition of what they intended to say than a verbal conversation could convey. Carmen would read and reread letters from her "students," trying to pick up the breadcrumbs of incomplete messages and interpreting other cues to discern the emotion left on the page.

In early 1966, Harry suggested that Marlon Brando, a long-time friend and activist in the civil rights movement, would be a good candidate for one of the roles in *Let There Be Light*. He forwarded his copy of the script to Marlon and set up an introductory meeting at a restaurant, intending that only he, Marlon and Carmen would attend. Perhaps he was not yet ready to share Joi with his good friend. Joi accompanied Carmen to the meeting, however, and she immediately charmed the moody actor.

Brando at a civil rights march in 1963.

After remarking about Carmen's distinctive perfume, which he liked, Marlon turned to Joi and said, "You're very young to have written such a mature script."

"I'm a very old soul," Joi replied.

Many years later, Carmen remembered the intensity with which Marlon Brando gazed at Joi after this remark. To her friend, Rayburn, she repeated his delayed but memorable response: "Not many people I know believe in souls any more, but I do. And I believe you are an old soul."

As the parties left the meeting, Montez recalled, Harry headed for his car. Marlon gently stopped Joi and, as Harry had done, inquired about her name. "Joi is an unusual spelling—J-O-I. Is it a pen name?"

"Yes, my real name is Cathy," the screenwriter replied, holding back her last name.

"If I were you," Marlon told her, "I would be 'Joi Sommers' with Harry and everyone else in this damn industry. Cathy is too ordinary for you. No one needs to know that name but me. Between *us*, though—Kitten. *Kit*."

"I like that name—*Kit*—between *us*. Does that mean we have a relationship?"

Marlon laughed as he thought about how "Kit" had asked that question, as if closing a sale.

Separate relationships immediately blossomed between Marlon and each of the women. Carmen became a confidante with whom Marlon could vent frustrations, share feelings, seek personal advice and give business counsel. Joi became both a creative collaborator, a muse, and something much more complex—a blend of untouchable lover and goddaughter. There is no doubt from his letters that Marlon fell in love with Joi, as Harry had. But paradoxically, Marlon had also developed a daunting sense of responsibility for her, as one might have for a goddaughter whose parents had passed.

Unfortunately, things started falling apart almost immediately. Within a few weeks, Joi learned that she was pregnant by Jim Mathews, who went into an emotional nosedive after getting the news. He soon stopped going to work, which created personal financial havoc. He tried to wager his way out of that mess but ended up with enormous gambling debts. His "creditors" began looking for him with baseball bats instead of paperwork. He abandoned Joi and fled to a small room paid for by a new lover, a married beautician named Chloe, whom Harry believed was a voodoo witch exercising control over his brother.

Like a sad country song getting sadder still, the drama continued spiraling downhill. Joi had a breakdown when Jim disappeared. She stopped eating. Jim's creditors threatened her with violence if she didn't reveal his hiding place, but she didn't know where he was. She feared for her child's future, questioned her own safety and started believing Jim had been killed.

Harry tried to support her, but 1966 was a tough year for him. Marital difficulties had tied up his finances, and he was going through a lean time professionally. When he couldn't talk Joi out of her desperation, he grew angry and tried to manipulate her into more positive behavior. Instead of letting herself be helped by him, she stopped talking to him.

That's where this chapter began—with the first letter in our possession from Harry to Carmen. In despair, Harry lamented that Jim had been overtaken with evil. He believed that Joi was doomed to die either by giving birth to the child or because Jim had emotionally destroyed her. Harry told Carmen that Joi's trust in Jim had been crushed and that she had come to despise the child in her womb, hoping that she would die before giving birth.

For the first time, Harry uncharacteristically confessed a hunger for revenge. He told Carmen that if anything should happen to Joi, Carmen should hunt down Jim and tell him that he was responsible for the death of Joi and their child, and that without Joi's forgiveness Jim was eternally damned. He insisted that Carmen write three words—*Yes, I promise*—on a piece of paper and send it to him as her pledge to honor his request. Before signing the letter, Harry wrote that he was very sorry about the entire situation because he had so badly wanted to be friends with his brother.

Harry's letters to Carmen are filled with disturbing visions and premonitions. About a month before Joi's child was born, Harry had a frightening vision of Joi lying in a street. Borrowing Marlon's car, he drove to Joi's apartment complex. Following his "radar," as he referred to his intuitive gifts, he discovered Joi bruised and unconscious near the building's swimming pool. He bundled her into the car and drove to a doctor friend's private clinic for off-the-record X-rays. Joi's injuries were mostly only bruises or internal obstructions caused by swelling, but the male fetus showed signs of a fractured back.

Joi told Harry that Jim had come to her apartment, and they had argued. She had fled her apartment to get away, but he had followed her. The sparring continued to a stairway where he'd angrily grabbed and shaken her, and she had tumbled down the steps to the pool level. She didn't remember anything else.

Harry's doctor friend urged Harry to take Joi to the hospital, but Joi refused, so Harry brought her to Marlon's house nearby. He watched over her all night, then took her home, urging her close friend Carmen to provide ongoing comfort and protection.

Furious that his brother would harm Joi and his own unborn son, Harry tried to contact Jim but failed. Joi went from despondent to desperate. In this depressed state she was easily persuaded by Harry to file charges against Jim, hoping it would force him into the open. Then suddenly she disappeared without a word. Harry and Carmen feared that the thugs chasing Jim might have kidnapped her, or worse.

Out of despair, Harry worked out an elaborate plan to coax Jim into helping to locate Joi. He sent Carmen an official-looking typed letter praising *Then There Was Light* and personally pledging unlimited funding for the movie production. He tossed in an additional $10,000 for pre-publicity expenses for another Joi Sommers property, *Walk a Lonely Road*.

September 2, 1966

Miss Carmen Montez
8949 Sunset Blvd.,
Hollywood, Calif.

Dear Miss Montez:

I am pleased to extend to you unlimited financing for your forthcoming motion picture production, "Then There Was Light". The beautiful and moving screenplay by Joi Sommers is one of the most timely original scripts it has been my pleasure to read in recent years.

I congratulate you on this property, and I am delighted at your consideration of me for the role of Euriah.

I am further able to offer you an investment in the sum of $10,000 for pre-publicity purposes for Miss Sommers and Miss Sommers protege, as previously discussed with Miss Sommers for the production, "Walk A Lonely Road".

Please contact Mr. Stein at the New York office immediately concerning the details of our agreement.

Again, thanking you for your dedication to the causes of artistic expression and social freedom.

Yours, Truly,

Harry Belafonte

HB:as

Harry Belafonte's letter pledging unlimited financing for a movie project.

That same day, Harry had a handwritten letter delivered to Carmen explaining that the typed business letter was a ruse. Fearing that the letter of intent could be binding, he clarified that he currently didn't have the funds to make good on his promise and that Carmen should not take it seriously. He gave Carmen a phone number for Jim at his hotel job and asked her to call Jim and read the letter of intent to him, then explain that without Joi the financing would fall through. Jim would understand that a portion of Harry's financing would go to Jim under his arrangement with Carmen, and that money could be used to pay off Jim's debts—but only if they could find Joi.

Harry longed to be reunited with Joi. In one heartfelt letter he told Carmen that he hoped God would return Joi to him one day. He blamed powerful forces unleashed by Jim's evil girlfriend, the "witch" Chloe, for seizing control of Jim, but expressed the belief that Carmen's spiritual strength might provide the jolt needed to "awaken" him.

Over the next several weeks, Harry arranged financial assistance for Joi's uninsured hospital expenses and bought some baby things. He worried about what might happen to the child if Joi wanted to put him up for adoption; if Joi had used Jim's name when she was admitted to the hospital, Harry had learned that she could not work through an adoption agency without Jim's permission. And he fretted over the fact that children of "mixed blood" were much more difficult to place than others.

But Joi was still missing. Carmen had not spoken with Jim yet, so the fake letter of intent remained unrevealed to him. Desperate, Harry rebuked Carmen for not trying hard enough to contact his brother.

Then, just as suddenly as when she'd vanished, Joi turned up at her apartment very ill and refusing to say where she had been. Harry spent the next twenty-four hours with her as she "hovered between life and death." She was so weak from not eating that she couldn't even get out of bed on her own.

The next day, Harry sent a letter to Carmen fretting that the unborn child could be born mentally damaged or physically defective from Joi's malnourishment. The only information he had learned from Joi was that the previous Sunday she'd left a note for Jim at his apartment explaining that she was going to kill herself and the baby, and that if he continued to ignore her it would be the same as an act of murder. In a dramatic closing plea, he begged Carmen to "get Jim" because Joi had lost her will to live.

The next day, after Joi failed to hear from Jim, Harry urged Carmen to reach Jim immediately because he was the only person who could save Joi, who was walking around now but was even more depressed. The letter revealed a man truly afraid that his loved one would "go buy some razor blades" the minute he left her alone.

That evening, Harry rushed her to the hospital. After five hours of labor, James M. Mathews was finally born on September 21, 1966.

Harry and Marlon took turns caring for Joi and "little Jim," knowing that Joi still loved Jim, the father of her child, but was deeply despondent over his withdrawal from their lives. Harry provided living expenses, and Marlon took care of the medical expenses for the baby and for Joi, who was struggling to regain her health. The relationship between Joi and Harry slowly grew more distant and business-oriented, as Joi's relationship with Marlon became deeper and more personal.

It always seemed strange to me that during the unfolding of such an intense relationship, Harry never knew Joi Sommer's real name. Toward the end of Harry's letters to Carmen, he sadly acknowledged that he had lost Joi, but if he ever would be granted the chance to "win her back," he'd give it everything he had.

He never had that chance.

It seems fitting that Marlon Brando's first surviving letter to Carmen was sent six months after "little Jim" was born. Marlon knew that Joi Sommers was the pen name of Cathy Kane, but he never called her by that name except when urging her at times to "be Joi," meaning to adopt the persona of the confident, accomplished, talented screenwriter named Joi Sommers. He also seldom called her Cathy. Instead, to Marlon she was simply "Kit."

In this first letter from Marlon we learn that Kit had been ill intermittently since the birth of her son, and for the previous ten days had been in the hospital with a serious case of anemia. Marlon had taken on the responsibility of "nursemaid" for the baby.

After Kit had been admitted to the hospital, she had betrayed her continuing obsession with Jim Mathews by making Marlon promise to investigate him more deeply. Marlon took his promise to heart and turned up some alarming information. Jim Mathews, he learned, had been married during his entire relationship with Kit. When Marlon told Kit, she went into shock "and almost died," he wrote to Carmen. He may have been exaggerating about this but explained that the news had caused Kit to become gravely ill, lose her vision and ability to speak, and come close to dying. He'd tried to comfort Kit by explaining that Jim had been separated from his wife for a long time during which he had seriously attempted to get a divorce. He told Kit that Jim had pretended to lose interest in her to avoid confessing the truth. None of these subtle details had eased her emotional state.

When Kit had charged Jim for physical abuse the night he injured her and the unborn child, she unfortunately had signed the papers as "Mrs. James Mathews." Marlon worried that the authorities would discover another Mrs. Mathews, and then Kit would be in serious trouble.

Marlon was also in trouble, he told Carmen. His wife, Tarita, had filed a complaint against Kit for alienation of her husband's affection. Marlon called it "ridiculous" but failed to deny the truth of it. Clearly, the talented but troubled Kit had cast a spell over both Harry and Marlon.

Over the next few months, Harry slowly withdrew from Kit's life and became resigned to the role of a career advisor. Marlon slowly realized that Kit's affection for him was not romantic, becoming less of a hopeful lover-in-the-wings and more of a loving uncle and matchmaker. I suspect, however, that he never completely abandoned his dream of a life with Kit.

***

After months of watching the painful, disintegrating relationship between Elvis and Priscilla—a woman he despised—Marlon suggested to Carmen that he had identified the perfect replacement to "fill Priscilla's shoes." It was someone both he and Carmen knew well—Kit. He told Carmen that "our spirit friend" (meaning Jeni, Elvis's deceased true love) had let Marlon know she'd been intensely unhappy because Elvis was suffering so much in his marriage. Lobbying for Carmen's support for his suggestion, he wrote that Jeni would be strongly in favor of Elvis exchanging Priscilla for Kit.

In a Brando letter sent January 1968, a physical description of Kit appeared for the first time. Marlon remarked about how much

Kit resembled Priscilla, and how Kit had been transforming her wardrobe toward the kind of flowing garments that Pris favored—a more modern and feminine look. In his opinion, Kit wouldn't have to work to fit into Elvis's world—she already was his type of girl.

Marlon reflected on the time that he, Harry and Carmen had spent trying to get Kit and Jim Mathews back together, and after Jim proved to be "worthless," how they all had thought Kit and Elvis might make it together. It's clear from the totality of his writing about the mysterious Kit that Marlon fantasized about a life with her, and though he never directly mentioned it to Carmen, I'm sure she knew.

One evening, while Kit was at Marlon's house waiting to go for a ride in the hills, Tom Jones called Marlon with a request. He was about to record some songs before a live audience and remembered that he was carrying around a written response to Carmen's most recent letter. He hoped Marlon could swing by, pick up the letter and get it to Carmen. He didn't want to lose it during all the costume changes for fear someone might find out about his relationship with her.

Marlon and Kit had to park a couple blocks from the studio. Leaving Kit in the car, Marlon went into the studio during preparations. Tom handed him the letter and said, "Why don't you join the audience? You can grab a seat down front before they let in the crowd."

"I've got a friend with me," Marlon replied.

"So grab two seats. But hurry."

Marlon dashed to the car, but Kit was reticent to go out in public because she was wearing a skimpy pair of red pants Harry had bought her. With some encouragement she relented. Marlon ushered her into the studio through the back entrance, and they took two seats in the front row.

The first two songs were big productions with staging and many dancers. Then a problem arose with the costumes, and the remainder of the taping had to be rescheduled on another day. Tom was embarrassed that the audience had been cheated out of a bigger show, so he offered to sing a couple more songs without the cameras. The audience erupted in appreciation.

During the first song, he glanced at the front row and saw Kit in her vibrant red pants. His face lit up. On the second number he danced over to Kit, then bent over and kissed her. Startled, she covered her face with her hands and Tom grinned, stepping away. A minute later he approached and kissed her again. As the song was nearing its climax, he kissed her a third time, but lingered after. Marlon told Carmen that Tom had whispered something to Kit before taking a bow.

After his impromptu performance, Tom escaped backstage, and Marlon asked Kit what Tom had whispered. Kit said that she had been invited backstage. Marlon accompanied her to Tom's dressing room, and they waited for him to shower and change clothes. By the time he emerged, scores of fans had surrounded the dressing room, making it impossible to get near the singer. Finally, Marlon yelled out Tom's name, which caused Tom to glance around and spot his friend. He signaled for Marlon to wait, but the actor was eager to continue his evening with Kit, so he motioned that he was leaving, then shouted, "See you later." Tom looked disappointed.

By this time, many of the fans had recognized the famous actor and surrounded him. For about five minutes, Marlon signed autographs and even introduced Kit as a writer, prompting one fan to ask for her autograph too.

On the way out of the studio, Kit noticed that the stitching on one of her gold shoes was coming undone, making it hard to walk. Marlon offered to get the car and pick her up. By the time he arrived at the studio back door, she had disappeared. A fan told him a woman wearing bright red pants had climbed into a Cadillac with Tom Jones. "Lucky woman," the fan said.

I can imagine what Marlon was thinking.

For hours, Marlon obsessively tried to track down Tom and Kit. He even called Elvis to ask where Tom might have gone. Elvis told him that Tom's manager, Gordon Mills, rented a bungalow at the Beverly Hills Hotel and Tom sometimes used it. Marlon called the hotel, and the manager told him that Mr. Jones had asked not to be disturbed.

Marlon was familiar with these hotel bungalows. He drove to the hotel and staked out Gordon Mills' unit. Through a thinly curtained window he could see that a light was on in the bathroom. Around five o'clock that morning the light went out, and so had Marlon's patience. He went to the bungalow's main door and started pounding. Nobody answered, which angered him even more.

Finally, Marlon went home and repeatedly called Kit's apartment. At eight thirty, in a rage, Marlon drove back to the bungalow and almost broke down the door with his fists. After a couple of minutes, Tom, cocooned in bedsheets, opened the door and Marlon pushed his way in. Clearly, Tom was alone, but two glasses of flat champagne stood together on a nightstand.

"Have you lost someone?" Marlon asked.

"Seems so."

"Where is she?"

"Marlon, what's this all about? She said she wasn't your girl. I wouldn't do that to you."

"She's not. Not really."

"Then what's all the fuss? I don't even know her name. I tried everything, but she wouldn't tell me. Do you know it?"

Marlon shook his head, a silent white lie. He knew that Tom was a good friend, and the innocent look on Tom's face was settling him down. Glancing around the room, he noticed a folded note on the bureau. Boldly, he picked it up and immediately recognized both Kit's handwriting and the object that slid out of the fold—Kit's antique gold pendant with two ruby hearts.

He looked at Tom, as if asking permission to read the note. Tom gestured to go ahead. Kit had written that she and Tom would meet again when things were different. In the meantime, she wanted Tom to have the pendant that her Welsh grandmother had given her so Tom would remember he would always be part of her.

"Part of her?" Marlon shouted. "You just met her!"

Tom must have known that Kit's words had infuriated Marlon because he snatched the pendant and the note away. "She gave it to me, not you. Am I right?"

Marlon answered by putting his fist into Tom's chin. The singer staggered backward but started grinning. "Mate, what'd I do to you? Tell me what I did."

Enraged even more, Marlon raised his fist again, but Tom would not defend himself, would not fight back. In the end, Marlon raced out of the bungalow before rearranging Tom's face.

In a letter to Carmen, Marlon rationalized his behavior as the result of disappointment that Kit had fallen for Tom after Marlon had decided she was the right match for Elvis. I think Carmen probably knew that fighting Tom said a lot more about Marlon's unconfessed love for Kit. Marlon said that he would never reveal how to find Kit or give her name to Tom, whom he still loved and admired despite his anger. Between the lines of this letter, I saw a plea for Carmen to do the same.

Lwli

Tom was not sorry at all, he told Carmen. The night of the taping he had seen this lovely girl in red pants and had suddenly been drawn to her by some irresistible gravity. He was not just hooking up with a sexy lady for the night. And he didn't believe in love at first sight. But even so, he felt compelled—psychically or emotionally or maybe spiritually—to possess this girl and not let go because they were not strangers. He was sure they both understood that, though neither could explain.

The intensity of Tom's rapturous expression in his letters took me by surprise. Here was a man of the world. At his young age, he had experienced many women and had just broken up with Mary Wilson of the Supremes. But his writing described how his soul "wept within me" as Kit touched his fingertips, and how he wouldn't worry about seeing her again because they'd find each other the way "two magnets are drawn together." He told Carmen that after meeting this girl with no name, a "dull pain went out of me," a pain he had not even known existed. He compared the merging of their souls to a scene in the movies where the ghostly image of a sleeping person rises out of the body. He told Carmen that was how he felt when he was with the girl with no name—like his soul would separate from his body and move into hers, and he would become a part of her, fastened there by "invisible chains."

Tom regretted that Marlon would never understand or appreciate the depth of his feelings and that Marlon would think he was just rebounding from a broken relationship with Mary Wilson. He didn't want to quarrel with Marlon and knew he deserved a punch in the face, but he'd been unrepentantly swept away by a Welsh girl who, for a short time, had made him feel "above all other men." Finding it awkward to have a girlfriend with no name, he decided to call her Lwli, meaning "baby" in Welsh.

Tom's letters do not reveal how he and Lwli got back together, but they did, and the relationship continued to intensify. Lwli must have revealed to Tom that she knew Carmen because he often referred to the women's friendship and occasionally asked Carmen to send letters to him via Lwli. In a letter written before Tom was returning to London, he told Carmen that "Miss Nameless" had taken hold of his mind and wouldn't let go. If he saw her before flying away, Tom wrote, he'd probably kidnap her on impulse and take her with him. Then, as if that notion had instantly taken root, he suggested that Carmen propose to Lwli the adventure of going with Tom to England. Tom would buy a ticket for her.

She didn't go to London with Tom, a decision Marlon applauded.

Marlon simmered for weeks over Kit's impulsive fling. He blamed Tom for abducting Kit "like he was a Valentino" and then grinning like the Cheshire Cat when Marlon caught him. He feared that Tom would break the heart of the fragile young woman Marlon cared for.

While Tom was in London, he and Marlon spoke via long distance and nearly came to blows over the phone. Marlon demanded to know why Tom had not opened the bungalow door right away when Marlon was pounding on it.

178

"That's my business, not yours," Tom said.

"You're a bastard, you know that?"

"Don't be so hypocritical. I'm sure you've slept with more women in your life than I've even looked at."

"I doubt that."

"There've only been three, besides my wife," Tom said unconvincingly.

"Well, I've seen Mary Wilson, and you've done a pretty good job of messing her up. I won't let you do that again with..." Marlon almost used Kit's name but stopped short.

There was an awkward pause, after which Marlon asked, "What are you going to do about her now?"

"I can't do anything without you knowing about it. And right now I'm in England—what can I do from here?"

"You say you can't do anything now, but I wonder what's going on in that mind of yours."

"You wouldn't like it," Tom responded. "Let's talk about something else. This gets us all riled up."

Marlon appreciated Tom's honesty and told Carmen that it hurt to fight with his friend, but he felt a sense of responsibility for Kit. After a couple of weeks, he and Tom stopped sparring, but I sensed a streak of jealousy between the lines of Marlon's ongoing letters to Carmen. A month later he wrote that Kit had asked him to include a small gift when Marlon sent his Christmas present to Tom. This exploded into an argument that Marlon regretted.

"So are you using me to send secret messages to Tom?" Marlon had asked. "Damn if I want to be in the middle of this thing you've got going."

"That's ridiculous. I suppose you X-rayed the cake I sent him."

On Kit's request, Marlon had earlier delivered a Welsh cake to Tom and a record of Welsh hymns from Tom to Kit. He confessed to Carmen that he had checked to see if the record was sealed. It was, which meant it didn't contain a message from Tom.

Over time, as Marlon witnessed the kindness and love that Tom showered onto Kit, his jealousy and suspicion waned, and Tom became even more obsessed with his enigmatic Welsh sweetheart, who still wouldn't share her name. But something else was also going on in Tom's mind. He shared with Carmen his growing belief that he and Lwli were possibly distant relatives.

One evening he and Lwli had been casually talking about their Welsh ancestors, which raised some questions in Tom's mind about common relatives. Tom vowed to explore the issue when he returned to Great Britain. He was sure it was not possible that he and Lwli could be as close as first cousins but wondered about other kinds of family ties. In fact, he wrote, the idea of a family connection seemed rather sexy to him, perhaps proving they were destined to be together—two unlikely souls, a Welsh girl trapped on the wrong continent and a lad who by rights should still be digging for coal meeting across the vast stretch of space and time.

He joked that such a story would be worth a fortune to Mr. Ripley.

Harry Belafonte was convinced that Joi/Kit/Lwli was Tom's first cousin, and his conviction prompted Marlon to consider this possibility more closely. Marlon told Carmen that he didn't approve of such a close mingling of bloodlines. It was not illegal, he knew, but even if one discounted the "old wives' tales" of damaged offspring, it just did not seem right. Beneath Marlon's ambiguous complaint, there may have been a notion that Harry's theory of relativity could be used to break up the smitten couple.

Suddenly everything seemed to point Marlon toward proof of this theory, even family photographs. In a letter, he reported to Carmen that he had encountered a photograph of Tom and his family that appeared on page twenty of an unnamed magazine. He painted a word picture of the photograph for Carmen. Tom's pregnant sister was in the foreground on the right side of the photo. Her husband was in the top left corner. Tom's mother, holding a leopard purse, stood behind Tom near her sister. Between his mother and aunt stood the mother of these two sisters—Tom's grandmother—with her hand on Tom's shoulder. Other relatives also crowded into the picture.

Marlon had seen a photo of Kit's mother and was struck by how much she looked like Tom's grandmother, the woman through whom Marlon believed Lwli and Tom were related. This picture seemed like verification.

At about this time, Carmen received a letter from Tom who said he was writing from his couch where he had been sitting with Lwli. It was while kissing her, he said, that he was struck by the absolute certitude that Lwli and he were of the same flesh and blood. He assured Carmen that he wasn't asking her to break any confidence but wondered if the reason Lwli would not reveal her name was because Tom could then easily learn they were relatives, and she feared his reaction.

If it was sinful to love a cousin the way Tom loved Lwli, he told Carmen, then he would continue to sin—and glory in it—because he had no power to stop.

I do not know how long the relationship between Tom and Lwli/Kit/Joi/Cathy lasted, or whether she ever told him her name, because Tom's letters ended before Christmas 1970, and Marlon's last surviving letter is from 1972. From one of Marlon's last letters, though, we learn that after almost three years Kit and Tom still felt like they couldn't live without each other.

Call me a hopeless romantic or a naïve fool, but I hope they had more time together than that.

And as for little Jimmy, wherever he is, I wish him all the best too.

Are You Lonesome Tonight?

After my first read of the Elvis letters, the depth of Elvis's confessed loneliness staggered me. He seldom spoke of it directly, but loneliness wafted from the handwritten pages and lingered like the perfume of an absent lover. I couldn't shake my sense of his despair, hopelessness and insecurity. It was hard to reconcile the author of these letters with the confident, magnetic on-stage performer who could conquer audiences with a shake of his hips or a curl of his lips.

I was also struck by the intensity of his relationship with Carmen Montez. I had read Elvis's letters perhaps a half-dozen times before I noticed a short remark in one of Elvis's last letters to her. He expressed his hope that God would someday "allow us to meet, here on this earth?" I was astonished! This 1972 letter made it clear that Elvis and Carmen had never physically met. How was this possible? How could a troubled man establish and maintain a relationship with a confidante and never physically spend time with her?

Nevertheless, his letters testify to his trust in her—and a growing dependence on her. For much of that time he didn't even know what she looked like, yet he longed to be with her. They both lived in the Los Angeles area, and certainly she had every career reason to strengthen a relationship with The King, but they communicated almost entirely through letters, which is our good fortune. They seldom spoke by telephone because of her insistence on written communication.

This must have posed a dilemma for Elvis because he seldom wrote in longhand, particularly long messages, and also because correspondence from Carmen could be discovered by his wife. Priscilla was intensely jealous and had found hidden letters to her husband from various starlets. In her autobiography, *Elvis and Me*, Priscilla describes how she found a note from Ann-Margret questioning why Elvis had broken off their relationship; Priscilla "tore it to shreds and flushed it down the toilet." While snooping in Elvis's closet one day, she found a bunch of notes and cards from various women; I'm sure Elvis learned not to keep evidence at home. Perhaps that's why none of Carmen's letters to him have ever turned up and why he was so secretive about his private relationship with her.

Elvis kept Carmen completely away from his circle of friends and associates except for Tom, Marlon and Harry, all of whom had similar emotionally deep but physically distant relationships with Carmen. Elvis, however, was obsessive about keeping Carmen a secret, a behavior that led to even greater loneliness. In numerous letters, he sets up dates with Carmen to watch one of his movies on local TV—he alone at his home and she alone at hers—only to betray his insecurity in the next letter by begging for scraps of praise for his performance while lamenting his flaws as an actor.

While reading these letters, I, too, vicariously shared these odd "date nights" with Elvis and Carmen and experienced an unrelenting loneliness. How could it be that Elvis was never able to share a sofa and watch a movie with the woman he called "Dear Sister"?

A Near Miss

In one series of letters, Elvis unveiled an elaborate scheme to finally meet Carmen. He planned to fly her to Las Vegas—with Carmen's friend Kit, as it turned out—to attend an Elvis concert at the International, an event mentioned earlier. I can imagine Carmen's excitement at seeing Elvis perform live for the first time, and Elvis's anxiety about whether or not his plan would work. If it worked out, perhaps they could meet after the show. To make sure that secrecy was maintained, Elvis could not use his staff to make arrangements, and to avoid media attention Elvis decided to book rooms for Carmen and Kit away from the International.

For several days, Elvis personally called numerous Vegas hotels trying to find available rooms. He didn't dare pull rank by identifying himself; news of Elvis Presley booking rooms for two women would certainly be leaked to the tabloids.

He finally found a room for two at an out-of-the-way motel. His patience exhausted, Elvis asked Marlon to book a rental car, buy the plane tickets and deliver them to Carmen. Because show parking would be difficult at the International, he coaxed Tom Jones into getting a parking sticker for the women.

Tickets for the show were so scarce that even Elvis couldn't get them. Tom was in Vegas, so Elvis prevailed on his friend again, confident in Tom's superior people skills. Elvis and Tom slipped away to the casino business office, and Tom entered alone. He emerged a few minutes later grinning broadly at Elvis with two tickets and a smear of lipstick on his face.

"It took nearly everything I've got, but I got 'em!" Tom said, waving the tickets.

Nearly forty years after Tom wrangled these tickets, I'm still surprised at how Elvis, arguably the most popular star of the era, relied on Tom to get tickets for Carmen. Insecurity, perhaps… or weariness of public attention? Maybe fear of being seen in public without a bodyguard? Regardless, throughout his letters he seemed to be descending slowly into his own insecure and lonely world.

After all the clandestine effort, Carmen and Kit flew to Las Vegas, stayed at the motel, drove to the casino and parked free, attended the opening-night show amidst countless celebrities on July 31, 1969… but never met Elvis.

Marlon also attended the show. Afterward, he wrote Carmen a note with his impressions of Elvis's performance. "Live and vital"… "a house afire"… "like electricity, throwing off sparks." He was moved by Elvis's rendition of the song "Memories" and suggested that it would be perfect for Kit's movie that he and Carmen were trying to get made. Knowing that Carmen could not attend the after-show party, Marlon described it for her, emphasizing how Elvis seemed to be glowing with delight at the enthusiastic response from the audience. He added an interesting anecdote about a comment Elvis's cousin Patsy had made to him at the party.

"I envy Elvis so much," she had told him. "He's too pretty to be a man. I spent the entire day at the beauty parlor, but Elvis has all that hair and just needs to run a comb through it."

Marlon also wrote that he had hoped Carmen and Elvis could have spent some time together, because in his mind that was the only way for people to really get to know each other deeply. He added that he'd also been hoping Kit and Elvis could have finally met after the show. Making a match between Elvis and Kit had been Marlon's long-term goal. He emphasized to Carmen that Kit needed a man like Elvis who was reliable but unsophisticated, open and honest, outgoing and in need of love. He was obviously lobbying Carmen for support. In closing, he asked Carmen to pray that Elvis would stay happy for a little while.

Visitations

I wondered, as Marlon had, how Elvis could gain such a trusting and dependent relationship with Carmen without having met her. A short passage from one of Elvis's letters written about eight months after he and Carmen had begun corresponding helped me understand. At times, he wrote, Carmen would make an out-of-body visit to him. He would enter a trancelike state that allowed him to discover the truth about previous events and sort out many of his perplexities. He begged Carmen to "visit" him again and help him explore his Indian heritage, an issue that had been haunting him for eight years since shooting the movie *Flaming Star*.

Elvis must have been aware that as a minister in the Universal Church of the Master, Carmen purportedly had the gift of mediumship, contact with the spiritual world, presumably allowing her to communicate with the living on a spiritual plane as well as the departed. Whether this knowledge suggestively contributed to a false belief that she made out-of-body visits or the phenomenon in fact was manifested cannot be proven, but in his letters, Elvis claims numerous times that such spiritual contact with Carmen occurred.

At this point in his letter Elvis made an astonishing claim. When he was younger, he wrote, an unscrupulous person had hypnotized him to explore this issue and others. This establishes that he may have been highly "suggestible"—easily influenced by suggestion—a trait that must be present for one to be hypnotized. While in a trance, he had revealed personal information that the hypnotist later used to blackmail him. Naturally, this had made Elvis afraid of opening up to other people. Since the hypnosis betrayal, he hadn't fully trusted anyone except Carmen. He was willing to fully share his thoughts and emotions with her because she had proven her trustworthiness.

If Carmen would agree to psychically visit and guide him on this spiritual journey, Elvis wrote, he wanted Marlon to also be by his side in case anything went wrong. This made sense to me because Elvis knew about Marlon's psychic experiences. Whether real or imagined, these experiences had made an indelible impression on both Marlon and Elvis.

In the chapter "Authenticating Elvis," I revealed that Marlon occasionally experienced "spirit writing" during which he would blank out while writing and another "spirit" would manipulate his hand, interrupting Marlon's original message to communicate something entirely different. And in the chapter "Brainwriting," psychologist/graphoanalyst Jane Hollis stated that the letter was physically written by Marlon, but the personality revealed by the handwriting was significantly different than Marlon's. Sometimes these messages were prophetic, at other times they reported events occurring some distance away. When the "spirit" left, Marlon would have no memory of what had been communicated until he read the spirit's inserted message in unfamiliar handwriting.

One explanation for this "spirit writing" is that Brando exhibited dissociative identity disorder (DID), also known as multiple personality disorder (MPD). A person with DID has at least two distinct and relatively enduring personality states, sometimes called "alters." Each of these alters presents consistent patterns of behavior, social relationships, emotional reactions, recalled education, memories of personal experiences and other characteristics. The features of one alter may contrast sharply with parallel features of other alters within the same individual, even physiologically. Each alter may exhibit different EEG reports, allergic responses, dominant handedness, vision characteristics and dermatological reactions.

Another explanation is that this phenomenon is just what I have labelled it, "spirit writing." For further insight into this kind of phenomenon I turned to Adrian Lee, author of the popular books about the paranormal, *How to Be a Christian Psychic*, *Mysterious Minnesota*, and *Mysterious Midwest*. A well-educated and straight-talking Londoner, Adrian had an immediate and visceral reaction to reading the letters, and he astonished our research team with the insights produced from his admittedly rarified point of view. The following are his own words:

"In Marlon's case, I wonder if his knowledge of Carmen's purported gift of mediumship and emphasis on a spiritual plane of existence had been one of the common bonds that drew him and Carmen together. Certainly, he felt free to send her letters containing "spirit writing" with no apparent fear of criticism and most likely the expectation of understanding.

"We have handwritten messages from two 'spirits' that occasionally seized control over Marlon. The first is Jeni, Elvis's true love, whom Marlon first encountered as a vision during a party in Elvis's home. In her 'spirit writing,' Jeni was eerily the first to report that Tom Jones had been in a serious automobile accident in the UK and had been paralyzed. Neither Elvis, Carmen nor Marlon had known about this accident before Jeni had used Marlon's hand to reveal the startling news. Jeni's 'SOS' message, proven later to be true, must have taken the threesome by surprise, even though all were believers in spiritual phenomena.

"The second 'spirit' that occasionally commanded Marlon's hand identified himself in a note as 'Chief Talking Eagle, Chief of the Cherokee Nation.' Among other things, the chief wrote, 'I who died for you am your brother, and Carmen is my sister, and my spirit is Elvis's spirit. Do you know me not? I am not dead.'" (Author's note: Under the assumption that these words were not written by Marlon Brando but by Chief Talking Eagle, I feel free to quote these words directly without fear of copyright infringement, though I'm sure the courts would find defining the authorship of this "spirit writing" problematic.) "It is understandable that Elvis would want Marlon present during a spiritual exploration of his Indian roots because both men believed Marlon had a psychic connection with Chief Talking Eagle.

"We know that Carmen had agreed to the visitation, but it never occurred. Five days after Elvis made his request, he canceled the event. Angry and depressed, he explained in his letter that he didn't care if he went on living or not. He had just learned that his estranged wife was pregnant a second time, dooming him to continue a relationship that would destroy his life and turn it into a 'living lie.'"

***

I have spent so many years with these deeply personal letters that it is hard not to consider myself a friend of both Carmen and Elvis. I have tried to imagine how Carmen responded to Elvis's numerous crisis letters and pleas for help, but the truth is I don't know. It has been frustrating to have only half the story. I do know that she helped Elvis; I know because he tells her. At times, despite lacking her presence in the unfolding events, I can almost feel the therapy she was delivering. For example, she somehow managed to get Elvis to confess his depression and loneliness, release the pressure to fulfill other people's expectations, and focus energy on helping his friends and meeting their needs. For a man who rarely wrote, writing these letters had become potent therapy indeed. Perhaps the lack of instant feedback from Carmen helped him explain things more fully and reflect more deeply.

There were times when Elvis wrote himself to sleep or into a trance: "Come to me soon, even if we can't talk." Other times he wrote so candidly it seems impossible that he could ever have *spoken* so freely: "If I didn't have you I'd explode." Like Tom and Marlon, he frequently passed on messages for his friends when they were on the move or buried beneath responsibilities. In this way they all stayed in touch.

Over time, Elvis's letters evolved from impersonal background about his life and business information to more personal matters, then pleas for advice or help. He confessed vain concerns about his on-screen weight in "Kid Galahad" and worried about his kidneys and various surgeries. He was scared to death of painkillers—didn't want to end up a "hophead." He complained freely of feeling numb, empty, like he was dying in pieces. At times he seemed perilously close to falling apart. When he was watching a show on TV he might fire off a letter to see if Carmen was watching the same show.

Carmen Montez spoke several times to her best friend, Carmen Rayburn, about watching TV movies with Elvis, mostly Elvis movies. But not until she read Elvis's letters did Carmen Rayburn understand that Elvis and Carmen were watching those movies alone but at the same time. I have no letters from Carmen Montez to Elvis, but I can imagine her asking, "Are you lonesome tonight?" In scores of letters back to Carmen, in a multitude of ways, he answered, "Yes."

Feud

If Elvis's behavior at times seemed eccentric or inexplicable, the causes may have been due to instilled fears or latent paranoia stirred up by something he'd just experienced. Every celebrity has some fears derived from bad experiences on the road or bizarre conduct by neurotic fans, and most have a set of evasive techniques to avoid awakening those anxieties. Elvis, though, was not just fearful—he was frequently controlled by his fears, or uncontrollable because of them.

His letters to Carmen Montez reveal the maze of danger, distress and outright abuse that had overwhelmed his life, much of it previously unknown. The effects shaped the later years of his life, a death spiral that almost everyone has misinterpreted because so many of the contributing factors have been kept secret. My chief motivation in publishing the facts contained in the Elvis letters, and those of his close friends, is to reveal hidden events that help us better understand the reasons behind Elvis's actions.

Jungle Sam

A chain of events leading to a brutal attack began in 1964 when Elvis was shooting the movie *Kissin' Cousins*, produced by Sam Katzman, "King of the Quickies."

Colonel Parker appreciated the sixty-four-year-old producer's reputation for aggressively slashing production costs to maximize profits. The budget of Elvis's previous movie, *Viva Las Vegas*, had unforgivably mushroomed out of control, threatening Parker's profit participation. Parker was looking for a producer who ruled with an iron fist and never let artistic sensibilities derail the budget.

For Katzman, who typically made movies for budgets of $250,000 or less—B movies like *The Giant Claw*, *Rumble on the Docks, Blackjack Ketchum,* and *Desperado*—an $800,000 budget was an opportunity to squeeze out some real money. In the 1940s and '50s, Katzman specialized in action/adventure serials with razor-thin margins, earning him the nickname "Jungle Sam." He was used to stars that worked for a few thousand dollars per picture and never complained.

This photo of producer Sam Katzman (holding hands with a chimp)
appeared in the March 23, 1953 issue of *LIFE* in an article entitled
"Meet Jungle Sam." Katzman is surrounded by veteran actors,
costumes and props from his many B-movie serials.

Just as Frank Sinatra was reputed to have Mafia ties, Katzman was rumored to be plugged into various criminal activities including narcotics and money laundering. Some crew members and actors whispered about goon squad tactics to maintain on-set discipline, blackmail threats and occasional job payment in chemical substances or untraceable cash. Even George Ramentol, Carmen Montez's husband, reported rumors that Katzman participated in "cash flow confusion" related to parking lot revenues. Carmen suspected her husband knew more than he had let on.

For decades, Katzman's reputation for stinginess and sexual harassment—he was an early "Harvey Weinstein"—was broadly known in the industry. In Boyd Magers's website *Western Clippings*, actress Linda Johnson (*Brick Bradford*) is quoted as saying: "I don't have anything nice to say about Sam. He was lecherous. Very. Anyway, there was a young girl, Helene Stanley, she was just darling, and she was fairly young, and Sam was just after her all the time... I don't mean anything serious happened, but he was just... crude."

Actor Billy Benedict (*Brenda Starr, Reporter*) said: "With Katzman, [you] were on a strict budget and got by just as cheap as they could. ...Katzman would hang around with his cane and beat the floor when things weren't going well. Maybe sometimes he'd even try to beat you!"

Actress Gloria Marlen (*Trouble Chasers* and *Sweet Genevieve*) revealed more about Katzman's smutty side. She said, "Katzman liked dirty jokes, he would go around and tell everybody dirty jokes... Also he had a terrible cane that had a finger on the end of it... if you bent over, I don't care who you were... and nobody would say anything."

Actor Ralph Hodges (*Superman, Sea Hound, Bruce Gentry, Mysterious Island*) confirmed the cane story. "He carried this cane that he nudged everybody with," Ralph explained. "I say *nudged* to be kind... 'The Fickle Finger of Fate.' Well, Katzman had one on the end of a cane."

House Peters, Jr. (*Flash Gordon*; *Adventures of Frank Merriwell*) added another malicious detail to the cane story. Katzman "had a walking stick with an electric battery in it," House remembered. "He got a great kick out of using that on people, especially girls."

House also reported that one day his agent asked Katzman for a twenty-dollar daily increase from the fifty-five dollars House was being paid. "I was standing outside the office door smoking my pipe and overhearing everything that was going on. Katzman would not budge. He insisted he didn't have any more money. Then he picked up the phone and dialed his bookie and put a thousand dollars on a horse! And he couldn't afford giving me a lousy twenty-dollar raise?"

In theory, Katzman and Parker, the carny huckster, were a matched set, both obsessed with milking each project for every cent, even at the expense of artistic merit. At the time, Parker thought he was cleverly saving money by signing Katzman to a two-picture deal. He knew that a producer credit on a successful Elvis movie could drive up Katzman's asking price for a second picture.

Kissin' Cousins

On October 14, 1963, Elvis arrived at the town of Big Bear in the San Bernardino mountains to begin location shooting. He probably had no idea that *Kissin' Cousins* would be his first true low-budget quickie. To save money, Katzman hired director Gene Nelson to a package deal. Nelson directed, wrote the screenplay, choreographed the dance numbers, and with music director Fred Karger selected all the songs. Nelson even played congas on the soundtrack. Katzman mercilessly slashed the production schedule to a meager seventeen days.

Kissin' Cousins was an unabashed rip-off of the Li'l Abner comic strip featuring Elvis in two roles—twin brothers, one of them blonde—and a band of man-starved girls called the Kittyhawks. On numerous occasions Katzman proved his skinflintedness. Startled by an animal wrangler's asking price for a dozen live chickens to populate a scene, he personally found a nearby farm and bought twelve birds for half the price. During production, Elvis's scenes with his "twin" had to be shot twice so Elvis could appear in each role opposite a stand-in. To make up some of the time to duplicate the shooting, Katzman shortened the time required for editing the complex scenes. In the released film an attentive viewer can glimpse the faces of the stand-ins.

Elvis hated the tedious shooting of his twin roles. Despite a respectful relationship with director Gene Nelson, he often clashed with Katzman about production details. Katzman's assembly line method of cranking out flicks in a few days began to fail when his high-priced star protested the script's idiocy and the producer's skimpy production schedule. On the set, Katzman openly hurled strings of obscenities at Elvis that described him in essence as the most uncooperative and unprofessional actor he'd ever worked with. Elvis used equally vulgar language characterizing Katzman as, well, insensitive and vicious.

Elvis swore he would never work on a Katzman-produced film again. Apparently, he didn't know about the two-picture contract Parker had signed with Katzman. A little more than a year later Elvis again found himself doomed to suffer through another Katzman production, *Harum Scarum*. He told Parker that the only reason he would appear in this picture was because his friend Gene Nelson was directing. Also because of the money, of course. Elvis was paid $1,000,000, and the rest of the cast shared $200,000.

Harum Scarum

Harum Scarum began production on March 15, 1965. Elvis was initially enthusiastic about this Baghdad adventure tale portraying a movie star who travels through the Near East promoting his latest film, *Sands of the Desert,* only to be kidnapped by a band of assassins. He had convinced himself that he could contain the Katzman problem. During the short rehearsal period, he paraded around his house in fanciful Arabian costumes and carved the air with prop swords. I'm sure it never occurred to him that the kidnapping plot of the movie would foretell real life.

"Whatever enthusiasm [Elvis] felt pretty much evaporated on the first day of shooting," Elvis biographer Peter Guralnick wrote, "as it became instantly clear that the story was a joke." Elvis withdrew mentally from the picture almost immediately, unable to stay focused on another sure-fire flop with predictably rotten reviews. Katzman quickly accused Elvis of acting while sedated and, more importantly to Sam, running up costs through production delays. Sparks flew.

Actor Will Hutchins (*Sugarfoot*; *Gunfighter*) said that while shooting the movie *Clambake*, "Elvis Presley... told me that *Harum Scarum* was his least enjoyable flick experience. Jungle Sam Katzman made him perform all his own stunts. Elvis said the sword fighting called for more rehearsal. Sam shouted, 'Time is money!' Elvis collected his fair share of sword conks on his knuckles— ouchville! Where was the Colonel when Elvis needed him?"

Feeling trapped, Elvis left the shoot whenever possible to spend time at the Lake Shrine retreat of the Self-Realization Fellowship in Pacific Palisades. The group had been founded in 1920 by Paramahansa Yogananda, a holy man from India, and Elvis had been introduced to it the previous year by his spiritual advisor/hairdresser Larry Geller. California during this time was a mecca for alternative spiritual movements that attracted millions of followers—at least temporarily. Elvis's fascination with this new spiritual path put him on an accelerated collision course with Katzman who had no openly declared spiritual interests at all.

To compensate for budget overruns, or perhaps just out of greed, Katzman recycled scenery from the 1925 colossus *King of Kings* directed by Cecil B. DeMille. He borrowed costumes from the 1944 film *Kismet*. Nothing seemed too small to scrounge. Elvis's dagger was purloined from the 1939 movie *Lady of the Tropics*. One studio hand said that every time it appeared the budget was threatened, Katzman tore out four pages of the script.

Sensing how badly the movie was going to turn out, Colonel Parker suggested a fix—adding narration by a talking camel. Better, he figured, that people would think the spoofiness was deliberate and laugh *with* the movie rather than *at* it. At the end of the shoot, Elvis gave director Gene Nelson an autographed photo with the handwritten words, "Someday we'll do it right."

Harum Scarum was an unmitigated disaster. After watching it, Colonel Parker exclaimed it would take "a 55th cousin of P. T. Barnum to sell this picture." In *The Sleaze Merchants*, author McCarty extended the Barnum reference, declaring that any fascination engendered by this movie was "roughly akin to gawking at the pickled cranium of a two-headed cow in a sideshow." Colonel Parker blamed Katzman for the *Harum Scarum* disaster, Katzman blamed Elvis and Parker, and a bad movie turned into a bitter, personal feud.

Parker defended his star, publicly laying all blame directly at the feet of Sam Katzman. Feeling betrayed and deeply wounded, Katzman appears to have taken a more private approach to tormenting Elvis and destroying the foundation of Colonel Parker's empire. His unholy, diabolical mission would unfold over the next five years and drive Elvis to the edge of insanity, if not over it.

Don't Be Cruel

Two years and nine months after completing his second picture with Sam Katzman, Elvis made a rare phone call to Carmen Montez. Lisa Marie was due to be born in a few weeks, so this should have been a very happy time for Elvis. But he was shaken by a package delivered to him that January morning. The parcel contained cassette recordings of Elvis having intimate conversations with some of the young ladies on the set of *Harum Scarum*. The most damaging content, according to Elvis, was his candid grievances about Priscilla, some of them deeply personal. He knew that the conversations could be interpreted as a man seeking "comfort" from impressionable young women, a common prelude to a sexual encounter.

On January 27, 1968, Elvis wrote a letter to Carmen revealing that the worst-case scenario had happened. The tapes had been sent to Priscilla. Her parents, who had always thought him incapable of being faithful to Priscilla, had also received copies. Now Priscilla and her family all had evidence they considered proof of their assumptions.

Adding to these woes, Tom Yohotam, the Japanese "boy" who served as a household man-Friday, had answered several disturbing telephone calls—long stretches of silence before suddenly hanging up. The previous day, Tom had also found a threatening note stuck into the mailbox. It began with the words, "We know you're alone…"

Feeling like a sitting duck in his own home, Elvis had attempted to have an "electric eye" installed on the property, but the electric gate shorted it out. Frustrated, Elvis had temporarily removed the gate. Now, he told Carmen, the landlord was refusing to reinstall the gate, leaving him even more vulnerable.

He wasn't so much scared by the calls, notes and tapes as he was suffering from reliving the past. He must have suspected that Jungle Sam Katzman and his cronies were behind the surreptitious recordings made during the filming of *Harum Scarum*, which dredged up the dreadful experience of that picture. He told Carmen that he had aged thirty years since shooting that movie. For Elvis to have suffered that amount of post-shoot stress, it's reasonable to assume that other threats occurred that we don't know about.

Charro!

On April 4, Dr. Martin Luther King, Jr. was assassinated by James Earl Ray on the balcony outside his motel room. Elvis was deeply disturbed that such violence had occurred in "his" city of Memphis. He wanted to speak out publicly about the assassination, but Colonel Parker forbade it. Two months later, Sen. Robert F. Kennedy was shot dead by Sirhan Bishara Sirhan in Elvis's other hometown, Los Angeles. Kennedy had just captured 172 delegate votes to win the 1968 Democratic nomination for president.

Though despondent over these waves of violence, Elvis was buoyed by the prospects for a new movie he was about to begin. Not since his earliest films had he looked forward to making a new picture. At one time he had complained to Carmen that with all the bikini-clad females in his movies, the next one was sure to be called *Elvis Presley At the Nudist Camp*.

The movie he was excited about was a pseudo-spaghetti western that would go through many working titles, including *Jack Valentine, Johnny Hang, Come Hell or Come Sundown* and finally *Charro!* Playing a straight dramatic role, Elvis wore a beard for the first and last time in a movie and didn't sing a note.

The role he played, Jess Wade, had been turned down by Clint Eastwood before it was offered to Elvis. Nevertheless, he felt energized by the thespian challenge and reported for rehearsals with a full beard. He liked the look and teasingly told a few friends that he might just keep it. Scenes were filmed in the Superstition Mountains near Apache Junction and at the Apacheland Movie Ranch in Arizona. To Elvis's delight, Jungle Sam Katzman was not the producer.

In the story, which was set in the 1870s, Jess Wade is a former outlaw riding through Mexico when he encounters two brothers from a previous gang, Vince and Billy Roy, who have an ongoing feud with Jess. The brothers' gang abducts Jess and takes him to a hideout where they have concealed the "Victory Gun"—the famous cannon used to liberate Mexico from Spain—that they had stolen to collect a ransom of about one hundred thousand dollars, a fortune in those days.

The brothers put Jess's face on forged "Wanted" posters offering a reward for the cannon thief. To make sure that Jess matches the description of the man suspected of the robbery—a gang member known to have suffered a neck wound during the raid—they torture Jess with a red-hot branding iron on the neck.

Elvis could not have imagined how his life would soon mirror the horror of this tale.

In a scene from *Charro!*, Elvis shows the neck wound inflicted by a hot branding iron.

199

Continuing the two-month pulse of public violence in America, the Democratic National Convention opened in Chicago on August 9. For days, ten thousand demonstrators protesting the Vietnam War's rising death toll confronted police in bloody battles. As the nation convulsed, Elvis, in my opinion, did some of his finest acting, though his long string of mindless B-movies made it difficult for critics to appreciate his work in *Charro!*

While Elvis was on location in Arizona, Marlon Brando couriered a short note to Carmen stating that after returning from an errand he found Priscilla in a cab at his front door. Priscilla handed him a letter surprisingly addressed to "Carmen Montez," asking him to give it to the "proper party," and then abruptly left. He sent the sealed letter to Carmen with his own note asking her to notify him if the letter was anything urgent.

I have never learned what Priscilla wrote to Carmen, or what Carmen did about it. I have also wondered how Priscilla learned about Carmen, and if Elvis knew that his wife had found out about his secret confidante.

The note from Marlon concluded with a frightening postscript. He explained that over the past week he'd had a "strange, nameless fear for Elvis." He couldn't define it, but he was troubled by his sense of impending disaster. "I wish you knew what it might be," he wrote hopefully. This fear seems eerily prophetic.

Three unsettling events occurred while shooting *Charro!* in Arizona. In hindsight they could have been connected to the source of the audio tapes sent to Priscilla. The first event occurred during a fight scene. Instead of faking a punch, one of the actors bashed Elvis in the stomach, really letting him have it. Afterward, the actor apologized to Elvis for getting carried away. Just then, the director walked up to Elvis and congratulated him on the extra realism he'd injected into the scene. The praise helped Elvis let the incident go, though he reported it to Carmen.

A few days later, Elvis had a close encounter with a rattlesnake in his trailer. It seemed suspicious, but we have no details. The incident was particularly traumatic because Elvis had grown up in

East Tupelo, Mississippi, which was choked with snakes. The cold-blooded critters would often slither into the family home and have to be killed by "Uncle" Vernon. Elvis frequently had nightmares of peeling back the covers of his bed and finding a coiled snake. All his life he was both fascinated by snakes and terrified of them. He wound up with a large body of knowledge about them, but he found working in Arizona rattlesnake country a big challenge.

The third event involved the same actor who had punched Elvis in the gut. The actor was supposed to point an unloaded gun at Elvis. Charles Warren, the director, explained how he wanted the scene played, but Elvis had another idea. Taking the gun, Elvis demonstrated. As he pulled the trigger, the supposedly unloaded gun fired a blank near Warren's face. Such a charge was not capable of killing anyone, but if fired close to someone's face could burn or blind the victim. Green powder sprayed Warren's face and caused minor burns. If the gun had been fired near Elvis's face, he could have been injured and forced out of the picture. Fortunately, Warren did not blame Elvis and after receiving first aid continued directing.

Elvis was shaken again by an event that threatened his infant daughter, Lisa Marie, back in Los Angeles. Weeks earlier, a man had tried to enter the nursery while Lisa Marie was asleep but was stopped before breaking in. Then, just before finishing *Charro!*, the police caught a woman breaking into the nursery. Elvis thought the woman might be connected to Katzman, or whoever was behind the audio cassette escapade, but dismissed that notion when the police told him the woman was mentally deranged. Elvis told Carmen that he had never met the woman, who claimed that she was Elvis's lover and Lisa Marie was her child.

Abduction

God help me, I wish that I didn't have to publish this section. It makes my skin crawl, but it explains everything about the problems Elvis had for the rest of his tragically short life.

By the end of August, 1968, Elvis had completed his dialogue "looping" on *Charro!*, a process of rerecording and replacing dialogue to improve the audio quality of the original location recordings. He threw a buffet dinner for cast and crew at the Goldwyn Studios to celebrate and then went to his home in Palm Springs for a rest, largely dropping out of sight until he flew home to Memphis on September 25.

For the first time, letters written to Carmen Montez tell what happened during those days following the *Charro!* shoot.

As revealed earlier, at his home in Los Angeles, Elvis and Priscilla had an argument that led to a driveway incident resulting in injury to Priscilla and the death of an unborn child. After she recovered, Priscilla went to Memphis, and Elvis visited his Palm Springs home to check on some construction work. At some point, Elvis drove from Palm Springs back to Los Angeles. The lease on his Bel Air home was about to expire, and he still had some possessions there.

It was important for Elvis to feel and act like a normal person whenever possible, so—according to Marlon's letters—Elvis had wrangled Marlon into helping him haul boxes out of that house. Many of these contained items that were special in different ways, and Elvis didn't want a moving company handling them. Elvis showed up at Marlon's house still sporting his *Charro!* beard. Marlon had rented a pickup, and after a late start the two men headed out. They picked up the boxes and transported some of them to Marlon's home for temporary storage while Elvis figured out where he wanted them. The rest they delivered to Elvis's Hillcrest home.

It was lunchtime when the boxes were finally carted into Elvis's garage. Priscilla was in Memphis, and Elvis's staff, expecting him to be in Palm Springs for an extended stay, was gone. Elvis was free of all encumbrances, except for his friend Marlon, who had just started rummaging through the refrigerator when a loud noise startled him—voices shouting, car horns honking and stones hitting the house near the dining room window. Elvis ran to the window with Marlon close behind.

Looking out, they could see two unfamiliar Cadillacs parked in the driveway. Just as Marlon turned from the window, he was knocked to the floor. He looked up to see Elvis defending himself against two assailants. A blow to the head stunned Elvis, and the two attackers overtook him. One of them pulled a gun.

Marlon immediately recognized one of the assailants as a member of the "Katzman gang," a term used often by Elvis and Marlon to describe a band of men who took orders from Sam Katzman. A year earlier, Marlon and Elvis had been baited into a violent confrontation with Marcus (a pseudonym), who was several years younger than Elvis.

"I'm going to whip you now, so lie down!" Marcus yelled at Elvis, then showed a short leather whip to prove he meant that literally.

Defiant, Elvis said, "You'll have to make me."

Marlon wished his friend would just cooperate. Karate could not get him out of this mess.

Marlon stepped menacingly toward Marcus, but the other assailant suddenly stuck the barrel of his gun behind Marlon's ear.

Elvis's large, silver belt buckle caught Marcus's eye. "Take off your shirt, and give me your belt," he ordered.

When describing this event to Carmen the next day, Marlon wrote, "That buckle could cut him to pieces."

Elvis glanced at the pistol menacing Marlon's head, then knelt and pulled his shirt out of his pants. As he loosened his belt, three more intruders entered the room. One of them was Shaul (another pseudonym), Marcus's older brother and clearly the leader.

"No!" Shaul shouted. "I don't want him beaten yet."

Sensing a temporary reprieve, Elvis stood up, tucked in his shirt and glanced at his friend. The gun was still pointed at Marlon's head.

Marlon had been waiting for an opportunity to launch his own attack, but the gun made it difficult. And now, with five against two, it seemed hopeless.

Shaul tugged at Elvis's beard and said, "OK, Mr. Elvis Presley, I want you to go into the bathroom and shave off that stupid beard."

The men all laughed. The two who had entered with Shaul drew guns and ushered Elvis toward the bathroom.

Marlon told Carmen later that if Elvis had owned a straight razor instead of an electric shaver, he probably would have slit their throats with it right there in the bathroom. He also wrote that forcing Elvis to shave was one of the weirdest aspects of the whole intrusion, the sense of which he never understood.

When clean-shaven Elvis and the armed thugs reentered the dining room, Shaul tore off leather "thongs" from Marcus's whip to bind Elvis's hands behind his back. He reached into a pocket and took out a small glass bottle containing clear liquid and forced Elvis to drink it—about two ounces, Marlon estimated. Elvis made a face when he tasted it, then turned to stare at Marlon.

To Carmen, Marlon explained that he was sure Elvis was trying to communicate something to him. Possibly he wanted Marlon to contact Carmen, he thought, because she was "the only one who's ever been able to rescue him from a tight place before."

Shaul motioned to the others. With guns drawn they herded Elvis and Marlon outside, shoving Elvis into the back seat of the first Cadillac with Shaul and another man on either side. Marlon was squeezed into the front seat between Marcus and the driver, Marcus's sidekick. Between the two cars Marlon counted eight men plus Elvis and himself. They drove to the entrance of Marlon's mansion on Mulholland Drive where they pulled Marlon out of the car. He looked back and saw Elvis with a "pleading look." He was "very white even under the tan." That was the last he saw of Elvis that day.

The presence of Marcus made Marlon's gut rumble. He knew that Marcus had personal reasons to punish Elvis, and this put Elvis at even greater risk. About a year earlier, Marcus—like Elvis, a student of karate—had been trying to deliver a message from Jungle Sam Katzman to Elvis, who took it as a threat. The two men got into a karate fight. At first it was just sparring, but then Elvis got the advantage and bloodied Marcus's nose. Elvis was really tearing into his adversary when Marcus's companion suddenly jumped into the fray, and this immediately drew in Marlon. By then, several onlookers had gathered. One of them yelled, "Call the police." Marcus and his sidekick apparently feared being publicly accused of molesting Elvis Presley and Marlon Brando, so they bolted.

Marcus and his buddy had waited for many months before retaliating—uncommon patience for hotheads. This attack on Elvis and Marlon clearly was not just Marcus's personal revenge.

Marcus and the gunman forced Marlon to unlock the front door and then marched him to his soundproof bongo room. A hard blow to the head made him woozy. After regaining his focus, he found his hands tied behind his back and a handkerchief stuffed and strapped into his mouth. It took him about three hours to get free and remove the pins from the door hinges.

The first telephone call he made was to Kit, hoping she could rally Carmen to the cause, but Kit didn't answer. He tried reaching Gee Gee, then the other Elvis regulars, but nobody was available. He called "Jungle Sam" to see if he could be reasoned with, but there was no answer at the old man's house. Finally, he called a private investigator he had used. This call went through, but when Marlon described the problem and mentioned Katzman, the PI refused to get involved.

Marlon worried endlessly about his friend. He considered this gang a bunch of "maniacs" whom he figured quite capable of killing Elvis, but even if they didn't, they could hurt him badly.

He wrote out a letter to Carmen and sent it to her via courier. He asked her what he and Carmen could do even if they found Elvis. This gang was brazen, he explained. There were many of them... and they had guns. Marlon couldn't imagine that these attackers hoped to go unpunished, but they didn't seem to care. Or maybe they believed they were somehow invincible. They had come to Elvis's Hillcrest house apparently knowing that nobody would be there except Elvis. Marlon had been a bonus.

Marlon closed his letter with the words: "Please tell me what to do. I'm frantic."

I have often wondered how Carmen Montez replied. But, of course, we don't know, just as we have no explanation for why Marlon did not immediately call the police after freeing himself from the bongo room. Perhaps he suffered from a common celebrity's instinct to avoid publicity at almost any cost; the tabloids usually picked up news of police involvement with celebrities immediately. Possibly Marlon feared personal retaliation from Katzman if he brought in law enforcement. It's also possible he sought some kind of personal vengeance and police scrutiny would make that difficult. I believe all of these issues were probably going through his mind as he wrote to Carmen and failed to call the police, but we can't know for sure.

The only response I am certain Carmen made to Marlon was the description of a local motel that might serve as a hangout for some of the brutes. How she came by this information we will never know; perhaps her source was George, her husband, who I suspect had underworld connections. After imprisoning Marlon in his own home, the gang took Elvis to a motel that fit Carmen's description. At least one of the abductors was living there.

As the two Cadillacs drove to the motel, nobody on the street noticed the famous star in the back seat. But when they pulled up outside the motel, the men saw several bystanders stare at Elvis as he exited the car and was pushed into a room containing another two occupants. The public attention alarmed the publicity-shy gang members, now numbering ten, who argued with each other until eventually deciding to return to Elvis's house, which they were sure would remain empty for several more days. It seemed the safest choice. Anyway, they almost certainly had more men and guns than any unexpected visitor to the Hillcrest home.

T-r-o-u-b-l-e

Song released in 1958, performed in the movie King Creole

Returning to Elvis's Hillcrest home, according to letters from Elvis and Marlon, they forced Elvis to endure nine hours of relentless misery. They stripped off his white shirt, black levis and boots, then bound him securely. They tortured him with lit cigarettes, then cut off some of his hair in front. Marcus placed that hair in a cellophane envelope as a ghoulish souvenir. The clear liquid Elvis had been forced to drink made him nauseated at first, but later seemed to enhance his memory and heighten his senses, especially to pain. Perhaps this was the intended effect.

The men consumed quantities of alcohol and soon were very drunk, which made their torture more audacious. A portly man plunged a large syringe into Elvis's arm. Soon many of the men were drawing samples of the icon's blood. Marcus extracted a sample, then squirted it into a glass of whiskey, turning the blood into a cocktail mixer. He forced Elvis, gagging, to drink the concoction. Like vampires, the others started sipping the whiskey-blood potion. Then someone else stuck a corkscrew into Elvis's leg and turned it.

The men who were not actively tormenting Elvis began trashing the house. They smashed dishes and lamps and ripped the drapes, cut up the upholstered furniture and broke the wooden pieces. They pulled out Elvis's clothes and shredded them, peed on the carpets, then smashed the automobiles in the garage, including Elvis's favorite white sports car.

Over a period of nine hours the gang sodomized him, all but Shaul and Marcus. Between rapes, some of the men put on Elvis's boots and took turns kicking him in the abdomen. They tried to make him cry out in pain, to curse them, but he wouldn't give them that satisfaction. Shaul supervised everything, making sure that Elvis's face was never marred, and his bones were not broken. It was a very professional job—maximum suffering with the victim left ambulatory and all the criminal evidence easily covered by clothing. If Elvis wanted to hide the severe shame of his abuse, he could do it easily.

By midnight, some of the men grew weary or bored. They left, leaving Shaul, Marcus and a couple of others to continue the torment. The men built a fire in the fireplace, then Shaul finally gave permission for his brother to whip Elvis with his belt and its massive silver buckle, leaving welts and several lacerations—a bizarre reimagining of the scene in *Jailhouse Rock* in which a policeman lashes Elvis's bare back.

Shortly after midnight, fueled by alcohol, Marcus started a fistfight with his older brother. Shaul wanted Elvis subdued but not unconscious. Marcus just wanted to beat the hell out of him. In the end, Shaul permitted his brother to rape Elvis, but this time the violent penetration caused Elvis to start hemorrhaging. Perhaps thinking they could cauterize the internal wound, or maybe just out of sadistic fury, one of them took the fireplace poker, plunged it into the flames, and then sodomized Elvis with it. The cries of pain seemed to intensify their pleasure.

Elvis passed out, but by early morning the men who had abandoned the party returned, and the torment continued. They tied Elvis's hands to two brass rings fastened to the floor of the fireplace. After moving a heavy mahogany table, they spread Elvis's legs and bound them around the legs of the table. The binding was so cleverly rigged that the harder Elvis tried to free himself, the tighter the binding became. He had about eighteen inches of leather cord to pull against.

Based on the rigging, Marlon summarized his assumption of their intent this way: "The sadistic bastards (excuse me) wanted him to have room to struggle without being able to get anywhere."

Finally, the gang left, leaving Elvis bound to the rings. After several hours of painful attempts, Elvis loosened his hands, but the ingenious rigging still did not allow him to reach his feet and untie the cords. He managed, however, to grab and tug the tablecloth. It fell to the floor, and along with it a telephone that had been resting on it. Perhaps the assailants had intended for him to eventually escape and call for help. Torture is one thing, murder quite another. Or maybe they had left the telephone there as a tantalizing but unattainable goal.

I Feel So Bad
Song released in 1961

Elvis called Marlon's house. Fortunately, Marlon answered.

"Where are you?" Marlon asked, frantic.

A creaking voice replied, "Home."

And then the line went dead. Marlon feared the gang might have caught Elvis using the telephone. He quickly drove to the Hillcrest house. Finding no cars in the driveway, he entered and found Elvis wrapped in the lace tablecloth and still restrained by the cruel rigging. He had passed out during the call, and the handset had fallen into its cradle.

Marlon untangled Elvis, careful not to touch the painful bruises and gashes, and Elvis slowly regained consciousness. Every movement caused intense pain. He recoiled when he saw Marlon hovering over him, unable at first to recognize him. By the time he was free of his bonds, he started to cry "without any tears," Marlon told Carmen. When Elvis tried to stand, Marlon could see a trail of dried blood on the rear of his legs originating from Elvis's rectum.

Marlon suspected significant internal damage. He called a doctor friend who arrived at Elvis's home minutes after the ambulance and explained that the nature of the wounds required a police report. Attempting to head off public exposure of the incident, Marlon called the Los Angeles police and was able to reach "Chief Ressoner." For over thirty minutes, Marlon explained the circumstances of the case and implored the chief to maintain confidentiality so as "not to subject Elvis to the misery of publicity."

In the end, the chief agreed that after receiving the doctor's report he would keep it in a special sealed file but warned that if the press asked about it he'd have to disclose the facts in the report. He also urged Marlon to hire a private investigator to make out a full report from Elvis's and Marlon's perspective. But he explained that this would be in addition to a full police investigation.

Elvis was taken to the emergency room and checked in, as usual, under an assumed name. Within minutes, Marlon was met by his PI friend, who insisted on interviewing Elvis that same day. This could not be done, though, until Elvis received emergency care. At last, Elvis was admitted to the hospital and X-rays were scheduled for the next day. Doctors told Marlon and the PI that Elvis was very weak, and they'd prefer he have no visitors until morning. The police came to the hospital later that day, but Elvis was not able to give them much information.

The next day Marlon wrote an extensive letter to Carmen detailing his brief conversation with Elvis. Without this letter, and many others to follow, we would not know about this horrific encounter. Marlon does not explain where he was when he wrote the letter, but I can imagine his despair after visiting his damaged friend.

During this visit, Elvis was hooked up to various tubes and monitors. As Marlon and the PI entered the hospital room, they found Elvis pale and weak, but his face was unmarked. His bruises and wounds were covered by sheets, so an unknowing observer might have mistaken him for a patient with influenza or any other medical condition. Marlon reported that Elvis was awake and coherent but clearly didn't want to talk about the atrocities inflicted upon him. He seemed withdrawn but not unresponsive.

"I could feel a part of him dying," Marlon wrote, adding that he could understand if his friend preferred to simply die. "I know how he feels... Maybe now for the first time I fully understand Elvis." Imagining a time after Elvis had healed, Marlon wrote that he wouldn't blame Elvis if he "got his gun and shot them all."

Finally, Elvis was able to answer the PI's questions about the aftermath of his abduction, but he spoke haltingly, without emotion—like "a robot" programmed to recite facts. He left out many of the uglier moments like the assault with a hot poker, which at this point Elvis had not even mentioned to Marlon. When Elvis was finished, the PI left, and Elvis seemed to zone out completely.

Knowing an old Elvis movie was going to play on TV the next day, Marlon tried to get his friend to perk up by pointing to a small TV mounted on the wall. "Carmen will be watching your movie with you on Sunday," he said. "You can watch it right here in your room."

Elvis "didn't bat an eyelash," Marlon wrote. By this time, Elvis had mentally and emotionally retreated from the conversation.

Marlon learned that the police investigation was underway. Sam Katzman had been contacted but had made no statement. Shaul and Marcus had not been located. Elvis was in no condition yet to review photographs of them or other potential accomplices. A kidnapping charge was potentially undermined, the authorities told him, by the fact that no attempt to collect ransom had been made. If this charge were to be dropped, with no formal charge of sexual assault by Elvis, the case would be reduced to illegal breaking and entering, assault with a deadly weapon and vandalism.

On Sunday morning, Marlon visited Elvis again on the way to deliver a letter to Carmen. He added a description of this visit at the bottom of his note. Elvis, he wrote, wouldn't talk to anyone. It's not that he refused to talk or protested anything—it's that he didn't even acknowledge visitors or staff, not even the doctors and nurses. He would stare *through* them as if they were invisible. "We don't seem to be in his world anymore," Marlon told Carmen.

Marlon was at a loss for what to do. He was exhausted, shocked into numbness and deep sympathy for what Elvis had endured. He was also feeling guilty. Shouldn't he have called the police immediately after the abduction? Wouldn't the police have gone to Elvis's home and interrupted the horror?

"I'll get this [letter] to you while I can still think straight," he wrote. "My head is spinning with a sickening disgust and fear and helplessness. That poor boy."

Several days later, Marlon sent another letter to Carmen in which he catalogs some of the doctors' findings and interventions. Marlon was not a medical professional, so he may have misinterpreted or erred in his recollection, but he reported that both of Elvis's kidneys were failing and blood clots had lodged dangerously close to his heart. The medical team had managed to dissolve the clots. They also had performed surgery on one of the kidneys and taken additional steps trying to head off a future kidney transplant, "which might fail anyway."

Remember, this was 1968.

Help Me Make It Through the Night

Song released in 1972

During this last hospital visit, Elvis was conscious. The painkillers had made him comfortable, but he was not talkative. The nurse said that a couple of small clots had formed close to his lungs that were cause for concern. Before Elvis was carted away for another procedure, Marlon had a short, one-sided talk with his friend. He showed Elvis a card on which Carmen had written an encouraging note. Then he urged Elvis to keep fighting.

Elvis's only response was to turn his head away and close his eyes, which angered Marlon.

Marlon grabbed Elvis by the hair and turned his head to look straight at Marlon. "Don't think you're going to get away with turning your head on me!" Marlon said sternly, then instantly regretted his behavior. He let go and gently explained that he knew how Elvis must feel—ashamed, disgraced, probably wanting to die. But if he died, certain people would literally get away with murder.

Marlon confessed to Carmen that he understood one unfortunate truth he could not mention to Elvis—that if this gang rape were to be made public, Elvis would go through "a public hell of the kind that will degrade him to death."

Marlon knew that the sodomy had caused irreparable wounds to Elvis's pride, his sense of masculinity, perhaps even his future relationships with women. The physical wounds would eventually heal, but the mental and emotional wounds would linger, maybe forever.

The police interviewed Sam Katzman based on Marlon's testimony. Marlon was furious that Sam had provided Shaul and Marcus with false alibis, swearing that the two main assailants had been fishing with the family patriarch near Arrowhead. Two witnesses corroborated the story, and Marlon was sure Sam had paid them off.

Sam seemed to have been counting on Elvis to keep the entire incident secret and not force the investigation forward. He likely had not expected Marlon to be at Elvis's when the abduction occurred.

Marlon was a wild card, and Marlon worried about what they might do to *tame* that wild card.

Vernon Presley, who Elvis called his uncle, told Marlon he was afraid that, after recovering, Elvis would track down and kill the men who had tortured him. Marlon wondered where it would all end. In a letter to Carmen, he made this comment: "But after 11 years, the past horror complete with nightmares is still with him [Elvis]. How long will it take to recover from this second horror?" Even having read these letters many times I had never noticed this startling assertion—that Elvis had endured another trauma eleven years earlier. The Katzman abduction had taken place in 1968, so this earlier incident would have happened in 1957.

I searched all the letters again for any mention of a traumatic event in 1957. In a letter dated March 9, 1969, I found it. Elvis was shooting the Universal Pictures movie *Change of Habit* with Mary Tyler Moore when he wrote the letter. He complained to Carmen about spending five hours in makeup to correct a few minor facial defects that other producers had ignored. Jokingly, he said that plastic surgery would have been faster and hurt less. He told Universal that he'd had the same face for all his MGM pictures and all those movies had made money. Besides, to his eyes he looked the same after makeup as he did before.

Colonel Tom Parker chats with Elvis during the production of *Change of Habit*.

The facial defects were scars resulting from a severe beating twelve years earlier. Since the letter was written in 1969, this drubbing would have occurred in 1957. Elvis mentioned multiple scars: beneath his lower lip, a scar approximately an inch long; a smaller scar caused by a deep gash between his right eyebrow and the bridge of his nose; scars on his left temple and his right upper lip; and a few other tiny scars.

There is no other mention of this event in the letters and none in the public record, but the incident affected Elvis deeply, otherwise he would not have mentioned it. A traumatic beating early in his career, at the age of twenty-one, could help explain Elvis's fascination with martial arts, which began three years later, as well as his longstanding phobia about hands and crowds.

Elvis had studied karate since a magazine article he'd read while serving in the US Army in Germany. The article featured a former marine named Hank Slomanski who took on 150 karate opponents in one day and beat them all. Elvis signed up for lessons three times a week in the Shotokan style with instructor Jürgen Sandal. Then, in early 1960, he witnessed a demonstration in Los Angeles of a new street-fighting karate technique invented by instructor Ed Parker. He signed up and in less than six months earned a first-degree black belt certificate after completing a five-hour test that included taking on two opponents at once.

For Elvis, a childhood fear of hands eventually transformed into a fear of crowds, an unfortunate phobia for a popular entertainer perpetually surrounded by hordes of fans and reporters. He confessed to Carmen his nightmares about crowds and a multitude of hands reaching out to touch him. He feared that when a hand touched him it was a premonition of something threatening or dangerous. When he was hemmed in by a crowd, he'd panic and struggle to stay rational.

One technique he used to calm himself down was to look at individual faces in the crowd—really study them—until he saw they weren't threats, only fans looking for autographs or a simple touch of the superstar. Unfortunately, his fear of being mobbed—or molested— intensified, and he also developed a fear of heights and of flying. He'd often drive long distances rather than fly commercially, which could put kinks into his busy schedule.

It must have been even more excruciating than I had imagined for Elvis to be raped by a gang of ten men—a multitude of hands clawing at him, punching him, pulling his hair—a twenty-handed mob consuming him.

At about six o'clock the next morning, Vernon Presley phoned Marlon a second time from Tennessee. He had just received a call from Elvis's doctor about an incident at the hospital. A nurse who had just come on duty had entered Elvis's room to check on him. He seemed to be asleep, so she opened the door to leave but then decided to get a closer peek at the famous star. She closed the door so she wouldn't be seen approaching Elvis. Apparently, Elvis was only feigning sleep. Just before the nurse entered he had been preparing to stab himself with an IV needle he'd removed from his arm. When he heard the door close, he thought the nurse had left the room and started raising the needle above his chest. Seeing this, the nurse screamed, startling him. He dropped the needle, and his eyes flew open. The nurse called for support.

The doctor told Vernon that Elvis seemed to be delirious and probably didn't know what he was doing. Marlon was not so sure. He remembered how the previous day Elvis's eyes had been staring at the IV drip— "Watching, thinking, not listening. His eyes were fixed on it, staring as if he were hypnotized by it." Marlon promised Vernon that he would check on Elvis frequently.

The next morning, Marlon visited Elvis and explained that Vernon wanted to come but couldn't leave Elvis's grandmother alone in Memphis. Elvis didn't respond. Marlon read out loud a letter from Carmen, hoping it would make Elvis feel better, but Elvis just closed his eyes. I have tried to understand the humiliation and degradation that Elvis must have been feeling at this time, but I'm sure I underestimate.

Marlon sat there wordlessly for a few more minutes before leaving. Medically, the hospital team was fighting to save one of

Elvis's kidneys that kept filling with blood, and they were concerned that peritonitis might set in.

It's Now or Never

Second-bestselling Presley single, released in 1960

Colonel Parker flew in from Texas later in the day. Marlon hated Parker, but he told Carmen, "He may exploit Elvis, and he's pulled a few fast deals and once played the sex angle—but he's ready to kill anyone who would do such a thing to Elvis. I think he'd like to beat each of them to death with his cane."

A couple of days later, as Elvis was sitting up in bed, he told the doctor it was difficult to breathe. Before this, he had been too dazed to identify specific aches and pains, so this seemed like progress. After a detailed examination, the medical team found that he had recently been burned inside his nose and into his head resulting in blocked sinuses. Elvis had no recollection of the gang violating his nasal passages, but he was drugged for much of the time.

On one lonely evening, as Elvis was lying awake in his dark hospital room, a visitor entered. He looked like an orderly. There is very little revealed in the letters about this event, but the "orderly" approached Elvis with a knife. Elvis, though weakened, reacted by grabbing the man's arm. They struggled for a moment, and Elvis fell out of his bed, smashing his head against a cabinet. Suddenly the door opened, and a nurse entered the room. The "orderly" pivoted and ran, nearly knocking down the nurse. When Marlon learned about the incident he was heartened that Elvis had fought to stay alive. Yet he knew that if Elvis's life was in peril, so was his.

In addition to feeling threatened, Marlon continued to struggle with his own personal catch-22. Letting Katzman and his gang get away with this crime went against every principle he believed in, yet bringing this sordid affair into the open could inflict on Elvis even more pain and suffering. Marlon's dilemma extended to Colonel Parker. He'd been told by Chief Ressoner that Parker had been relentlessly pressuring the police department to close the investigation and keep the whole thing under wraps. Ressoner was in favor of going after Katzman, but Parker's influence was extensive. Marlon wanted the incident kept secret, too, but in his heart wanted Katzman to be formally charged.

By the weekend, Parker had managed to get Elvis moved to a psychiatric ward because of the attempted suicide. Marlon felt this was shifting the blame from Katzman to Elvis, so he called Parker to vent his feelings.

Parker gruffly countered that "someone who does the things Elvis has done lately is not completely right in the head." As evidence, he listed the attempt to stab himself with a needle, and secondly, "Elvis told me himself when I was there that he wanted to die, and could I help him."

"Look, Elvis was anxious to get out of the hospital," Marlon said.

"You think I'm blaming Elvis? I'm not blaming him. He's been driven out of his head. He doesn't know what he's doing. I've received threats against him at my home that Elvis doesn't know anything about. The world is filled with crazies. There's only one way to deal with people like that, and it isn't the police."

Marlon asked what that meant, though he already knew.

Parker replied, "Some of Elvis's closest friends and me have formed a kind of citizen's committee to give 'em back what they've given to Elvis. If you were a true friend you'd join us and put your argument out there the way it'll do the most good."

The idea of vigilante justice had some appeal to Marlon, but he also feared an all-out war. "I don't know that that's what Elvis wants," he said. "I think you're thinking of yourself, not Elvis."

"Well, suit yourself. I just don't expect the police to do the right thing where Katzman is concerned."

Marlon was getting angry at Parker's know-it-all attitude. I also think that Marlon suspected Parker's pressure on the police to close down the investigation was partly intended to reduce scrutiny of the citizen committee's activities.

"If you hadn't been pressuring the police like they worked for you they might have done something by now," Marlon said.

This infuriated Parker. He didn't like being accused of making mistakes. "Apparently you don't know what they did to Elvis."

"I'm the one who found him at his house all beat up and called the ambulance. He was a mess. Of course I know."

"No, you don't. If you did, you'd be leading the committee on this. He didn't tell you because he went through it because of you, and he was too ashamed. Do you know how they stuck a red-hot poker up his ass, and when he was writhing in pain they had improper intercourse with him? Of course not."

Marlon was stunned. Speechless. The damage to Elvis, sickening as it was, had been much more devastating than he had known, and he was hurt that Elvis had shared more details with Parker than with him.

Parker wasn't done. "And you say they don't deserve to get it back? Do you think I'm going to let those sadists have their satisfaction with him and do nothing about it?" Suddenly he was shouting. "Do you? You say I'm not thinking of Elvis? I won't stand by and see any human being, even an animal, hurt like that, let alone Elvis. If I've pushed him, it's because his work is all he has, and if he's left to sit around and brood he's not going to need friends—he's not going to need anybody but an undertaker."

Marlon had little respect for Colonel Parker, but he had never heard him get so emotional about Elvis. In a letter to Carmen, he confessed that at that very moment he believed what Parker was saying and suddenly became "angry like I haven't been since M. King was killed."

His anger and frustration overcame his good sense. After he hung up, he drove to Sam Katzman's mansion. The front door was unlocked so he barged in and found Sam on a sofa in the sitting room with "a guy who works for him." He suspected this guy might have been part of the mob that had nearly killed Elvis. Marlon bluntly said he knew what had happened and that Katzman's gang was responsible.

With a sly grin, Sam denied everything. "Those boys would never do anything like that," he said. Then he stood up, accused

Elvis of being queer, "and put another word I can't mention in front of it."

Marlon told Carmen that Katzman called him a liar and ended up propositioning him right there in his home. This was too much for Marlon, who punched Sam in the face. "I'd have done it before if the guy weren't such a fat slob," Marlon told Carmen later.

Katzman sat back down on the sofa holding his chin. His hired thug lunged at Marlon. The two men brawled for a couple of minutes before Sam motioned his man to back off. Marlon's right eye was already blackening, and the other one was already swollen. Marlon used the moment to hurl some insults and then march back to his car. Back at home, he wrote a long letter to Carmen summarizing the dramatic events of the day and declaring that he still felt like pulling someone apart with his bare hands. He told Carmen that Elvis wanted him to pick up a letter he'd written for her and deliver it, but he didn't want Elvis to see him so roughed up, "so you might get it late."

Marlon reflected on how difficult it was for Elvis to stand up when Marlon had found him after the beating. Now he understood what Elvis had experienced, and the emotional trauma, though Elvis had kept the horrendous details secret except for Parker. Even when Elvis had been in the hospital close to death, someone had tried to attack him. "God knows what I would do if I were Elvis," Marlon wrote. "Maybe it is up to me, and to others who care, Carmen?"

It was a question.

The next morning, Marlon took a chilling phone call from Marcus telling him to keep his mouth shut or Elvis would die. "You won't know where or when," Marcus said, "but it's going to be nice and slow, and we'll let you watch." Marcus boldly bragged about how he had almost killed Elvis in his home after most of the others had left for the night and would have if his brother hadn't stopped him.

Marlon wrote that Marcus and the others were probably "shaking in their boots" because of the police investigation, but these words struck me as false bravado. While Marcus was making threats, Marlon's own rage was mounting, "making it almost impossible for me to hold back from doing everything possible to have him punished." And then Marlon used some very suggestive language: "Yet I know there will be other vengeance." He closed with the words, "They can't be allowed to get away with it. They just can't, Carmen. They can't."

All Shook Up

Eventually, Elvis was able to go home, though the Hillcrest house triggered nightmarish memories. He asked Marlon to stay with him and his cousin Gene for a few days. Marlon described Elvis's first evening home in a letter to Carmen. Elvis was restless and seemed "very haunted." He sat down to write a letter to Carmen but couldn't focus his thoughts or get his writing hand to work. He had lost eleven pounds in the hospital and was having trouble sleeping. Gene and Marlon tried to get him to eat something, but he couldn't, so they suggested he go to bed.

Before Marlon turned in for the night, he checked on Elvis and found the bedroom empty. Frantic, he went from room to room and finally found Elvis in his pajamas standing motionless in front of the kitchen sink. Not wanting to startle Elvis, Marlon watched him for a moment. Elvis was staring at an open drawer containing a row of steak knives. Recalling the incident with the needle in the hospital, Marlon spoke out before Elvis could do anything foolish.

Elvis reflexively turned and said, "I wasn't doing anything." His knee-jerk defense betrayed the guilt of almost yielding to temptation. Suddenly, his face contorted in pain. Marlon took his arm to help him back to the bedroom, but Elvis stood there shaking his head, his jaw clenched, unable to speak. Marlon thought the atmosphere of this torture house might be too much, so he asked Elvis if he wanted to go to Marlon's home.

Elvis took a deep breath, shook his head and squeezed out a few words. "I'm on my own now."

Stand by Me
Song released in 1967

For several days Marlon stayed at his own home but checked on Elvis regularly. Then, one evening, he went to the Hillcrest house to watch *Jailhouse Rock* on TV with Elvis and then stay overnight. After going to sleep, Marlon had a comical dream about himself and Carmen chasing mice around the house with butterfly nets. The dream was interrupted by a scream. He woke up instantly and ran to Elvis's room, switching on the light. Elvis was sitting straight up glancing suspiciously around the room. He swore that he'd seen a figure clad in black by the bed. It had been trying to fit a noose around his neck.

After convincing Elvis it was just a nightmare, Marlon told Carmen, "I was more than willing to go back to the mice!" Marlon tried to get some rest, but Elvis repeatedly moaned in his sleep and called out for Carmen. Unable to sleep, Marlon decided to sit in a chair and watch Elvis toss and turn.

Around daylight, Marlon was sure he smelled the fragrance of Carmen's perfume in Elvis's room, which he believed was a sign that Carmen had psychically come to relieve him and look after Elvis. I would have been spooked by this, but Marlon reported the phenomenon matter-of-factly, as if it had been no more unusual than a physical visit from a concerned friend.

With the faint fragrance wafting over him, Elvis settled down, and Marlon returned to the guest room.

Elvis was fortunate that he had a few weeks off after the abduction, except for some minor obligations. In late September he flew home to Memphis with Priscilla and Lisa Marie, escaping to the movies almost every night for two-and-a-half weeks until returning to Los Angeles. When it was time to resume his busy schedule, he outwardly pulled himself together. Few people knew what he had gone through. Parker's plan to keep it all under wraps was working.

But beneath the surface, Marlon told Carmen that he could see a deep sadness in his friend. He knew that Elvis was profoundly disturbed, suffering from shame and trying desperately to conceal his distress from everyone around him.

The Trouble with Girls

Looming on the horizon was another movie project with the working title *Chautauqua*, which would be changed before release to *The Trouble with Girls (And How to Get Into It)*. Elvis complained that he didn't have the motivation or resolve to undertake another picture. As Marlon told Carmen, he just didn't want to do anything anymore. Unfortunately, he knew that he'd likely be sued for breach of contract by MGM if he didn't perform. Besides the cost of litigation and damages, Parker warned, his reputation as a reliable star in the movie industry could suffer irreparably, lowering his market value.

Grudgingly, Colonel Parker tried to make MGM angry with Elvis so they would pay him off and hire a different actor. After announcing Elvis as the star of this picture way back in 1961, the studio had already switched the lead to Dick Van Dyke, sold the property with Van Dyke attached to Columbia Pictures in 1964, and then reacquired the movie rights and reattached Elvis as the star in 1968. Parker calculated that MGM could easily make another change under the right circumstances, and Elvis would still be paid his large fees.

Marlon believed that abandoning the job could be the worst thing Elvis could do. He admitted to Carmen that he understood Elvis still felt "as though he's under one big dose of anesthetic, and he's no good at anything." Marlon became so frustrated with Elvis's quandary that he went to church and prayed about it. It may be hard to believe Marlon Brando going to church and praying, but in his own words, he really prayed. "I mean, *really*—not just the repetition of some automatically learned prayers," he wrote.

The answer he got back stressed the importance of work to one's well-being, the importance of friends fighting for Elvis when he didn't have the strength to fight for himself, and helping Elvis understand that he still had something left to give. Marlon was discouraged when he entered the church. He wrote, "…but I came out determined" to be both brother and father, and he begged Carmen to be not only Elvis's "sister," but mother as well.

He and Carmen must have prevailed because on October 22, 1968, Elvis began pre-production on the movie. The very next day Elvis's film *Live a Little, Love a Little* opened nationwide to poor ticket sales and bad reviews. Even the Elvis insiders who screened it on opening day returned with definitive thumbs down. Their reports made Elvis despondent. Elvis expressed the depth of his despair to Carmen. Before this, he had not shared the details of his abduction and torture with Carmen, perhaps to spare her the horror, but suddenly his emotions poured out. He was losing his battle against depression, he wrote. Despite Marlon's advice, he was finding it impossible to connect with himself. The only part of him left was the "professional me"— enduring wardrobe fittings and makeup sessions, studying the details of another tour the Colonel was hoping would distract him. He felt that no one understood how raw, unsettled and confused his feelings were.

The Colonel told him he'd be himself again if he'd just get some girls and have some fun. Marlon encouraged him to "talk to God." Elvis explained to Carmen that his sense of morality prevented him from the former, and regarding the latter, he felt too undeserving and estranged from God to have a conversation with Him. He was deeply worried that he was psychologically damaged, otherwise why wouldn't he be attracted to all the Hollywood women around him? Could the brutal acts of sodomy, he wondered, have been a response to unconscious homosexual signals he'd been sending out? Something in him must have prompted that attack.

He wrote that it would probably take something radical, something extremely powerful, to erase those ugly experiences from his memory. He was going insane remembering all the horrible details. He felt degraded and ashamed and only half-alive. He told Carmen that he almost didn't write to her because he had nothing left to give her. He felt guilty selfishly pouring out his feelings all the time, but he just couldn't keep them inside any longer. He was obsessed with the belief that everyone knew what had happened to him. He could feel eyes following him at the movie studio and could almost hear whispers of "he asked for it" or "he must have done something to deserve it."

Uninspired and emotionally numb, he labored on with the picture, though once in frustration he walked out on director Peter Tewksbury, something he had never done before. Marlon saw *The Trouble with Girls* when it opened a year later and said it was easy to see what Elvis was going through at the time by looking at his face on the screen—sunken cheeks, sleepless and pained eyes, tightly drawn mouth. "Looking at him revived all those days when we kept constant vigil over him," he told Carmen. As for the movie itself, Marlon wrote that calling it bad was the understatement of the year.

Shortly after finishing the movie, Elvis discovered Gee Gee and Priscilla together in his guest house and threw Gee Gee out, an incident described earlier. This humiliating event must have been a final blow to his masculinity, a confirmation that he could not even be a satisfactory husband. He told Carmen that he was feeling increasingly desperate and needed someone to show him "the way." Then he apologized for burdening her with his problems without even inquiring about her life.

About this time, Elvis learned that Shaul was in jail on a narcotics charge, accused of leading a nationwide drug ring. He must have felt that some justice had been served, though the charges had nothing to do with the assault on him. If Elvis held a personal grudge, it certainly would have been against Shaul's brother, Marcus, who had personally tortured and raped him.

Peace in the Valley

EP released in 1957

In January 1969, clearly seeking peace from the tumult swirling around him, Elvis attempted suicide again. We know about the unsuccessful attempt because of references to it by several authors in their letters, though no description of the event was ever provided.

The next month, Elvis apologized for his attempt by telling Carmen not to be so worried about him, but then he planted more concern by declaring, "What is in me nobody else can help." He felt completely empty and fatalistic, he wrote, and was just coasting along, doing whatever he was told to do. Marlon had told him he was brainwashed, but Elvis said that was impossible because his brain and all his emotions were dead already.

Elvis's letters reveal that he had also attempted suicide in 1967. A couple months after the 1969 attempt, he mentioned it to Carmen. He believed she was sent to save him—not his body, but his soul. Then he referred to a night in the "lonely desert" in November 1967 when he might have been lost forever were it not for Carmen. The timing of this incident corresponds to his introduction to Carmen during the shooting of *Stay Away, Joe*, near Sedona, Arizona.

Suicide seemed never to be far from Elvis's mind. We know this not only from his letters to Carmen but by more recent revelations. Joe Esposito, Elvis's friend and road manager, revealed shortly before his death in 2016 that he had found a suicide note next to Elvis's body the day Elvis died, but he had burned it to protect Elvis's family from the shocking contents. In 2018, radar.com published an article revealing a just-discovered suicide note Elvis purportedly had written in January 1977, seven months before he was found slumped in his bathroom. In the note, Elvis had written, "I need a long rest. I'm sick and tired of my life." He goes on to write, "My willpower is almost gone." Elvis's stepbrother Rick Stanley called the note, which was so similar in tone to many of the letters written to Carmen Montez a few years earlier, "...a clear indication that suicide was on his mind."

The night of that 1967 suicide attempt, Elvis reminded Carmen, he had been literally out of his head. After just six months of marriage he had become deeply depressed and had fallen into a trance-like state in which he felt devoid of all reason. Somehow, out on that desert, Carmen had intervened, and Elvis credited her with his salvation. Later, he asked a minister if he would have been pardoned by God should he have died, and the minister told him yes, God always forgives a person if they ask.

I have always wondered if Elvis considered his 1968 abduction and torture to be his punishment for this first attempted suicide, and if the certainty of forgiveness had made it easier to try again as we know he did in January 1969.

Suspicious Minds

On March 13, 1969, Elvis for the first time told Carmen about the hot poker. He had given her a partial rundown of the gang's acts of torture but could not bear to put into words the gang rape and poker atrocity.

The stimulus for writing the letter was having just learned that Marcus, the "fiend" who had tortured and anally raped him, had been found dead—violently beaten with his skull crushed—in a canyon near Culver City. Worrying that he could be suspected of seeking revenge by killing Marcus, Elvis told Carmen that he could never have done or even ordered such a thing because he despised violence. In Elvis's view, whoever had murdered Marcus had doomed himself just as Marcus had been doomed for his cruel acts of torture, but the way in which Marcus had burned Elvis was nothing compared to the way Marcus's soul was burning in hell today.

Elvis confessed that when he was experiencing the "searing pain" of the poker's penetration, he had wanted to tear Marcus apart. He reminded Carmen that he could explode a man's head with one lethal karate blow, and he would have felt justified in this case. Vengeance still lived in his heart, so he hoped he would never meet any of his assailants alone for fear of what he might do.

Marlon revealed more details about the murder. In Marcus's wallet, the police had found an envelope containing clippings of hair. Marlon was sure the hair was Elvis's, a souvenir of that brutal evening of torture. He feared that if the police could determine the hair was Elvis's, they would view the killing as vengeance and investigate Elvis for the crime.

Elvis was glad he had not told Marlon about the poker incident. If he had told him, Elvis would have worried that Marlon was responsible for Marcus's death. He had only told one person that detail, and he didn't identify that person to Carmen. We know, of course, that the person he told was Colonel Parker because it was Parker who told Marlon that gruesome detail.

We will never know if Parker's citizens' committee had somehow organized or encouraged Marcus's death, or if Marlon had joined that vigilante group. Giving credence to a theory of Parker as capable of murder, however, is information unearthed by author Alanna Nash and published in her book *The Colonel: The Extraordinary Story of Colonel Tom Parker and Elvis Presley.* Born Andreas van Kuijk in Breda, Holland, he disappeared suddenly from his hometown leaving everything behind. He soon arrived in America as an illegal alien. A woman he knew was found murdered in Breda that same month. Nash builds a persuasive circumstantial case pointing to van Kuijk aka Parker as the murderer.

Nevertheless, it is hard to imagine Parker ordering or permitting physical and emotional damage to his meal ticket without getting something of equal or greater value in return. As for Marlon, I can understand his rage and need for vengeance, but I am only left with suspicions about whether he acted on those emotions.

A Mess of Blues

Song released in 1960

A few months after the murder of Marcus, there was another abduction. This time, Tom Jones and his manager Gordon Mills were the targets. I suspect this kidnapping was retaliation for Marcus's killing. The Katzman gang may have assumed that Elvis and Marlon had organized the slaying of one of their bunch, so had decided to reciprocate by targeting one of their close friends.

According to several letters from Tom, he and Gordon had just completed contract discussions at Caesar's Palace in Las Vegas. As they were walking out of the casino to visit the Flamingo where Tom had often performed, numerous people recognized the singer, and a crowd quickly gathered around him. He signed autographs and gave rehearsed answers to many questions, taking time to give his fans the attention they craved. When Tom and Gordon departed, two men broke off from the crowd and followed them out the side entrance.

Outside, two thugs pulled guns and marched the celebrities across the street where they were joined by two more armed men. Tom and Gordon were escorted to their rental car and forced to get into the back seat. It is not clear that this gang was the same one that had kidnapped Elvis, but Marlon, knowing that Elvis had shared the previous attack with Tom, implied they were when he wrote, "He [Tom] said he was afraid that they were going to try to attack him the way they did Elvis."

The captives were driven to an abandoned mine in the desert where they were greeted by two more armed men. They all entered the ruins of an abandoned mining office where Tom's and Gordon's hands were tied to an overhead beam. Tom told Marlon that all six gang members seemed high on a "speed drug." Intensifying Tom's fears, the men stripped off his clothes—down to his famous red undershorts—and then tore the clothes off Gordon Mills. They tried to force Tom to swallow a clear liquid. When he fought off their attempts, one of the men drew a knife and made superficial wounds on Tom's abdomen, left thigh and left upper arm.

Tom told Marlon later that he started praying the roof would fall in. As he pulled down on the rotten overhead beam and desperately jumped up and down, the creaking floor gave way, and Tom fell into a pit where no one could reach him. His weight had cracked the overhead beam. A section of it tumbled into the pit and narrowly missed him. His body was twisted, and he had wood splinters everywhere. Every time he tried to pull himself up, the beam to which he was still bound got caught on something. Escape seemed impossible, and even if he had gotten out, there was no escape from the gang.

Angry that the subject of their attention was out of reach, and perhaps sensing the personal peril of trying to liberate Tom from the pit, the gang turned its wrath on Gordon. They began by pouring a liquid on his bare skin that made him writhe in agony for hours but did not leave any burns. Then they gang-raped him and forced some of the fiery liquid into his bowels before savagely beating him. At last they stole their captives' wallets, jewelry and shoes, then left both men half-dead in the ruins.

Semi-conscious for a long time, Gordon finally woke up about four o'clock in the morning to the sound of Tom scuffling about in the pit below. Tom had managed to get his hands free, push the beam section upward, and with great difficulty claw his way to the surface. With the little strength he had left, Gordon painfully reached into the pit and grabbed Tom's hand, giving his friend an extra hold to pull himself up.

After resting for a bit, the two survivors dressed in the shredded remnants of their clothes and limped barefoot across the rocky desert to a road about five miles away. It was nearly ten o'clock before they flagged down a highway patrol car.

Gordon had received the brunt of the attack and wound up in the hospital for a few days. Tom's wounds were more superficial, except for recurring nightmares.

It Keeps Right On A-Hurtin'

Song released in 1969

The next attack came at a surprise summer send-off party for Elvis, who was soon leaving for another concert series in Las Vegas. About fifty people gathered on Elvis's patio for the celebratory farewell: a handful of musicians who would be backing Elvis in Vegas, their girlfriends and wives, a few close friends, the inevitable party crashers and a few others. The event started loudly with the band jamming for about ten minutes before Elvis appeared to raucous applause and tried out a couple of numbers from his upcoming show. Then Elvis introduced Tom Jones. They joked around, then improvised an old Elvis song with the band. Before long, the two friends were trying to outdo each other with playful histrionics.

It was very hot outside. Elvis wiped his forehead with a handkerchief and said he was going to save himself for Vegas. He took a seat at a table to Tom's right. The audience was standing in a semi-circle around the singer. Marlon was standing in the front to Tom's left.

Tom tried to politely turn the improvised show back to the band, which was vamping in the background, but the audience wanted more. He was standing there, probably wondering what to do while giving his best Tom Jones smile to the crowd, when suddenly he lowered his head and nearly doubled over. The audience thought he was preparing for one of his Tom Jones moves, but he continued to stand there motionless for a few seconds. Slowly the cheering quieted.

Above the music, Marlon heard Tom say, "I've been shot."

Marlon wasn't sure he had heard correctly. There had been no gunshot, no spatter of blood, but he rushed to his friend along with one of Elvis's bodyguards and a second man. Elvis didn't seem to know anything had happened until the men helped Tom sit down. Marlon didn't even know at that time where Tom had been shot.

Elvis suddenly bolted from his chair and raced to Tom, who looked up and calmly said, "There goes another pair of pants."

Someone called a doctor, and Tom insisted that his manager, Gordon Mills, be called immediately. Tom's leg had started to bleed, so Marlon and the bodyguard quickly moved Tom inside. Within a few minutes, the police and the doctor had arrived, but most of the women guests had already left. No one else was allowed to leave until they were questioned. The doctor discovered that the bullet had struck high up on Tom's thigh near the groin and fortunately had not hit any bone or major arteries, so no surgery would be required. The doctor dressed the wound and gave Tom instructions to stay off the leg for at last a week and have it reexamined in a couple of days. The police found the bullet lodged in the patio floor and said the music had probably masked the sound of the gunshot, or maybe a silencer had been used. After the shock had worn off, Tom found that he was able to put weight on the leg and take a few steps without a lot of pain.

Two letters were sent to Carmen later that day, the first by Marlon and the other by Tom, who anticipated Marlon having already written to her. "I'm all right," Tom wrote. "Don't worry. I was more taken by surprise than anything else." He was 99 percent sure that the Katzman gang was responsible for the shooting and considered it a brazen and stupid act. The police, however, were operating on the theory that the shot was fired by a crackpot who couldn't crash the party or hated Tom's music.

Tom felt lucky that the shot had gone cleanly through his leg with minimal damage. He figured the shooter wasn't aiming for his leg, but he had moved, and the gunman had missed a more vital spot. Elvis believed the gang didn't want Tom going with him to Las Vegas. The shooting, however, had made Tom more committed than ever to go. Tom closed his letter with an expression of concern for Elvis. "I pray Elvis rests tonight. He's quite upset."

Devil in Disguise
Song released in 1963

During July and August of 1969, Los Angeles was haunted by the specter of a Satanist cult. At four different locations over several weeks the cult had viciously murdered nine people including actress Sharon Tate, supermarket executive Leno LaBianca, and Rosemary, his wife. Everybody in southern California was on edge, and it is likely that the crimes committed by the Katzman gang seemed even more frightening to Elvis in the shadow of the unknown serial killers.

During this time, another related event was revealed in letters by Tom Jones. I have not been able to solve the mystery these letters presented because the details are murky, but I share them here.

We know that in May of 1969, Tom Jones and Gordon Mills were kidnapped, driven into the desert outside of Las Vegas and brutally tortured. Then, in a letter written in the summer of 1969, Tom made an alarming reference to a weapon he had possessed. The letter makes clear that he had mentioned the knife to Carmen earlier, but we have no record of that remark. In the letter we have, he explained that he had thrown away the knife while traveling between the US and the UK. The main reason for taking a trip home to England, he explained, was to make sure the knife was deposited "where no one will ever be able to find it no matter how long or how hard they look." Remember, this event happened in 1969, long before terrorists caused travelers to endure rigorous searches prior to boarding planes or ships.

Clearly, the knife he discarded held great peril for him so long as it was in his possession. Even worse, he explained to Carmen, his understanding was that British law allowed a person to be convicted of a violent crime based on circumstantial evidence even when a weapon had not been found. He was relieved that he would not be bringing the knife to his London home where his wife might accidentally find it. He got chills when he woke up at night realizing that he could "get hung in London or imprisoned in America" because of that knife.

When I first encountered Tom's reference to the knife, it seemed likely it had been used in a violent crime. I wondered how Tom Jones, world famous pop singer, had come to possess it. At the time, I was reading the letters out of sequence because of dating issues and had not yet read descriptions of the horrible kidnapping and torture of Gordon and Tom. When I came across those accounts, I suspected that Tom's zealous ditching of the knife was connected somehow to that abduction.

Then I came across another Jones letter in which he revealed a shocking development in the knife saga, one that terrorized him. The news media had reported that the body of a man had been found partially buried in the "Nevada Flats." I believe this referred to a stretch of desert northwest of Las Vegas called Frenchman Flat used until 1968 for underground nuclear testing. It's likely that the area between Frenchman Flat and the town of Indian Wells is where Tom and Gordon were tortured and where the body in the shallow grave had just been found. I believe the road to which Tom and Gordon walked after their kidnapping was Highway 95, which leaves Las Vegas and runs northwest to Interstate 80.

The news report that made Tom so nervous reported that the man had died about two months earlier of a knife wound in the chest. Tom quickly wrote a letter to Carmen. The opening lines of this letter were hastily scratched out as if he worried that he had shared too much information, but the content can still be deciphered. He wrote that he was comforted that the victim was "described as being older," but older than what? He does not say, but that incomplete thought implies that Tom may have meant to write "older than the man I know was killed out there."

Tom also wrote, "It may not be the same [man], but I've been shaking in my boots ever since I heard. Elvis is jittery, yet there can't be anything to tie us in. There can't be, yet I feel very uneasy. (Please destroy this letter before you leave.)" Fortunately for us, Carmen didn't destroy it.

A letter from Tom revealed to Carmen his anxiety about a corpse found in the desert and its possible connection to Elvis and him.

235

When Tom wrote that there wasn't anything to "tie us in," was he referring to the knife that he had dropped where "only Davey Jones and I know"?

These brief comments suggest a connection between the knife, the abduction of Tom Jones and Gordon Mills, and the corpse in the desert that may or may not have been a member of the Katzman gang. But without more details, we are left with tantalizing speculation.

I Got Stung
Song released in 1958

Throughout the summer of 1969, Marlon noticed that Elvis's behavior had become more erratic than usual. In late September he came up with the notion that someone might be adding poison to Elvis's food—not enough to kill Elvis right away, but enough to cause emotional and mental disruptions. Marlon suspected Colonel Parker or possibly one or more of the Memphis Mafia who were supposed to be looking out for Elvis. Marlon convinced his friend to save samples of meals he had been served at home. While visiting Elvis, Marlon personally took small samples of many different foods from the kitchen, including a bottle of Sucaryl sweetener, then delivered all the samples to a chemist. For the next few days, Elvis ate some meals at Marlon's home as a precaution.

The wait for the chemical results stoked Elvis's paranoia. He grumbled to Carmen that he was afraid their food search might have missed something. He wrote that he couldn't imagine living out his life in constant fear of being poisoned.

The results of the tests were devastating. As Marlon explained, the chemist had found enough "acid" in the Sucaryl "to kill an army battalion." Marlon didn't identify the specific kind of acid to Carmen but had asked the chemist if someone could have spiked the sweetener with acid out of revenge, maybe to burn Elvis's vocal cords.

The chemist explained that a dose of the spiked Sucaryl sufficient to sweeten a cup of coffee would contain enough of the acid to kill the recipient. The chemist called the poison a "slow acid," meaning the recipient could have finished his sweetened cup of coffee—maybe even washed and put away the cup—before noticing the effects. An autopsy could have discovered the cause of death, but because of Elvis's frequent bouts of depression and history of suicide attempts, a medical examiner might easily conclude that the singer had finally succeeded in killing himself.

At first, Marlon suspected that Elvis's cousin Gee Gee was the perpetrator. Elvis had thrown Gee Gee out of the house, so the former bodyguard could have been seeking revenge. Since the acid seemed designed to finish what it started, however, simple revenge seemed an unlikely goal. There was bad blood between those two cousins, but it was hard to see Gee Gee as a murderer.

Marlon's suspicions turned to another insider, but then Elvis remembered that it was Colonel Parker who had prodded him to use Sucaryl as an aid for weight control. What may have saved Elvis was that he seldom drank coffee or ate cereal. For breakfast, he was a steak, eggs and milk kind of guy. So why spike the Sucaryl? Stupidity, perhaps. It would have been just like Parker to be oblivious to Elvis's eating habits.

Marlon hired a private investigator who found two sets of identifiable fingerprints on the Sucaryl container: Marlon's and Kit's. Many other partials were smudged. Marlon remembered that when he had taken all the samples home, Kit had rummaged through them. Not taking Marlon's investigation seriously, she had come close to using the Sucaryl for her cereal before Marlon grabbed it away. Remembering how Kit had come so close to tragedy horrified Marlon now.

Mean Woman Blues

Song released in 1957, performed in the movie Loving You

The year 1969 continued with more acts of violence that rattled Tom, Elvis and Marlon. In early October, Tom was leaving a recording studio in Los Angeles and heading for his parked car when he saw a small group of fans and a couple of photographers positioned to ambush him. An attractive blonde girl caught his attention by approaching him with a bouquet of mixed flowers. Tom prepared to accept the flowers and then sign autographs.

Smiling broadly, the girl suddenly dropped the flowers and threw out her arms as if offering an embrace. Suddenly, someone yelled, "Look out, Tom!" At the last second, Tom saw the glint of a straight razor in the girl's hand. He flinched, and the blade, arcing toward his jugular, nicked his black wool turtleneck. A photographer leaped on the girl, and a fan wrestled the razor away from her. The police arrived within several minutes and hauled the girl away.

Tom hired a private investigator, Mr. Gilbert, to find out more about the girl, but the PI insulted him by insisting on interrogating Lwli, whom Tom wanted to keep part of his secret life. Within days the PI resigned. A week later, the police apprehended four "hippie types" associated with the razor girl. Tom learned that this group was "connected with Charles Manson," but a full understanding of what that meant was not yet possible. Tom vented his frustration by writing, "All I need is a third set trying to get rid of me."

In searching newspaper archives for any information that might shed light on this bizarre incident, I discovered an "Exclusive" article in the *Los Angeles Herald-Examiner*. Under the sensational headline "Ghastly Tortures Planned for Stars," staff writer William Farr reported an interview he had conducted with a cellmate of Susan "Sadie" Atkins, one of the notorious followers of Charles Manson. The thirty-seven-year-old cellmate, referred to as Mrs. Virginia Graham, told Farr of plans, revealed to her by "Sadie" Atkins, to murder various stars in various gruesome ways. The stars included Liz Taylor, Richard Burton, Frank Sinatra, Steve McQueen and Tom Jones.

"Sadie" Atkins, according to her cellmate, resented Tom Jones because he had become famous as a singer while her idol, Charles Manson, a wannabe singer/songwriter, couldn't even get a record deal. Atkins confessed that she had a problem with the plan to kill Jones because she was attracted to him sexually. She apparently resolved this quandary by plotting to force him into having sex with her before she "slit his throat." We can't be certain that Susan "Sadie" Atkins was the razor girl who attacked Tom Jones outside the recording studio in 1969, but Tom certainly was a man marked by the Manson gang for having his throat cut.

Ghastly Tortures Planned for Stars

EXCLUSIVE

By WILLIAM FARR
Herald-Examiner Staff Writer
Copyright 1970 Los Angeles
Herald-Examiner

Deep resentment also apparently smouldered against pop singer Jones, as Mrs. Graham relates:

"She resented Tom Jones' voice. He didn't sing as well as Charlie, according to her. Yet he had all that success and Charlie couldn't get his voice on record even.

"This murder was a problem for Sadie, she told me. She didn't really want him killed, or at least she had second thoughts because she was sexually attracted to Jones.

"What she wanted to do is to get him in a position and force him to have sex with her at knife point, and . . . she was going to slit his throat.

A 1970 article in the *Los Angeles Herald-Examiner* describes a plot by the Charles Manson gang to murder Tom Jones by cutting his throat.

Dirty, Dirty Feeling
Song released in 1957

Tom's letters suggest that another crime had occurred in Las Vegas before these months of violence. Few details were reported, but the outcome of the crime was made clear. Elvis, Tom, and at least two of the Supremes, a popular vocal trio, were out together on the streets of Vegas when they were confronted by three men. We don't know what words were exchanged, but Tom Jones told Carmen that singer Mary Wilson, his former lover, had been "slashed down the stomach and under the bust… like that girl was murdered in Beverly Hills." By "that girl" he was referring to Manson victim Sharon Tate. Apparently, Cindy Birdsong, the other Supreme, was not harmed, nor was Tom or Elvis.

Tom was sickened by the senseless mutilation of Wilson, and the violence sent him into a nauseating swoon as he recalled the terror he'd endured during his kidnapping. He was certain there was a connection between the slashing of Mary Wilson and his recent abduction. Was it the same men who perpetrated both crimes? He struggled to remember the kidnappers' faces, but the trauma of the two events prevented him from putting the pieces together.

On October 18, 1969, Diana Ross and the other Supremes— Mary Wilson and Cindy Birdsong—hosted the Hollywood Palace TV Show featuring Sammy Davis Jr., ventriloquist act Willie Tyler and Lester, and the first national television appearance of the Jackson 5. Michael Jackson, future husband of Lisa Marie Presley, made his solo debut. Elvis told Carmen that this was Mary Wilson's first appearance since the attack in Vegas. Elvis hoped Mary would do well because he knew she was feeling self-conscious and fearful of appearing in public. He understood that feeling.

I Say a Little Prayer
Song released in 1967

A couple of days after the Supremes performed on TV, someone took a shot at Tom Jones. He was climbing into a limousine and Gordon Mills was getting in beside him. Gordon had just lowered his head when a shot whizzed by. If it had not narrowly missed, Tom told Carmen, "he could be a dead man today."

Even though Tom had been shot in the leg earlier that year, Elvis wondered if this bullet might have been meant for Gordon. Killing Gordon would have been a twisted but ingenious way to torture Tom because Gordon was Tom's sherpa. Tom would be devastated personally and career-wise without him.

The police did a bullet trajectory analysis and calculated the position from which the shot was fired. They reported that it was probably intended to strike Tom's abdomen, not his head or Gordon Mills, but simply missed. Their operating theory was that a fan's jealous boyfriend had taken a potshot at Tom.

Elvis concluded that the trajectory meant the shooter was not aiming to kill Tom, but to wound him, perhaps badly. Small comfort. Tom took it as a reminder that he was not safe no matter where he was.

Anxiety was quickly stoked again Tuesday night, December 2, 1969, when Cindy Birdsong was abducted at knifepoint from her Hollywood apartment. The abductor forced Birdsong to bind two male guests with neckties and an electrical cord, stole a hundred dollars from Birdsong, and drove away with his captive in Birdsong's own car. The guests quickly freed themselves and called the police. Word of the abduction spread swiftly to the other Supremes and to Tom and Elvis, who must have suspected the Katzman gang at work again.

Fortunately, Birdsong escaped unharmed from her abductor when he inexplicably slowed the auto on the southbound Long Beach Freeway near the Pacific Coast Highway. After jumping from the car, Birdsong ran along the shoulder of the freeway against the traffic and was picked up by California Highway Patrol officers and treated for minor stab wounds and abrasions. Hours later, Charles Edward Collier, the custodian of Birdsong's apartment building, called the police and confessed after fleeing to Las Vegas and gambling away all but two dollars of the stolen money.

Elvis and Tom were relieved that Collier had no known affiliation with Katzman, but the incident frayed their already ragged nerves.

The year had begun with an attempted suicide by Elvis and gone downhill from there, with violence visited upon more of Elvis's band of close friends. Surely, things would settle down in 1970. Striking an optimistic tone not supported by recent events, Elvis scribbled on a Christmas card to Carmen, "May you be blessed this Christmas with the richest of gifts: peace, joy, and love."

CHARLES E. COLLIER, 26, is escorted to Clark County Justice Court in Las Vegas by Sgt. Jack Phillips. Collier turned himself in Wednesday several hours after Cindy Birdsong of the Supremes said she was kidnapped Tuesday. Collier waived extradition to Los Angeles.

—AP Wirephoto

A news article about the Birdsong abduction from the *Long Beach Independent*, Dec. 4, 1969.

Only the Strong Survive

On March 3, 1970, Elvis checked into the Baptist Memorial Hospital in Memphis for three days to diagnose and treat chronic eye problems that had worsened. Doctors discovered he had glaucoma in his left eye, a condition that can lead to blindness, sometimes suddenly. According to *The Ultimate Elvis* by Patricia Jobe Pierce, Elvis "cried for hours and could not sleep" upon getting the news.

Then, shortly after his discharge from the hospital, Elvis received a letter that forced him to relive past torments and promised new miseries to come. That disturbing letter came at a time of great vulnerability for Elvis, almost as if timed to produce the greatest impact. That letter was not preserved, but we know it had a big impact on Elvis, though in a way the author could not have anticipated. Instead of crumbling beneath the weight of remembered horrors, he instead embraced a new direction for his life to eradicate the shadow that had been cast over it.

On March 8, Elvis sent a letter to Carmen revealing his new personal goal. He had decided to abandon his career within the next two years and become an evangelist like the man he believed was his biological father, Virgil Presley. He was sure the name Elvis Presley would attract audiences, and if he could just help one soul out of thousands know God better each night it would be worth it. He might use a little wiggle or a holler to get them into the big

243

tent, he wrote, but that didn't matter as long as they showed up and listened to God's truth.

He told Carmen that the personal tribulations of the past year had helped him grow closer to God, and he would no longer let anyone stir up his dark side. He'd been taught from childhood to believe in God but had drifted away and stopped trusting in the Almighty. He was sure, though, that God had not forgotten or abandoned him and had even delivered a miracle by sending someone to touch his life and help him survive the darkest days. As a way of thanking both God and Carmen, he had just recorded a new album called *He Touched Me*, and he hoped she would like it.

At that point in his letter to Carmen, his mood abruptly changed, and he referred to a new threatening letter that had propelled him into depression. He called it "soul-shattering." As much as he'd tried to erase all those bad things from his mind, he told Carmen, the letter resurrected fear, anger, even remorse for allowing "them" to regain such control over his emotions. Reading that letter, he wrote, was almost beyond suffering. "Dying is one thing, but that's another."

He closed his letter by remembering his "Mama," who he knew was "rooting for him." He called his mother and Carmen a solid team, with one member here and the other in the world of spirit. He closed with the words, "so I'm trying, Sis." Perhaps Elvis was giving himself a badly needed pep talk in this letter. He remained at Graceland into May, deeply depressed despite his uplifting but unkept decision to become a preacher, sleeping twelve hours each day, and believing he would be blind by the end of the year.

More trials came and went for Elvis over the next several months, most of which I've described in earlier chapters. But none of them could top the new horror that occurred during the summer of 1970. Finally convinced by his aides that he was not going blind, Elvis began rehearsing at MGM for his late-summer opening at the International Hotel in Las Vegas. In 1969, he had performed 114 concerts at the International and was booked for another fifty-eight concerts beginning August 10, 1970. He had become a Vegas fixture, a sharp turn from his early days.

Elvis normally enjoyed rehearsals, but there was additional stress this time. He had become obsessed with improving the show, giving the audience something new and fresh and perhaps fending off lingering fears and depression. Adding to his anxiety, a movie crew directed by Denis Sanders, a recipient of two Oscars for documentaries, was shooting the rehearsals for an upcoming concert film, *Elvis—That's The Way It Is*. The crew was everywhere, peeping into corners and looking for poignant emotional moments featuring The King. Shooting would continue in August when Elvis opened at the International.

On Friday, July 17th, Elvis and Priscilla flew to their unassuming Palm Springs home on Chino Canyon Road and spent the day relaxing. Elvis was restless that evening. Few knew it, but according to a letter written by Elvis, Priscilla was pregnant again. Typically, he went to bed after Priscilla was asleep. Despite the strain of rehearsing and filming, he fell asleep easily about one thirty a.m. with Priscilla at his side and several staffers sleeping in other bedrooms.

The Presley home in Palm Springs.

At 4:20 that morning, Elvis woke up. Had he heard something? The house was quiet. He looked at the clock on his bedstand. There had been many days when he was just going to bed at that hour. The only sound in the room was Priscilla's soft breathing. Strangely disturbed, he

245

was afraid that he wouldn't be able to go back to sleep, so he coaxed himself along. Finally, he drifted back to sleep, deeply this time.

* * *

It was an odd sensation, like a dentist clanking around in his mouth with cold metal instruments. Elvis knew that feeling; he had suffered most of his life with tooth problems. But this was different. Something cold and hard was pressing down on his tongue, making him gag. Saliva was running down his cheek. He tried to wake up, but his mind felt numb. He turned his head and rolled onto his back, but the steely object moved with him. A nightmare? Too real. He bit down and his teeth ground against smooth steel.

Slowly, he forced his eyes to open. This couldn't really be happening. He tried to sit up but couldn't. The cold protrusion forced itself down his throat.

Panicky now, Elvis focused his eyes. A large hand blocked his view, a hand knotted into a fist—no, not a fist. The hand was holding something. A gun. The hand held a .45 caliber pistol, and the barrel was jammed into Elvis's mouth. Elvis sucked in his breath. A cold shudder rippled through his body.

He refocused his eyes down the gunman's arm to a sneering face in the dim light. *Two* faces. There were two shadowy creatures in the room. Elvis recognized both of them, cutthroat thugs who worked for Jungle Sam Katzman. They had helped abduct and torture him back in 1968.

The accomplice shook Priscilla, who woke up irritably until she saw the two men. She gasped, but the accomplice silenced her with a broad palm across the mouth. Her eyes darted around until she saw the gun barrel in Elvis's mouth. She emitted a muffled whimper. And then the accomplice spoke in a hoarse whisper: "Make a sound and we'll blow his guts out from the inside." Clearly, they wanted to avoid waking others in the house.

The man with the gun quietly told Elvis, "Don't even move your head or I'll blast you and cut her open and take the baby." The threat of such brutality horrified Elvis, I'm sure, but he also must have been stunned that they knew Priscilla was pregnant.

Quickly the intruders whipped the covers off Elvis. They tore Priscilla's nightgown. They brutally forced Elvis to roll face down on top of his pregnant wife. There was another gravelly whisper. "Remember how Mary Wilson got cut up over in Las Vegas?"

Elvis remembered how Wilson had been brutally slashed and had gone through numerous plastic surgeries.

The accomplice climbed onto the bed and squatted closely behind Elvis, who braced himself for the sting of a blade. But there was no knife. Elvis heard the horrible whine of a zipper, and then felt as if he were being torn in half as the man viciously penetrated him. With each thrust, the weight of Elvis and the accomplice came crashing down on Priscilla. Elvis whirled through a kaleidoscope of emotions—fear, humiliation, rage—until he felt he would explode. This was the supreme indignation—a savage violation of his home, his body, his psyche. He was being violently and painfully abased in front of his wife. His unborn child was being crushed inside its mother.

Priscilla was nearly mad with fright.

When the torture appeared to be over, the gunman pointed the pistol at Elvis's head, watched Elvis grimacing in pain, then mumbled something about having only two bullets in the gun. Slowly, he squeezed the trigger. It was like a game of Russian roulette. Elvis could feel his own heartbeat drumming in his temples. It seemed like each beat might be enough to set off the trigger. The finger kept squeezing. Suddenly the gun jerked forward... and clicked.

The chamber was empty.

Elvis sighed, but then realized the terror was not yet over. The gunman moved the pistol maddeningly around to point at different parts of Elvis's head. With a faint grin, he again slowly began to apply pressure to the trigger. This was a new game—*Let's see how long it takes to click the trigger.*

Priscilla was trembling uncontrollably. Elvis squinted, waiting for an explosion, praying for a click. The finger moved as if in slow motion, and the gunman's sly grin seemed to light up the room. What were the odds that two chambers in a row would be empty?

Click.

The accomplice laughed.

It was too much. Elvis lunged at the men. They were stunned at first, but before Elvis could land a karate chop, the gun barrel crashed onto his head. Then he heard screams. They seemed to echo in his head.

Finally, Elvis refocused. Priscilla was holding his head, screaming and crying.

"The baby... the baby!"

Elvis struggled to sit up. The two men were gone. The sudden impact of Priscilla's words hit him hard.

The baby.

Somehow, he had to get Priscilla to a doctor. But he couldn't think clearly. Everything was hazy, distant. He looked at Priscilla, her face streaked with terror and tears, clutching her abdomen, saying those words: *The baby!*

Afterward he could barely remember his next steps, but he got dressed and lifted Priscilla off the floor. He recalled others in the house opening their bedroom doors, watching silently. He carried Priscilla out of the house. She was unconscious before they reached the car. Miraculously, they arrived at the hospital without an accident.

Even though he was in pain, he could not bear to explain what had happened to himself. The physical pain now seemed no worse than the psychological pain he had been enduring for years. Suddenly there were many people around him, and he thought he was going to be ill. All the fears and trauma of the past years seemed to crystallize in this moment. And Elvis knew this wouldn't be the last time.

Because Priscilla had not been with Elvis after the abduction and gang-rape in 1968, she had never truly believed what had happened to her husband. Marlon spoke with her after the Palm Springs ordeal and told Carmen that she definitely believed it now. Priscilla was still shaken when she talked to Marlon and broke down crying on the phone. "I just didn't understand such things could happen," she said. "I don't know why they didn't kill both of us." Then she sobbed again and blurted out, "They even tore my negligee, the one I had on my honeymoon."

Amazingly, Priscilla did not miscarry immediately. Marlon reported to Carmen that Priscilla went through false labor for about twenty-four hours, then became hysterical, and the doctor almost had to take the baby. After she calmed down, she left for Graceland.

Sometime during the next several months, Elvis became aware that his wife was no longer pregnant. It may seem strange that a husband and wife would not share all the details about a pregnancy, but this was Elvis and Priscilla. They seldom discussed anything personal except accusations.

Four months later, perhaps answering a question, Elvis told Carmen that his wife rarely showed signs of pregnancy in the past, so most people didn't know she was pregnant. With Lisa Marie, he wrote, she had kept to her normal weight until the last minute when she finally gained seven pounds. It would have been hard to tell when she had lost the baby. I think Elvis must have questioned whether Priscilla was really pregnant at all or making it up to gain leverage over him.

When I first read the account of the home invasion, two perplexing details troubled me. As Elvis described it, he and Priscilla were asleep in a "dim" room, but upon waking Elvis claimed to recognize two men who were among his kidnappers back in 1968. How could he recognize these men in a darkened room? Well, we don't know how dim the light was, of course. Elvis could have meant "not fully illuminated but just light enough to recognize faces." Some people sleep with nightlights on, or with shades open to let in moonlight. The invasion happened just a few days before a full moon, so presumably there was enough light coming into the bedroom to "dimly" illuminate faces.

A thornier detail is the gunman's seemingly clairvoyant knowledge of Priscilla's unannounced pregnancy. How could he have known about it? In rereading all the letters chronologically I was reminded that prior to the home invasion, food and milk had been poisoned in Elvis's home, possibly the work of an aide on Katzman's payroll. Certainly, news of the pregnancy would have been known to household staff, and this information could have been passed on to Elvis's tormenters. I also have had to remind myself that memory is not perfect, and all accounts of past events probably contain some factual inconsistencies and rearrangements of facts to make them tell a more compelling story.

Somehow Elvis began his concert series at the International to enthusiastic audiences just three weeks after the Palm Springs home invasion. After some initial jitters, he found some comfort in the familiar routine of shows. But then, four days after, a Los Angeles waitress named Patricia Ann Parker filed a paternity suit against Elvis claiming that she had given birth to a son fathered by Elvis during his previous Vegas concert series. The papers were handed to Elvis by a server who had deceitfully claimed to be an Elvis fan seeking an autograph. Elvis, who confessed to aides that he'd had sexual flings from time to time, must have been deeply concerned about Lisa Marie, whom he adored, suddenly gaining an illicit half-sibling. Out of anger, or possibly to head off unflattering publicity, Elvis commented on the paternity suit from the stage the following night. There is no doubt, though, that this development must have felt like the universe was "piling on."

An even more troubling event occurred just two weeks later. According to the public record, the security office at the International received an anonymous call on Wednesday, August 26, with information about a plot to kidnap Elvis. On Thursday, a similar call was placed to Colonel Parker. The next day, Joanie Esposito, wife of Elvis's road manager, received a call for her husband who was not available. Stressing the urgency of the message, the caller told Joanie that he had information about an attempt to assassinate Elvis that would occur during the Saturday evening performance, so she had better make her husband Joe available quickly. Forty-five minutes later the caller reached Joe

Esposito and offered the name of the would-be killer in exchange for payment of $50,000 in small bills.

Biographer Peter Guralnick in *Careless Love* discloses that Elvis's lawyer, Ed Hookstratten, believed the plot was related to the paternity suit. He called in the FBI and set up a meeting of close Elvis advisers including Jerry Schilling, Red West and Ed Parker. When Red arrived from Memphis, Guralnick reported that Red told him Elvis was so distraught, "he just stumbled into my arms and hugged me."

Understanding how this event occurred after many other stressful events, including the violent home invasion in Palm Springs and the razor attack on Tom Jones by a Manson groupie, it's easier to appreciate the emotions that drove Elvis's orders as reported by Guralnick: "If some sonofabitch tries to kill me, I want you guys to kill him, I want you to rip his goddamn eyes out. I don't want him sitting around afterward like Charlie Manson with a grin on his face, saying 'I killed Elvis Presley.'"

A newly created security detail scrambled to take up strategic stations around the venue. Sonny and Jerry "joined" the orchestra, and Red and Ed Parker each took a position on one side of the stage. They all carried concealed weapons. Elvis hid a pistol in each boot. Newly hired plainclothes police officers scattered through the audience. The hotel doctor created a makeshift ER backstage equipped with oxygen and blood supplies. An ambulance parked outside the closest exit.

The show began, but nothing happened until the midway point when someone in the balcony called out, "Elvis!" Everyone flinched. Was this it? But the man simply wanted Elvis to sing his favorite song. By the end of the show, the entire team was emotionally exhausted. Elvis's inscrutable reaction confused Joe Moscheo, singer-manager of the Imperials, who said, "It was crazy. It was like he was disappointed that he didn't get shot!"

After everything Elvis had been through, Moscheo may have been onto something. Nevertheless, no other calls or incidents occurred during the concert series, though the security detail of the International remained on high alert until the Elvis shows were finished. The FBI declared the calls a hoax. I think Elvis wasn't so certain.

* * *

In November, Elvis discovered another chemical tampering in his house, this one less dangerous than the acid in the Sucaryl. Elvis's dentist had been giving him some special tooth powder. Early in 1970, Elvis had started to complain that there was something wrong with it. A fresh can always started out normal but then deteriorated in texture and taste, making him light-headed when he used it. Each time Elvis returned the powder, the dentist gave him a quizzical look along with a new can. No other patient, the dentist said, had reported a problem like this. And each time Elvis got the new supply of tooth powder home it was fine for a couple of weeks then went bad again.

In November, Elvis returned his tooth powder with an angry outburst. He believed the tooth powder was making him shake uncontrollably at times, and for weeks food had been making him ill. He was feeling so strung out that he couldn't sleep, and because of Elvis's previous irresponsible use of barbiturates, his doctor wouldn't let him keep sleeping pills at home.

This time the dentist sent the tooth powder to a laboratory for chemical analysis. The lab reported that one-third of the tooth powder had been replaced with cocaine.

Again, the letters do not reveal a solution to the mystery. It's clear, though, that Elvis had become hooked on the cocaine and probably suffered withdrawal when the perpetrator had no more tooth powder to mix into it. This intrusive act of betrayal seems like an attempt to disrupt Elvis's life and career. An out-of-control cocaine addiction would have made it impossible for Elvis to sustain a concert series or complete a movie, ruining his reputation. This tends to rule out Colonel Parker as the wrongdoer because an incapacitated star would be bad for business. Then again, cocaine could make Elvis more vulnerable to influence, and this could be good for Parker.

At any time, the perpetrator could have notified the police that Elvis possessed cocaine at his home, setting up a drug bust with enormous legal consequences. The fact that the drugging went on for many months leads me to believe that *misery* or *control* was the goal, not the ruination of Elvis's career. More likely the responsible party was someone with a grudge who worked for Elvis and had access to the house, or maybe someone in the household who was on the payroll of an adversary with a vendetta.

A Paranormal World

The letters written by Elvis and his friends to the spiritualist Carmen Montez are filled with accounts of paranormal and supernatural activities, or at least a belief in them. In hindsight, as I first plunged into the private worlds of Elvis, Harry, Marlon and Tom, I should have immediately focused on how these compatriots understood the world around them. If I had, everything would have made more sense. Instead, I took the long way around. Since the beginning of this quest I have always felt a sense of unease, but never entered seriously into any speculation about Satanism or witchcraft until recently, when, for various reasons, I was persuaded to pursue this line of inquiry. After seeking the opinion of London-born ghostbuster Adrian Lee, I sometimes wonder what on earth I was walking into with this project. As you read on you may find the hair on the back of your neck rising—something that happened to me after consulting with Adrian Lee.

When he was thirteen, Elvis moved from Tupelo, Mississippi, where he became rooted in mystical Christian fundamentalism, to Memphis, a city brimming with voodoo shops and black musicians still connected through their families to the witchcraft of Africa and the traditions of southern American folklore. Anyone with Elvis's background easily could have had the tools to practice dark magic—or be practiced upon.

Elvis's twin brother, Jesse, was stillborn. P. G. White, Ph.D., a twins researcher and the author of a website called *The Sibling Connection*, claims that Elvis suffered from intense guilt at being the surviving twin and probably blamed himself for Jesse's death. "Many twins feel this way," White wrote. "As an adult, Elvis spoke to his brother as if he were praying. He visited his brother's unmarked grave and had it moved to Graceland, where he created a private cemetery for him and his mother."

White also stated that Elvis believed his brother was his guardian angel. Apparently, Marlon knew of this belief, writing to Carmen in a letter dated just a month after the 1968 kidnapping: "In less than a full year he's had enough to crack an even stronger person. He has a stubbornness about him that has saved him so far. That and a guardian angel."

Another of our letter writers, Harry Belafonte, at the age of eighteen months was transported on a banana boat by his father, Harold, from the poverty of New York City to the penury of Jamaica. There, in the warm embrace of his grandmother, he received an abundance of love but also full immersion into the magical world of Jamaican voodoo. In his July 1966 letter to Carmen, he exposed his reliance on this spiritual upbringing when describing his attempt to confront a woman he believed was corrupting his half-brother, Jim Mathews. "I used my knowledge of voodoo," he wrote, "to bring the girl Chloe here to where I was, each of us in spirit."

Apparently, Harry also sought some help of a non-spiritual nature from Carmen. What he had in mind we do not know, but he tucked a note inside a Beverly Hilton envelope and had it hand-delivered to Carmen. The note, written on a scrap of paper, contained only the address and phone number of the beauty salon where the "witch" Chloe worked.

The envelope and note written by Harry Belafonte contained Chloe's
work address and phone number.

The more worldly Marlon Brando, however he acquired spiritual instincts, firmly believed in the afterlife and the concepts of mediumship and channeling. He participated repeatedly in "spirit writing," whether channeling the spirit of Jeni and Chief Talking Eagle or exhibiting the behaviors of dissociative identity disorder. He witnessed the ghost or mirage of Jeni, Elvis's dead girlfriend. He demonstrated clairscentency—a psychic power that uses scent as the medium for transmitting a message—when he detected the fragrance of Carmen Montez's perfume in Elvis's bedroom though she had never physically been there.

While the Tom Jones letters never show Tom expressing an interest in paranormal or spiritual matters, he described to Carmen a frightening brush with the occult in the form of a woman with a straight razor who obsessed about having sex with him. Susan "Sadie" Atkins, a member of the infamous Charles Manson "Family," was also a follower of famed Satanist Anton LaVey in San Francisco. Manson was linked to a satanic church called "The Process" and mixed its teachings with science fiction and Scientology concepts to produce a murderous belief system that he implanted into his followers. Some Christian fundamentalists go so far as to believe

Manson was infested by demons—perhaps even being a case of "perfect possession" in which a demon is in full control of the individual.

Tom confessed to Carmen an experience that may have been paranormal, though he wasn't sure that he might not have been dreaming or under the influence of hospital drugs at the time. The event took place a few days after an attempt on his life was foretold by Marlon in a letter "spirit written" by "Jeni." While recovering from a serious automobile accident, Tom was awakened one night by the sensation of a needle going into his arm and a night nurse "caressing me" under the sheets. Still weak from his condition, Tom tried reaching for the call button, but the nurse prevented him from summoning help by pressing a pointed scissors against his neck.

"Suddenly, I swear, something green and luminous and without shape seemed to swoop down," Tom explained, "and the lady went flying, picked herself up from the far side of the room where she landed, and fled in terror." Tom's manager said he was sure the event was a drug-induced delusion, but nevertheless moved Tom out of the hospital immediately. Marlon believed the green shape was Jeni who had been watching over Tom since the accident and reporting Tom's progress through spirit writing.

What is indisputable is that these four friends confessed in writing to Carmen that they were deeply affected by paranormal circumstances, and three of them believed deeply in spiritualism and psychic phenomena. They certainly were not skeptical of unexplained events, perhaps because they could explain them in familiar spiritual or psychic terms. Events appearing to be paranormal may have been so commonly experienced by Elvis, Harry and Marlon that they could comfortably describe them to a fellow believer such as Carmen Montez while remaining more guarded with others.

While many readers may easily dismiss paranormal events as a plausible explanation for some of the more mysterious events and behaviors in the letters, no one should dismiss *belief* in the paranormal sphere as trivial. Belief in witchcraft can cause the witch to practice witchcraft. Belief in the effects of magical spells can have profound effects on the spellbound believer. Belief in demons can cause the believer to see signs of possession in the natural world. In his book *The Biology of Belief,* former medical school professor and research scientist Bruce H. Lipton, Ph.D., explains scientifically how belief can even change a person's physiology.

Of course, many readers may believe in the occasional intersection of a spiritual and physical realm, psychic powers and other paranormal phenomena. This is a complex subject. Because of the abundance of "woo woo stuff" in the letters—a term used by my skeptical publisher—I felt compelled to explore this dimension. Since I am no expert in the paranormal, however, I reached out to a true believer and experienced researcher for some clarification of what may be going on here.

Adrian Lee is one of the leading experts in this field. He graduated from Kent University in 1992 and attended London University. He studied art history and history methodologies for his master's degree, and more recently religious humanities. Currently he lectures on all aspects of the paranormal including ghosts, hauntings, UFOs, psychic development and angels.

I got to know Adrian Lee well while editing three of his popular books: *How to Be a Christian Psychic*; *Mysterious Minnesota: Digging up the Ghostly Past at 13 Haunted Sites*; and *Mysterious Midwest: Unwrapping Urban Legends and Ghostly Tales from the Dead.* I shared with Adrian pertinent letters from our collection, as well as a draft of this manuscript, and then asked him to apply his extensive knowledge of paranormal phenomena to help me understand the scattered assortment of bizarre events reported to Carmen Montez. He came back to me with a remarkably coherent theory.

"Elvis Was an Empath"

Adrian declared to me with great conviction that "Elvis was an empath." He seemed to believe that this statement would immediately fill in a lot of gaps in my understanding, but it didn't.

"Empaths just know stuff without having prior knowledge," Adrian said. "It's a 'knowing' that goes way beyond intuition or gut feelings, even though that is how many people would describe the 'knowing.' As an empath becomes more attuned, more receptive, his gift grows stronger."

Adrian pointed out a passage in one of the letters to Carmen in which Elvis wrote, "I know I have ESP," a clear summary, Adrian said, of how many empaths feel.

"For an empath," Arian continued, "being in public places can be overwhelming—places like shopping malls, supermarkets or stadiums where there are many people around. These can fill the empath with the turbulent emotions that are stirring around in the crowd. Imagine feeling other people's emotions and taking them on as your own. That would be quite traumatic, wouldn't it?"

I remembered Elvis's admissions to Carmen of having a childhood phobia about hands that grew into a panic-inducing fear of crowds and how he'd struggle to stay rational when surrounded by people.

"Some empaths will only feel emotions from people who are nearby," Adrian said. "But others can also sense the emotions of those who are a vast distance away. A particularly adept empath will be able to not only sense the emotions of others, but also negative thoughts that are directed at him. As an empath, Elvis would have known when someone was being dishonest, but I'd expect him to often dismiss this when the signals came from friends and family because the pain of knowing a loved one is lying can be so intense."

Adrian's remarks stirred up the dramatic scene of Elvis looking for Priscilla at home and finding her missing. Almost immediately he had known she was with his trusted aide Gee Gee in the guest house.

"Is this making sense, Gary?" Adrian asked, knowing it did.

Nodding, I replied with a new line of inquiry. "Elvis suffered from an assortment of physical ailments. He had weight issues, hypertension, a compromised cardiovascular system, a chronic colon condition, back pain…"

Adrian nodded. "All those things are common to empaths. They can suffer with digestive disorders and lower back problems. The solar plexus chakra, which is the seat of emotions, is in the center of the abdomen. This is where empaths feel the incoming emotions of another person. A flood of arriving emotions can weaken this area and eventually lead to anything from stomach ulcers to IBS and many other digestive conditions."

"What about Elvis's weight gain?"

"Well, Elvis's reported diet didn't help much. But in general, empaths are prone to carry weight without necessarily overeating. Excess weight can be a kind of physical barrier to lessen the impact of negative incoming energies. Many empaths can sense the energy of food. They don't like to eat meat or poultry because they can feel the vibrations of the animal—especially if the animal had suffered."

Adrian explained that lower back problems can develop from being ungrounded. "If you have no knowledge of being an empath then you will always be ungrounded. Grounding activities tend to be undertaken by default. In the same way pregnant women may crave food their bodies need, an empath will be unconsciously drawn to grounding activities that will benefit him. These could be swimming, walking, being alone in nature…"

As Adrian spoke, I thought about a moving passage in a letter to Carmen from October 1968 delivered shortly after Elvis's kidnapping and torture. "Something powerful and new has to happen to erase this memory or I'm going to go crazy remembering," he wrote, "like running around the ocean in full dress or going swimming at three a.m. or running out for a walk in the rain, or just throwing a party— not to impress associates, but because you love a few people and want to sing and play music for them."

Adrian got his second wind just as I thought he'd exhausted his summary of the empath's common characteristics. "Empaths are always looking out for the underdog. A person who is suffering emotionally or is the victim of bullying draws the attention and compassion of an empath. Unfortunately, some people, even strangers, instinctively try to offload their problems onto an empath because they are such easy dumping grounds. When the dumping overloads the grounds, an empath may become addicted to alcohol, drugs, even sex to barricade against the junk of others. When these self-protection measures don't work, the empath may become so drained of energy that even sleep doesn't help. A lot of empaths are diagnosed with ME—myalgic encephalomyelitis—a condition that mimics the energy-sapped empath."

These points seemed to be illustrated by Elvis's letter to Carmen dated August 25, 1968, in which he wrote, "The musical coordinator told me I looked sleepy and mechanical, and my eyes looked tired. Remember when I felt bad and I was so tired I didn't know how to stand up or hold up my head?"

Adrian wasn't finished. "Empaths typically are very creative people who sing, dance, act, draw or write. They have vivid imaginations and an irrepressible desire to please people and make them happy."

In a letter to Carmen from October of 1968, Marlon Brando summed up Elvis the empath this way: "The funny thing about Elvis is, as unhappy as he himself may be, he has a way of making others around him feel like their lives were standing still before he arrived on the scene. Something happens—people begin having fun and acting alive when Elvis is around—on the set, at a party, or just at home—it's always the same way. Elvis brings a certain vitality with him that lights up the whole scene or environment. And it's catching."

Adrian finished with a flourish from his field of expertise. "Empaths are intrigued by anything of a supernatural or paranormal nature, and they don't surprise or get shocked easily. They get frustrated easily, though, when their questions go unanswered, which drives them to find explanations. And this can result in information overload. When they downshift, they can appear moody, shy, aloof, disconnected, quiet, unsociable, even miserable."

I couldn't argue with Adrian. Elvis certainly seemed like a classic empath.

The Native American Connection

Elvis's letters, and references by his friends, repeatedly orbit around his connection to Native American culture and spirituality. His great-great-great-grandmother was a full-blooded Cherokee. He often referred to his "Indian sixth-sense" or his uncanny intuition by saying "an Indian knows these things." He pleaded with Carmen to help him psychically explore his Indian heritage.

Adrian pointed out that Native Americans recognize the existence of empaths with the word *Hevoka*. A Hevoka possesses the traits of an empath but also functions as both a mirror and a teacher. The Hevoka often uses extreme behaviors to mirror others, thus forcing them to confront and examine their own doubts, fears, hatreds and weaknesses. Their power to heal emotional pain comes from having experienced shame. They often sing of shameful events in their lives and behave like clowns, provoking laughter in distressing situations and causing fear and chaos when people feel complacent and overly secure.

Hevokas serve an important role in shaping tribal codes. Unbound by societal constraints, they can freely violate cultural taboos and critique established customs. Paradoxically, though, by breaking norms and taboos, they help to define the accepted boundaries, rules, and guidelines for ethical and moral behavior. They are among the few who can ask "Why?" about sensitive topics. They use satire to question those in positions of power and authority, including the guardians of sacred knowledge.

Individuals who are authentically open to the Hevoka's healing energy will feel peaceful, relaxed and loved while in their company because they are operating on the same frequency and resonating strongly. Adrian suggested that this may be why other empathic and psychically sensitive individuals like Marlon, Harry and Carmen, would be attracted to Elvis and develop a meaningful relationship.

Hevokas, like Elvis, are unpredictable and unconventional, Adrian said. They do not adhere to society's expectations, abide by rules, uphold cultural conditioning or follow the masses. They are loose cannons—much like Elvis, who invited a fourteen-year-old fiancée to live in his home for years despite society's disapproval; who enraged parents with his thrusting pelvis, spastically jack-hammering thighs and defiant sneers; who appropriated black music during an intensely racist era; who broke industry rules while shattering sales records; and who inflamed religious leaders by rallying the passions of youth.

Spells and Demons

Because of his empathic nature, Adrian speculated, Elvis would be more susceptible to spells and demons sent by practitioners of voodoo, hoodoo and witchcraft. Whether these entities were real or not, Elvis certainly believed in the power of spirits and ill intent. The ease with which he had been hypnotized by a blackmailer, as confessed to Carmen, demonstrates that he was highly suggestible.

Adrian Lee, an ardent advocate for the "reality" of the supernatural and paranormal, believes that Elvis may have been exposed to a suicide or death demon, an entity conjured from darkness and sent to Elvis through the use of black magic. As evidence, he pointed to a letter from Marlon in August 1968 in which the actor, while staying at Elvis's home after the brutal kidnapping and torture event, was awakened by Elvis screaming. After rushing into Elvis's bedroom, Marlon said that Elvis "was sitting up in bed and swore he'd seen a figure in black standing by his bed trying to get a rope around his neck." This did not surprise Marlon. He wrote, "Carmen, for a week now I've had a funny—a strange, nameless fear for Elvis. I don't know what it is, but I'm afraid of something. I wish you knew what it might be."

Adrian also referred to another letter in which Marlon reported finding Elvis in the kitchen staring at an open drawer of knives. And he reminded me that Elvis, by his own admission, had attempted suicide three times.

Adrian explained that dark magic directed at Elvis would cause him to act in a manner very unlike himself, see the entities attacking him, experience physical pain and emotional struggles, and lapse occasionally into a trance-like state. Adrian had catalogued passages in the letters illustrating these behaviors. On one occasion, Elvis's face changed and started to twist as if in pain; then he shook his head and couldn't speak. Another time, in the hospital, Marlon had found Elvis staring at the IV drip, "Watching, thinking, not listening. His eyes were fixed on it, staring as if he were hypnotized by it." Yet another time Marlon tried to take the phone away from Elvis and turn him over in the hospital bed. "He jumped up like he'd been shot," Marlon wrote, "those bleary eyes going wild and all ready to defend himself. So he's apparently scared to death to go to sleep."

I asked Adrian who he thought might have been directing dark magic at Elvis. "In the 1960s in Memphis and Los Angeles, just about anybody," Adrian said, reminding me of the Manson Family's reign of terror and Harry Belafonte's conviction that a voodoo witch named Chloe had seized control of his half-brother, Jim Mathews, and had likely cast a death spell on her competitor for Jim's affections, Joi Sommers. But when pushed for a candidate to use dark magic against Elvis, Adrian mentioned a name: Sam Katzman.

Voodoo Rituals

Adrian theorized that producer Sam Katzman, whose Jewish parents had come to America from Russia, was a practitioner of witchcraft, and when Katzman's feud with Elvis intensified, Sam had turned to dark magic.

In my manuscript, Adrian stressed, I had already pointed out the eerie parallels behind the story of *Charro!*—the movie Elvis had finished shooting just before the kidnapping—and the actual facts of the abduction and torture. Adrian believed the script had inspired the actual crime. "If I'm right, in some of Katzman's other films we should be able to find links to ritual magic and events that transpired during Elvis's torture," Adrian said. "It wouldn't be surprising if Katzman slyly inserted his belief in dark magic into the storylines of his films—a wicked joke on the public."

In preparation for our conversation, Adrian had studied Katzman's body of works and offered some prime examples of his theory. In one of Katzman's earlier films, *Voodoo Man*, released in 1944, a villain played by Bela Lugosi captured young women and transferred their body fluids and life essences into his long-dead wife. In a 1942 film called *The Corpse Vanishes,* an abducted victim was taken to an isolated mansion. "Imagine Elvis's mansion here," Adrian suggested. In the film, glandular fluid was extracted from the victim with a syringe and then injected into the villain's vein but aged wife to renew her youth and beauty.

Next, Adrian showed me a poster for *Jungle Jim*, the 1948 Johnny Weissmuller movie that gave Katzman his nickname, Jungle Sam. The story centered around the discovery of a vial of potion that may be a deadly poison used by a witch doctor. *Fury of the Congo,* released in 1951, depicted a rare type of drug extracted from an okongo (half-antelope and half-zebra). The 1952 film *Voodoo Tiger* portrayed sacrificial voodoo rituals. *Devil Goddess* in 1955 depicted a tribe that sacrificed humans to appease a fire-controlling demon. In 1953, *Serpent of the Nile* told a story about Cleopatra that ended with her using a poisonous snake to commit suicide.

"What does the snake have to do with Elvis?" I asked.

The Ouroboros

"In magic, a strong tie exists between serpent mythology and the cycle of life, death, and rebirth." Adrian explained that the circle of life is often depicted with the symbol of a snake eating itself (Ouroboros) and fertility, which is linked to the number of eggs laid by a snake. Connections between snakes and babies, especially rattlesnakes and copperheads, are common in ritual magic. "If you kill a snake, then a baby will die, because both are magically connected," Adrian said. "Your manuscript tells of a rattlesnake that was placed in Elvis's trailer during the making of *Charro!*, which was shot in the desert. I believe the snake was not put there to kill Elvis, but to entice Elvis to kill the snake. This would cause the death of Lisa Marie, who had been born a few months earlier. Or maybe the intended victim was Priscilla's unpublicized child in utero that had been conceived a few weeks after Lisa Marie's birth."

I was intrigued by the notion that Elvis may not have been the target of the rattler.

"If you want someone to get sick and die," Adrian continued, "you use a snake with an intended victim's hair tied around it. Then you kill the snake and bury it in the person's yard. The target will get sicker each day because the snake has that person's hair tied around it. The connection between snakes and hair has existed for millennia, as shown in the ancient Greek tales of the Medusa. I'll bet if someone had looked closely at the rattler in Elvis's trailer they would've seen someone's hair tied around it."

"Why target an innocent child of Elvis?" I asked.

"Katzman's goal was to torment Elvis and drive him crazy. Causing the death of someone Elvis loved so dearly would be extraordinarily painful." Adrian paused, then added, "There's another eerie connection between Katzman and serpents."

I nodded for him to go on.

"Another magical tradition is to pound the ground with a stick or cane until a serpent emerges. I recall your reporting about how an actor in Katzman's early movies said that Katzman was famous for carrying an ornate cane that he'd use to goose people when they weren't looking."

"I see where you're going with this," I said. "The actor Billy Benedict recalled that Katzman would beat the floor or the ground when things weren't going well."

"Another odd coincidence, perhaps," Adrian offered.

I suggested, "I'm thinking about all those old Katzman movies you mentioned. It seems to me that, maybe, instead of Katzman's films being evidence of his belief in dark magic, it's the other way around. It could be that Elvis, who was a movie fanatic, watched Katzman's old films and a lot of other B-movies about voodoo and demons and witchcraft. Those stories might have inspired dreams or visions about such things, and then Elvis confused those delusions with reality and wrote them down in letters as if the dreams had actually happened."

"Except for one thing," Adrian said. "Katzman's gang abducted and tortured Elvis ritualistically, performing many of the rites used in the practice of dark magic."

This assertion stunned me. "You'll have to explain," I said.

"OK, let's go back to the time when the Katzman gang first abducted Elvis and Marlon in Elvis's home. In your manuscript you wrote that one of the oddest things that occurred was when Elvis was forced to cut off his *Charro!* beard."

"True," I said. "I have no explanation for why they did that."

"Well, I believe this odd behavior was part of a 'goofer' ritual that involves removing hair from a person you want 'goofered,' which is a silly term that means 'made to suffer or die.' Goofer dust, a traditional hoodoo hexing concoction made of natural ingredients, is mixed in a jar with the intended victim's hair. Then, after poking holes in the lid, the jar is thrown into a lake, river or swamp. As it sinks, the victim begins to waste away. It's like using a voodoo doll, which also requires the hair or nail clippings of a victim for the curse to work."

I recalled that when the Katzman gang was torturing Elvis with lit cigarettes, they cut off some of his hair and Marcus put a lock of it into a cellophane envelope—as a souvenir, I had surmised. Later, when Marcus was found in the desert with his skull crushed, the police found a sample of what may have been Elvis's hair in his wallet. After listening to Adrian's theory, I decided that maybe this hair sample was more than a souvenir.

"The letters say that the gang forced Elvis to drink a mysterious liquid," Adrian said. "He made a face when tasting it, and it made him feel nauseated. In American folk magic and hoodoo, goofer dust, which is made up of graveyard dirt, sulfur and other unpalatable substances, is sometimes mixed into food or drink to destroy health and cause terrible pain. Obviously, this would taste awful and produce all kinds of digestive issues."

"So, you really think that some kind of dark magic was being used against Elvis?"

"Well, either that, or there are an unlikely number of coincidences. And speaking of that, let me give you another odd 'coincidence'—the moon."

I couldn't think of any reference to the moon in the letters, so I just gestured my confusion.

"In dark magic, a full moon illuminates the earth," Adrian explained, "providing greater gravitational pull for negative energies to cause heightened distress for their victims. That's why practitioners of dark magic often time their spells and actions to coincide with a full moon. It can take patience… and sometimes good luck for everything to align."

Adrian's comment caused me to recall an event communicated by Carmen Montez in which Marcus and another thug had baited Elvis into a street fight that backfired by Marcus being beaten. Adrian had copied out of my manuscript this description of that event: "Marcus and his buddy had waited for many months before retaliating—uncommon patience for hotheads, but typical of their boss, Sam Katzman."

I wrestled with the puzzle pieces that Adrian was assembling into a coherent picture. "Marcus's retaliation came in the form of the abduction and torture of Elvis," I said, searching through the scattered pieces. "Are you saying that he and Katzman had timed the kidnapping to coincide with a full moon?"

"Like I said," Adrian replied, "they would have been looking for a full moon that coincided with many other factors, such as Elvis's empty mansion. And let me remind you... you calculated that the abduction occurred on September 7, 1968. That evening was a full moon. And in pagan and occult practice, September represents Virgo, a sign associated with the bowels. If used in a negative way, dark magic could ruin careers, reverse healing, and reinforce bad habits such as the abuse of medications. Certainly, during the torture ritual, Elvis suffered a direct attack on his bowels."

"Still," I said, "the abduction occurring during a full moon could be just a fluke."

"Yes, it could. There would be a one-in-thirty chance of that happening. But what about some of the other so-called flukes, then?"

"Like what?"

"Well, let's go back to just a month earlier. In a letter dated August 8, 1968, Marlon caught Elvis staring at an open drawer of knives as if contemplating suicide, and then later Elvis had a vision of a dark figure with a noose. These events occurred just a day after a full moon, and exactly a lunar month before the abduction of Elvis and Marlon. To me, this is evidence that a suicide demon had been conjured and sent to Elvis."

"Does this demon have a name?"

"Yes, but to speak it is to summon the demon—a dangerous idea."

"This is pretty creepy stuff, and frankly quite hard to believe."

"You asked me for an alternative explanation for some of the mysteries in your book. I'm giving you an explanation that seems plausible to me. Have you had enough, or do you want to hear about the blood ritual?"

"The what?"

"Just as physical birth involves bleeding, blood rituals in occult practice represent a *symbolic* death and rebirth. I was fascinated by how the gang withdrew Elvis's blood with syringes and then drank it. The drawing and ingestion of Elvis's blood would represent, of course, his symbolic death and a renewal of strength for the person who drank it. The spilling of blood also intensifies ritual magic. As an offering to demon spirits, it is integral to the casting of spells."

"Instead of a vicious feud, you've painted a picture of a battle between good and evil."

"That's what I think was going on here. You wrote that Elvis had wanted to preach and evangelize the word of God. With this conviction, Elvis found the strength to fight against the darkness he found within himself. And I think he was winning. He had drifted away from what he'd been taught in his childhood but was struggling to trust again in the Almighty."

"He had found Carmen Montez," I added, "who helped him realize his potential to promote goodness and the cause of God."

"Marlon Brando possessed a kind of rough-hewn spirituality," Adrian said, "and was fully aware of the effect of evil. As I recall, he wrote to Carmen pleading with her to 'break the circuit of evil' and make plans for the forces of darkness to go awry. Marlon actually documented the internal fight within Elvis between good and evil, which became frighteningly tangible when an evil force disguised as a hospital orderly came at Elvis with a knife."

"If this was a battle between good and evil," I wondered aloud, "does the early death of Elvis mean that evil eventually won?"

For the first time in our conversation, Adrian had no reply... or didn't want to give it.

Return to Sender

The frequency of letters sent from Elvis dropped off considerably late in 1970. We have only a few signed letters from 1971 and 1972. It is possible that Elvis and Carmen continued to correspond regularly, but the letters were lost or destroyed. It could also be that some letters were returned to the senders at their request because they had become concerned about the secrets revealed in them.

I believe, however, that as with most pen pal relationships, this one—and Carmen's associations with Tom, Harry and Marlon—simply waned with the passing of the years. Each of these celebrities had survived a tumultuous period in his life. In the end, I think, they all just moved on. Carmen's movie producer ambitions collapsed despite her high-level contacts. Elvis staged a comeback but began suffering from frequent emotional outbursts that prescribed medication could not control. Marlon found renewed fame and industry attention with the *Godfather* movies. Harry deepened his activist and advocacy efforts.

The few letters we have from 1971-72 regrettably demonstrate that Elvis continued to be plagued by bizarre and suspicious events. Some of these may have been perpetrated by the Katzman gang, and some not.

In early 1971, Elvis told Carmen that for a few months he had enjoyed a respite from the campaign of terror being waged against him. His life in Los Angeles was quiet temporarily with the Colonel gone and no concerts or recording sessions, but he had an eerie feeling that trouble was brewing. His "Indian sixth-sense" had caused him to believe something had "stayed their hand"—a reference, I presume, to the Katzman gang—"but not forever." He told Carmen that for some reason "they" had become afraid to move against him, but he could still feel them out there waiting for the right opportunity. He felt like he was living on "borrowed time."

I can't imagine the stress of living with the prospect of another surprise attack.

On the anniversary of the assault against Elvis and his wife, these thoughts were still weighing heavily on his mind. Elvis couriered another letter to Carmen in which he claimed that he had just experienced an epiphany while staring into the blaze of his fireplace. The sadistic gang had been loosed on him, he suddenly grasped, not for revenge but to prey on his past fears and "drive me crazy with fear and shame and pain." He was astonished, he said, that he had not seen this truth before.

For the first time he felt the full force of genuine hatred for the men who had tortured him, "animals suddenly uncaged" who were supposed to be human but had resigned their humanity. "There are no words in me now," he told Carmen, asking her to pray for him because "I need help. Right now."

I wonder if the horrifying memories, the intense hatred they repeatedly stirred up, and the guilt arising from his desire for vengeance continued to fester in him until his premature death in 1977. I think so, but I hope not.

Still, Elvis toiled on. In mid-1972, his "Indian sixth-sense" proved correct. He could never prove that the Katzman gang was behind a new threat, which he narrowly survived. The incident was revealed when Elvis called Marlon from Las Vegas and said the previous evening he'd had a dream in which Carmen came to him in the desert wearing a turquoise nightgown. She warned him that his car needed a check-up and then suddenly vanished. Elvis explained to Marlon that Carmen had "saved" him in 1967 while he was in the desert shooting *Stay Away, Joe*, though we have no details about how that happened. That 1967 contact had been their first encounter. Now, it seemed, Carmen was trying to save him again.

In the morning, fretting about Carmen's warning, he asked the diminutive Charlie Hodge, a close friend and aide, if he knew if anything was wrong with the car. Charlie said that the points were going bad, but he knew of no other problems. Even so, the dream still troubled Elvis. He instructed Charlie to take the car in for a thorough check-up. Elvis expected to have the car back before an interview at a Vegas radio station at seven o'clock that evening.

The mechanic called Charlie back a couple hours later, his voice quivering. He had just discovered a time bomb under the hood set to go off at 6:40. The police had come to dismantle it.

Obviously, someone had known about Elvis's interview at seven and expected him to leave about six-thirty to make the twenty-minute drive before checking in at the station. He would have been in the car at 6:40 when it blew up.

After that, Elvis told Marlon, he'd be taking taxis around Las Vegas.

* * *

One of the most bizarre sequences of events tormenting Elvis during this time involved an impersonator. Not a performer who mimicked Elvis's looks and mannerisms on stage, but a double who impersonated Elvis in real-life and may have even duped Priscilla.

The first allusion to an Elvis double appeared in a 1970 letter written shortly before he and Priscilla were attacked in their Palm Springs home. Elvis was rambling on to Carmen about the child that Priscilla was carrying, the one they had told no one about. And then Elvis asked Carmen a strange question. "Do you think it is dishonest to not tell her about the child?"

The first time I came across that question, I wondered what kind of information about the child he was withholding. Elvis told Carmen that he had not revealed this information to Priscilla to protect her "outlook" and "for the child's sake." Clearly, he believed he was doing the right thing by not telling Priscilla the facts as he knew them. But what was this information?

Elvis went on about how Pris must have been really drunk, and probably "thought I was drunk." But what could these statements mean?

Then Elvis made a remark that brought this confusion into focus. He said that no matter how two people might look the same, "no two people kiss alike." He wrote that Priscilla's senses had been off lately, and this probably was why she didn't know "the difference."

Suddenly it became clear that Priscilla, thinking she was having sex with her husband, may have been unwittingly seduced by an Elvis look-alike. I think that Priscilla may have made some reference to events that occurred the night this child was conceived, and Elvis, having no recollection of that, suddenly knew the truth. Somehow, he must have known the existence of his double, but I doubt Elvis had ever imagined the doppelganger interfering so personally in his life.

In a letter written later, Elvis referred to a party at which Priscilla showed up with his double. Tom Jones also attended that party but arrived after the couple had left, otherwise Elvis was sure Tom would have exposed the impersonator. Elvis told Carmen he'd heard rumors that he was suffering from a bad cold that night and had even worse "lingo." The double had also been seen alone at other venues around the city making a scene in Elvis's name.

After hearing stories about Elvis's double roaming loose in society, Marlon told Carmen about an unexpected break in the mystery. His wife Tarita had been watching the Art Linkletter show on television and suddenly called for Marlon to come in and see a man who looked exactly like Elvis Presley. The man was modeling western clothing for Nudie's Rodeo Tailor on Lankershim Blvd. in North Hollywood, which coincidentally was Elvis's tailor and had outfitted some of his costumes.

Marlon called Linkletter's office and spoke with Art about the Elvis look-alike. Linkletter told him the model's name was Ronnie

Bisset, but he wasn't sure of the spelling. It was probably a stage name anyway. Apparently, the segment was taped a few months earlier but was put on hold by someone and finally released.

Marlon did some checking and found out that Bisset was also a musician and had played off and on with a combo at "that Western place over there in the Valley." Bisset played several instruments, Marlon was told, but none exceptionally.

"I want this guy exposed for the sake of El's reputation as well as his life. The guy's trying his hardest to ruin both," Marlon wrote to Carmen.

* * *

In early 1972, Elvis invited karate champion Mike Stone backstage after a Las Vegas show to meet with him and Priscilla. The meeting ended with Elvis suggesting that Priscilla, who had expressed interest in karate, take lessons from Stone. The teacher-student relationship grew into a romance that eventually split up Elvis's marriage and threatened his custodianship of Lisa Marie.

The Elvis letters to Carmen finally trickled to a stop in early 1973 so far as we know, but threats to his life did not. At the midnight show at the Las Vegas Hilton on February 18, 1973, four men violently stormed the stage targeting Elvis. Since the assassination threat of 1970, the Elvis team had prepared for such an event, so they were not surprised. Biographer Peter Guralnick documented what happened next. Red West tackled the first assailant, and then, from a karate stance, Elvis knocked the second man off the stage. Bass player Jerry Scheff, Jerry Schilling and the rest of the "security" team neutralized the other two. Elvis was so worked up that "uncle" Vernon had to race onto the stage and restrain him with a bear hug. Someone told Elvis, "Think of the show, the audience." Elvis slipped out of Vernon's grasp and turned to the audience as if to apologize.

"I'm sorry, ladies and gentlemen," Elvis said with a defiant edge. "I'm sorry I didn't break his goddamn neck is what I'm sorry about." And then he went on with the show, the consummate entertainer.

Authorities declared the "assailants" to be overzealous fans, but I'm convinced that to Elvis they represented the boys who scarred him back in 1957: Marcus and Shaul and all the thugs who worked for Sam Katzman; whoever was responsible for Jeni Pearson's death; and Mike Stone, the karate champion who had inflicted the freshest wound by "winning" the competition for Priscilla's affections. It was Stone, though, who stuck in his mind, and he began to convince himself that the four "assailants" had been hired by Stone to kill him.

By the next day his staff began to panic when Elvis told Sonny West, one of his bodyguards, that there was only one solution to the problem. In Elvis's words as reported by biographer Guralnick, "You know it, Sonny. There is too much pain in me, and he did it. Do you hear me? I am right… Mike Stone [must] die. You will do it for me—kill the sonofabitch, Sonny, I can count on you. I know I can… He has no right to live."

His staff called a doctor who gave Elvis an injection of a sedative, then another, but no amount would calm him down. The next day he coerced Red into getting a price from a contract killer. Red contacted someone who had a friend who knew someone who might be interested. Right before the evening show he told Elvis a hit on Mike Stone would cost $10,000. Red didn't know if he could contact the assassin should Elvis order the hit—he'd never been asked to do anything like this before.

Elvis grew silent after Red told him the fee. It was almost time for the show to begin. At last he turned to Red and said, "Aw hell. Let's just leave it alone for now. Maybe it's a bit heavy. Let's just leave it off for now." He never brought it up again.

Elvis died in 1977 after pulling away from many of the people, including Marlon, who had tried to help him. Marlon, apparently embittered by Elvis's rejection of his attempts to help and suffering from his own crises—a suicidal daughter, a son convicted of murder, and career and financial setbacks—eventually turned on his old friend with cruel public remarks, calling Elvis a "bloated, over-the-hill, adolescent entertainer." Marlon Brando died in 2015. Harry

Belafonte and Tom Jones are still alive but have not responded to our invitation to participate in this book. I can understand deciding not to relive so many bitter memories.

Exactly one month after Elvis died, Carmen Montez received a mysterious letter from The Florida National Bank and Trust Company in Miami, an institution that had been established in 1931. The letter stated that she had been named as beneficiary of two million dollars from a trust that had been set up by an anonymous benefactor. When I came across this letter, its date—September 15, 1977, just thirty days following Elvis's death—and the staggering amount of money mentioned led me to believe that Elvis may have set up a trust for his spiritual mentor, the disbursement of which would be triggered by his death. What an astounding conclusion for this story that would be.

But then I noticed some peculiar details about the bank's letter. In describing the amount of money that Carmen would be receiving, the letter's author wrote "TWO MILLION ($2,000,000,000) dollars." Suddenly the amount had grown to two billion dollars. It would be quite an error for a bank officer to wrongly add three zeros to the number of dollars held in trust for a beneficiary. Certainly, typographic errors like this occur in official documents occasionally, but this one is unusual indeed. In studying the signature on the letter, I also found it odd that the officer's name was Ms. Janice Doe.

Really? Jan Doe?

This could be a real name, of course. In searching Google and Facebook I found numerous individuals with the name "Jan Doe" or close renditions of it. Still, I found the name suspicious.

Adding to the mystery is the stunning lack of assets at the time of Carmen's death. There were no savings accounts or investments. If she had received a trust of two million dollars, where had the money gone? In all the years that Montez and Rayburn had known each other, Montez had lived very frugally.

THE FLORIDA NATIONAL BANK
AND TRUST COMPANY
at Miami

TRUST DEPARTMENT
P. O. BOX 010625

TELEPHONE
373-1171

MIAMI, FLORIDA 33101

September 15, 1977

Rev. Carmen Montez,
Beverly Hills, California

Re: Money in Trust

Dear Rev. Montez:

This letter is to inform you that you have been elected
Beneficiary to an estate of which the Benefactor wishes
to remain anonymous. Florida National Trust Company has
in its possession, at this time, complete control of assets
for disbursement per instructions submitted by the Benefactor, in which you have been indiciated as sole Beneficiary in this estate.

We are proud to inform you that all of the assets of the
aforesaid estate are your sole property. A substantial
fee of 2% for estate administration is to be deducted for
processing of documents and another 2% for Federal Income
Taxes. After deductions have been made we estimate that
the total amount of cash (to be submitted to you in check
form) amounts to close to TWO MILLION ($2,000,000,000) dollars.
This check shall be forwarded to you upon full completion
of investigation into the Benefactor's estate, which cannot
be determined at this time as the Benefactor has not yet
entrusted us with notable assets.

We shall continue to keep you abreast of upcoming events
in connection with the above Trust. If you have any
questions, please keep them until we contact you personally.

Yours very truly,

Ms. Janice Doe
Vice President & Sr. Trust Officer

JD:zh

cc: Benefactor

The bank letter informing Carmen Montez that she was the
beneficiary of two million dollars from an anonymous benefactor.

Is it possible that this bank letter was a scam, a pre-Internet-
Nigerian-prince ploy to bilk money from Carmen? If so, the
perpetrator had not done his homework because Carmen didn't
have enough money to make the scheme worthwhile. If the letter
was authentic and Carmen never received the money, why not?
Questions abound, but answers do not.

The FBI files we obtained through numerous FOIA requests paint a startling picture of the final threat Elvis would face. In early 1977 the FBI began assembling a team to conduct a covert campaign called Operation Fountain Pen (OPFOPEN) that targeted professional White Collar Crime (WCC) thieves who were ripping off tens of millions of dollars around the world.

Two con men, Philip Karl Kitzer, Jr. and Alfredo Proc, who used the alias Frederick Peter Pro, were the principal ringleaders of a larger group of con men financiers known as "The Fraternity." The group creatively crafted and executed complex scams usually involving securities transactions or leasing schemes for high value assets owned by wealthy people. Kitzer was the con man's con man. His specialty was creating phony Caribbean banks to provide worthless bank documents—letters of credit, certificates of deposit, et cetera—that other swindlers could use in their scams. Soon he had graduated to running his own cons. The FBI calculated the losses to individuals, banks and other financial institutions through Kitzer's con games at between ten and fifteen billion dollars.

The FBI successfully placed undercover operatives inside Kitzer's "Fraternity" and soon learned of a plot to use one of Elvis's airplanes to defraud the entertainer. Elvis owned three aircraft including a Lockheed Jetstar he had purchased for $900,000. The scam started when "Freddie" Pro approached Elvis and Vernon Presley with an attractive business proposition, a complex sale/leaseback transaction that eventually, Pro promised, would pay for itself and produce a nice monthly annuity for Presley.

Kitzer used an international telex cable system to fraudulently confirm to Vernon Presley that the intended purchaser, Pro's bankrupt firm, had "in excess of $500,000 US on deposit" with a financial institution in London. No such account existed, of course. Elvis agreed to invest a large sum to be used by Pro and Kitzer to refurbish the Jetstar so it would qualify for a special FAA maintenance program essential to the deal. Pro took possession of the aircraft, but the work was never done.

Elvis's Lockheed Jetstar, named "Hound Dog II," on display at Graceland.

The Fraternity used the money for other nefarious purposes, and during the six months the Jetstar was in its possession used the plane as fraudulent collateral for other bank loans. The October 26, 1977 edition of *Today* reported that Elvis eventually lost more than twelve million in the intricate fraud.

In August 1977, Freddie Pro and Kitzer were involved in a deal to help the Vito Genovese and Joseph Colombo crime families of New York take over the Brookhaven Mortgage Company and use its assets to finance loan-sharking operations. Bill Beeny, in 1977 the owner of the Elvis Is Alive Museum in Wright City, Missouri, claimed in an interview with classicbands.com that Elvis was scheduled on August 16, 1977 to testify before a grand jury about the Kitzer/Pro scams and possibly the involvement of other confederates and Mafia figures. On that day, Elvis was found dead in his bathroom.

A few weeks later, Frederick Pro was placed into the witness protection program and moved to California with a new identity, Frederix Peter DeVeau. In April of 1981, he and his family were moved to San Antonio for unspecified reasons. A month later, Pro fled Texas, claiming the government had blown his cover as a protected federal witness. Yet he continued to be shuttled around the country testifying in fraud cases of over a hundred known con men and Mafia figures. He died in 1990.

Of all the stubborn unknowns, Elvis's death remains the biggest mystery of his life. Some observers think the FBI did not protect Elvis from those who may have wanted him dead. Others believe they did… by making him disappear. If so, I wonder if Frederick Pro met Elvis again in witness protection. That would have been a memorable reunion.

The Boy from Tupelo

The five-year stretch of Elvis's life exposed through his letters were filled with manipulation, marital discord, betrayal, loneliness, humiliation, fear and terror, some of it self-inflicted, but much of it imposed upon him by outside forces. But the letters also reveal bonds of friendship and loyalty that sustained Elvis during his many crises and demonstrated his own capacity to care for others.

The portrait of Elvis that emerges from these letters shows a deeply spiritual and introspective young man who had extraordinary talents but was overwhelmed and transformed by a complex world of deceit and power. He was not the caricature of the bloated, drug-abusing entertainer magnified by the events of his final days. That was merely the heartbreaking outcome of a tortured life.

Like others who have read these letters, I have been challenged at times by the credibility of Elvis's reporting of events that seem so extreme. We know that Elvis's mental and emotional state was deteriorating under the pressures of fame, depression and drug use, voluntary or otherwise. But I have been swayed by the convincing testimony of Marlon, Tom, and in some cases second-hand comments by Priscilla, corroborating these events and most of the details.

In the end, all we are left with is the testimony. Is it possible that some people make up stories when they write to their spiritual mentors? Yes. Is it possible that the letter writers experienced *folie à deux*, a psychiatric syndrome in which symptoms of a delusional belief and sometimes hallucinations are transmitted from one individual to another? Perhaps. Is it possible that Carmen Montez, whose guidance to her acolytes is entirely missing from this story, somehow encouraged false memories? Possibly. But I keep coming back to Occam's razor, the scientific rule that states the simplest of competing theories is usually the correct one. In this case, the simplest explanation is that the corroborated testimony of a group of friends honestly expressed their concerns for each other while reporting events that are certainly not unprecedented in society. All I can offer is the testimony as reported by Elvis Presley, Marlon Brando, Tom Jones and Harry Belafonte to their close friend.

I have become an expert on Elvis and an expert on these letters but am no closer to the absolute truth than I was on the first day I read them. My nightmares probably will continue. This journey has provided the education of a lifetime, thrusting upon me a view into human nature that I did not seek to explore. Yet we are left with unsolved mysteries. Without mysteries, of course, we have nothing to think about, nothing to explore, nothing to solve. Marilyn Monroe lives on in our thoughts because of doubts about how she died and who may have caused her demise. JFK lives on because of the continuing mystery about whether a lone wolf or a conspiracy was responsible for his assassination. Elvis lives on because of the undying mystery surrounding his real or feigned death.

I am both blessed and cursed to have been the only person in the world who could have written this book. There will be no more letters from the stars—all correspondence will now be electronic, and this book will be read primarily on electronic devices. There will be no call in the future for experts on handwriting, perhaps only on writing style, but here we have it—these letters were written to Carmen Montez by the real Elvis Presley, not his double, and that's a fact.

In a letter to Carmen written in March of 1970, after reflecting on his failed suicide attempt two years earlier, Elvis penned a more astute and honest appraisal of himself than I could ever write. He told Carmen, "I feel so used sometimes. All this is just too much for me. I'm still a boy from Mississippi. I've learned to polish, to be professional, but my heart is still the same."

I choose to remember Elvis as that talented, irrepressible boy from Tupelo before the world devoured him.

Timeline

1901

July 7   Sam Katzman is born.

1926

March 11   Carmen Rayburn is born.

1930

June 9   Carmen Montez is born.

1935

January 8   Elvis Aaron Presley is born to Vernon and Gladys
                Presley in a two-room house in Tupelo, Mississippi,
                the second of identical twins. His brother was
                stillborn. In a letter to Carmen Montez, Elvis
                claims that his father was not Vernon but Vernon's
                identical twin brother, Virgil, who died when Elvis
                was several years old.

1946

January 8   Elvis receives his first guitar purchased by his
                parents for $7.90 at the Tupelo Hardware store. He
                had wanted a rifle for his eleventh birthday, but his
                parents couldn't afford one.

1953

July 18	After moving to Memphis, Tennessee, Elvis makes a demo acetate disc of "My Happiness" and "That's When Your Heartaches Begin" at Sun Records.

1954

January	Elvis makes a demo acetate at Sam Phillips' Sun studio.

1955

August 15	Elvis signs a management contract with Colonel Tom Parker for one year plus renewals.

1956

January 27	Elvis's first RCA single, "Heartbreak Hotel," is released, becoming the first Elvis single to sell over one million copies. The lyrics were inspired by a newspaper article about the suicide of a lonely man who jumped from a hotel window.
September 9	Elvis makes the first of three appearances on television's Ed Sullivan Show, attracting the highest ratings ever for a television variety show.
November 15	"Love Me Tender," Elvis's debut performance in a movie, opens and is the only time that Elvis doesn't receive top billing, which went to Richard Egan and Debra Paget.

1957

March 19	Elvis buys Graceland Mansion in Memphis, Tennessee.

Unknown date   Elvis is physically assaulted and suffers permanent scars on his face.

1958

March 24   Elvis is drafted into the US Army and then posted to Germany.

1960

March 5   Elvis is discharged from the army and soon begins shooting his first post-army movie, *GI Blues*, for Paramount.

1963

October   The roots of an intense feud between Elvis and Sam Katzman, producer of the movie *Kissin' Cousins*, began sometime during the seventeen-day shooting of the movie.

1967

May 1   Elvis marries Priscilla Beaulieu in a private ceremony in Las Vegas.

June   Carmen Montez is introduced to Harry Belafonte to discuss a screenplay written by her protégé "Joi Sommers." The growing relationship with Harry helps facilitate relationships between Carmen and Marlon Brando, Tom Jones and Elvis Presley.

October   Sometime during the location filming of the movie *Stay Away, Joe*, Elvis attempts suicide. In his letters he credits Carmen, whom he has never met, with saving his life through a kind of psychic influence.

1968

February 1   Elvis's daughter, Lisa Marie, is born.

July 8   Elvis begins pre-production on *Charro!*, the only movie in which he wears a beard and does not sing a song.

August 28   Elvis completes audio looping for the movie *Charro!*, and it is released. The historical record is dark about this period, claiming simply that he spent the next several weeks relaxing at his Palm Springs home. His letters to Carmen Montez, however, tell a different story. Now we know that he was abducted, tortured, sodomized and then secretly spent time recovering in an LA hospital. The extremity of the assault was kept from the public because during this period in history male-on-male rape would have sullied any machismo star's standing with fans and industry executives.

September   While recovering from the assault, a hospital nurse reported interrupting a semi-conscious Elvis who appeared to be attempting suicide in his room.

December 3   His career waning, Elvis appears on an NBC special that becomes known as "The '68 Comeback Special." It became NBC's highest rated show of the season with 42 percent of the total viewing audience.

1969

January   In early January, according to letters written to Carmen, Elvis attempted suicide for a second time.

July 31	Elvis begins a series of shows at the International Hotel in Las Vegas, setting attendance records and spinning off his first live album. Tom Jones and Elvis arrange tickets for Carmen Montez and "Joi Sommers" who drive to Vegas for the show but are never able to meet Elvis.
September	After completing his series of concerts at the International in Las Vegas, an exhausted Elvis checked into a hospital under an assumed name, then disappeared and woke up in Nancy Sinatra's hotel room with no memory of how he had gotten there.

1970

July 18	Early in the morning, two men invade Elvis's Palm Springs home and assault Elvis and Priscilla in their bed.
July 31	Elvis begins a series of shows at the International Hotel in Las Vegas, setting attendance records and spinning off his first live album.
November 11	"Elvis, That's the Way It Is," a documentary of Elvis on tour, opens to good reviews. He begins wearing the famous jumpsuit and cape outfits on stage.

1972

February 23	Elvis and Priscilla separate, and she moves out.

1973

January 14	Elvis makes television and entertainment history with his "Elvis: Aloha from Hawaii" TV special via satellite. It is seen in about forty countries by up to 1.5 billion people. The concert album hits No. 1 on the Billboard pop album chart, his last No. 1 album on that chart.
August 4	Sam Katzman dies.
October 9	The divorce between Elvis and Priscilla Presley is finalized.
No date	Toward the end of the year, Elvis is hospitalized in Memphis with serious health problems including an increasing dependency upon prescription drugs. He is back in the hospital in early 1975 and April 1977.

1977

June 26	Elvis makes his last concert appearance in Indianapolis.
August 16	Elvis Presley dies at Graceland, found on the floor of his bathroom by fiancée Ginger Alden.

1982

May 8	Carmen Montez dies.

1984

March 17	Carmen Rayburn buys a suitcase full of letters at an auction of Carmen Montez's personal belongings and discovers personal letters of Elvis Presley, Harry Belafonte, Tom Jones and Marlon Brando.

1988

February 17 | Gary Lindberg receives a call from a friend, Bill Mack, asking him to participate in a writing project based on the letters from Elvis and other celebrities.

1992

April 9 | Gary Lindberg and Bill Mack collaborate on a massive book proposal and visit New York to present to major publishing firms.

1993

April 9 | Gary Lindberg and his wife travel to Apple Valley, California, to visit Carmen Rayburn at her ranch. It is the first time that Gary meets Carmen face-to-face. The purpose of the meeting is to gather additional information from personal interviews that will facilitate publication of the book without a major New York publisher. Unfortunately, funding the project proves to be impossible.

1997

July 6 | Carmen Rayburn dies. The project collapses.

2004

July 1 | Marlon Brando dies.

2015

June | Having co-founded a publishing company, Calumet Editions, Gary Lindberg and Ian Graham Leask decide to resurrect the Elvis book project. It will still take over three years to complete the manuscript and find a legal path to publication.

Help Us Solve These Mysteries

Letters from Elvis introduces a number of new Elvis mysteries. Some we have solved, others remain unsolved. You can help us fill in the blanks by telling us what you know. Here are some of the mysteries that continue to occupy my mind.

Who Was Elvis's Father?

In one of his earliest letters to Carmen Montez, Elvis makes the startling declaration that Vernon Presley, who was universally considered his father, was actually his uncle. Elvis claimed that Vernon had an identical twin brother named Virgil (twins were common in the Presley family). If you have information about Virgil Presley, who would have been born on April 10, 1916, please contact us at elvis@calumeteditions.com.

Who Was Carmen Montez?

The historical record is remarkably scant concerning Carmen Montez, the secret confidante of Elvis, Marlon Brando, Tom Jones and Harry Belafonte. We would like to confirm her place of birth and learn details of her early life. We would also like to hear from her friends and students. And, of course, we are eager to learn what happened to the mysterious trust fund of $2,000,000 that she was promised by an anonymous source. If you have information about Carmen Montez, please contact us at elvis@calumeteditions.com.

What Sparked the Feud?

We think there are people out there who have information about what started the violent feud between movie producer Sam Katzman and Elvis Presley. If you have information about the cause of this hostility, the members of the "Katzman gang," or about feuds Katzman may have had with others, please contact us at elvis@calumeteditions.com.

Who Was Jeni Pearson?

To Elvis, Jeni was the perfect love who got away. To Marlon, she was a ghost in a blue dress he saw manifested at Elvis's home and a spirit he channeled in his letters to Carmen. But who was she, really? If you have information or photos of the historical Jeni Pearson, we would like to hear from you at elvis@calumeteditions.com.

Who Was the Girl with Four Names?

Cathy's last name is our best guess. Belafonte called her Joi Sommers. Marlon called her Kit. Tom Jones called her Lwli. All of them were in love with this charismatic screenwriter friend of Carmen Montez. What we know about her, unfortunately, comes only from the letters to Carmen, and we want to know more about her and her lost screenplays. If you have information about the girl with four names, please contact us at elvis@calumeteditions.com.

Who Was Jim Mathews & Son?

In a letter to Carmen Montez, Harry Belafonte startled us by stating that he had a half-brother named Jim Mathews, and that Jim had fathered a child with "Joi Sommers," which was a pseudonym of Cathy Kane, a friend of Carmen Montez. We are interested in obtaining more information about Jim Mathews and finding out what happened to the child, who was also named Jim. If you have any information about this, please contact us at elvis@calumeteditions.com.

What Happened During the Filming of Charro!?

The movie *Charro!* was shot immediately before Elvis and Marlon were abducted. In letters to Carmen Montez, Elvis described several unnerving events during production that may or may not have been connected to the "Katzman gang." If you have any information about these events, or know of other strange occurrences during the shooting of this movie, please contact us at elvis@calumeteditions. com.

Who Beat Up Elvis in 1957?

Elvis claimed that he was beaten badly in 1957, an incident that left permanent scars on his face. If you have any information about this event, please contact us at elvis@calumeteditions.com.

Bibliography

Adler, David and Ernest Andrews. *Elvis My Dad: The Unauthorized Biography of Lisa-Marie Presley.* New York: St. Martin's Paperbacks, 1990.

Belafonte, Harry and Michael Shynayerson. *My Song: A Memoir of Art, Race, and Defiance.* New York: Vintage Books, 2011.

Burk, E. Bill. *Early Elvis: The Humes Years.* Red Oak Press, 1990.

Bolig, Lorina. *Ancestors of Elvis Aaron Presley 50 Generations Revised and Edited Edition.* Self-published, CreateSpace, 2007.

Choron, Sandra and Bob Oskam. *Elvis! The Last Word.* New York: Carol Publishing Group, 1991.

Clayton, Rose and Dick Heard. *Elvis Up Close: In the Words of Those Who Knew Him Best.* Atlanta: Turner Publishing, Inc., 1994.

Dundy, Elaine. *Elvis and Gladys.* University Press of Mississippi, 11 April. 1985. Kindle edition.

Dunleavy, Steve. *Elvis: What Happened?* New York: Ballantine Books, 1977.

Goodman, Charles and Charlie Hodge. *Me'n Elvis.* Memphis: Castle Books, 1988.

Greenwood, Earl and Kathleen Tracy. *Elvis: Top Secret.* New York: Penguin Books, 1991

Greenwood, Earl and Kathleen Tracy. *The Boy Who Would Be King*. New York: Penguin Books, 1990.

Guralnick, Peter. *Last Train to Memphis*. New York: Little, Brown & Company, 1994.

Guralnick, Peter. *Careless Love: The Unmasking of Elvis Presley*. New York: Little, Brown & Company, 1999.

Guralnick, Peter and Ernst Jorgensen. *Elvis: Day by Day*. New York: Ballantine Publishing Group, 1999.

Hopkins, Jerry. *Elvis: The Final Years*. New York: Berkley Books, 1981.

Hopkins, Vernon. *Tom Jones Just Help Yourself*, Second ed. Iponymous Publishing, 11 Dec. 2013. Kindle edition.

Jones, Sir Tom. *Over the Top and Back: The Autobiography*. Blue Rider Press, 24 Nov. 2015. Kindle edition.

Lacker, Marty, Lacker, Patsy and Leslie S. Smith. *Elvis: Portrait of a Friend*. Memphis: Wimmer Brothers Books, 1979.

Latham, Carol and Jeanne Sakol. *"E" Is for Elvis: An A-to-Z Illustrated Guide to The King of Rock and Roll*. New York: Penguin Books, 1990.

Loper, Karen. *The Elvis Clippings*. Houston: 1977.

Malone, Aubrey. *Still Rockin': Tom Jones, A Biography*. Y Lolfa, 2010. Kindle edition.

Manso, Peter. *Brando: The Biography*. New York: Hyperion, 1994.

Pierce, Jobe Patricia. *The Ultimate Elvis: Elvis Presley, Day by Day*. New York: Simon & Schuster, 1994.

Presley, Beaulieu Priscilla and Sandra Harmon. *Elvis and Me*. New York: Berkley Publishing Group, 1985.

Riley, C. Julian. *The Roots of Elvis*. Memphis: Paw Pad Printing, 2010.

Shaw, Arnold. *Belafonte: An Unauthorized Biography*. Philadelphia: Chilton Company-Book Division, 1960.

Strausbaugh, John. *Reflections on the Birth of the Elvis Faith*. New York: Blast Books, 1995.

Stanley, Billy. *Elvis, My Brother: An Intimate Family Memoir of Life with the King*. New York: St. Martin's Press, 1989.

Stanley, Rick and Paul Harold. *Caught in A Trap: Elvis Presley's Tragic Lifelong Search for Love*. Dallas: Word Publishing, 1992.

Surhone, M. Lambert, Tennoe, T. Mariam and Susan F. Henssonow (Ed.) *Sam Katzman*. Betascript Publishing, 2011.

Thomsa, Tony. *The Films of Marlon Brando*. New York: Carol Publishing Group, 1992.

Tillery, Gary. *The Seeker King. A Spiritual Biography of Elvis Presley*. Wheaton: Theosphical Publishing House, 2013.

Tracy, A. Kathleen. *Elvis Presley: A Biography*. Greenwood, 30 Nov. 2006. Kindle edition.

Wilson, Mary. *Dreamgirl and Supreme Faith: My Life as a Supreme*, Updated ed. Cooper Square Press, 11 Jan. 2000. Kindle edition.

Worth, L. Fred and Steve D. Tamerius. *Elvis: His Life from A to Z*. Chicago: Contemporary Books, 1998.

Zmijewsky, Steven and Boris Zmijewsky. *Elvis: The Films and Career of Elvis Presley*. New York: A Citadel Book, 1983.

Photo Credits

Images on the following pages are in the public domain, used by permission or licensed as specified below.

Page 77: Photo by Mike Kelly, used by permission.

Page 111: This file is licensed under the Creative Commons Attribution-Share Alike 4.0 International license.

Page 115: This work is in the public domain in the United States because it was published in the United States between 1923 and 1977 without a copyright notice.

Page 120: This work is in the public domain in the United States because it was published in the United States between 1923 and 1977 without a copyright notice.

Page 137: This work is in the public domain in the United States because it was published in the United States between 1923 and 1977 without a copyright notice.

Page 164: This work is in the public domain in the United States because it is a work of the United States Federal Government under the terms of 17 U.S.C. § 105.

Page 166: This work is in the public domain in the United States because it is a work of the United States Federal Government under the terms of 17 U.S.C. § 105.

Page 199: This work is in the public domain in the United States because it was published in the United States between 1923 and 1977 without a copyright notice.

Page 213: This work is in the public domain in the United States because it was published in the United States between 1923 and 1977 without a copyright notice.

Page 245: This work is from the Carol M. Highsmith Archive collection at the Library of Congress. According to the library, there are no known copyright restrictions on the use of this work. Carol M. Highsmith has stipulated that her photographs are in the public domain.

Acknowledgements

This book, which has evolved over several decades, has attracted many contributors, all of whom have been a necessary part of the process at different times. Each of them shares credit for the fact that this book exists. At last, with the often-abandoned project finally in print, I can express my sincere gratitude to those who have contributed their time, craft, perspectives, contacts and critiques. In particular, I wish to acknowledge the following individuals:

Bill Mack, who introduced me to the mysterious cache of letters and invited my participation in a project that would consume me for years.

Ian Graham Leask, my publisher at Calumet Editions, who prodded me into resurrecting this project after years of neglect and then, as developmental editor, collaborated tirelessly on improving the manuscript beyond my own high expectations; Rick Polad, my superb copyeditor, who relentlessly vanquished countless writing mistakes and made important suggestions for enhancement; John Zelman, for hours of expert proofreading in search of typos and errors; and also Lynn Ness, fact-checker extraordinaire, who not only verified information but uncovered other astonishing facts that have enriched the book.

Annemarie Osborne, our senior publicist, who endured with me the many disappointments and challenges on this journey and provided unflagging encouragement during the darkest times; Rachel

Anderson, publicist, who assisted mightily in getting the word out; Marc Kramer, my very close friend, who contributed in so many ways I can't list them here; Mike Kelly, director of operations at Calumet Editions, who smoothed the path forward during the final sprint to publication; Josh Weber, publishing associate, who helped close gaps in the manuscript with his research and organization of the letters; and Sue Skelton, whose obsession with the veracity of the book challenged everyone on the team to articulate the facts and alternative explanations more precisely.

There have been many others who have contributed significantly to this project, and I want to publicly thank them here: Jim Barnum, who provided critical advice at exactly the right time to successfully change the direction of our publishing effort; the late Elayne Lindberg, my mother, whose handwriting analysis of the letters originally encouraged me to embark on this endeavor; Bonnie Lindberg Carlson, my sister, who always stepped in at critical junctures with ideas, contacts, encouragement and sometimes solace to keep me going; Adrian Lee, for his invaluable insights about paranormal experiences; Jane Hollis, for her contributions in analyzing the handwriting of the celebrity letters; beta readers Jim Barnes, Lynn Nodland and Doug Nodland for their useful comments; and Phil Dell who contributed his marketing expertise and wise counsel on numerous matters.

Finally, and most importantly, I wish to thank the person who contributed the most to this project, my wife Gloria Lindberg. Gloria endured with me every swing of emotion, faced the same terrors of legal and financial risks, suffered through long periods of abandonment caused by my obsession with the book and for some unfathomable reason stayed with me. To Gloria I owe not only a debt of gratitude, but an apology and a promise to never again let a book become my mistress.

About the Author

Gary Lindberg has spent forty years as a filmmaker and the last ten years writing and publishing books. As an author, he has written four consecutive Amazon #1 bestselling novels: *The Shekinah Legacy*; *Sons of Zadok*; *Deeper and Deeper*; and *Ollie's Cloud*. With his mother, Elayne Lindberg, he co-authored a nonfiction book entitled *The Power of Positive Handwriting*. He is the co-founder of Calumet Editions, a publisher of fiction and nonfiction.

As a filmmaker, he has written, produced and/or directed countless corporate films, TV commercials, music videos and entertainment movies. He co-wrote and produced *That Was Then, This Is Now*, a Paramount feature film starring Emilio Estevez and Morgan Freeman. He has won over one hundred national and international awards for his work in media, including two Grand Awards from the New York International Film Festival.

The Power of Positive Handwriting
Elayne V. Lindberg, MGA and Gary Lindberg

The theory behind graphotherapy is simple: change the handwriting stroke and you change the associated handwriting trait. Graphoanalysis has proven that each stroke in your handwriting means something about you and your personality. This book will give you the tools to build the positive and productive life that is your birthright. You will learn to retrain yourself, to lose negative habits and establish new, positive ones.

The point is this: if you follow the suggested exercises for thirty days, you will see a change in your personality. New worlds will open up for you. This book cannot answer everyone's needs, however. It is, by necessity, a toolbox with a terrific set of instructions for building a new you.

Graphotherapy will not give you a better body or turn you into the world's greatest lover by Saturday. One of the areas it will help you understand is the mental side of your sex life. I can help you work on traits that may be standing in the way of greater fulfillment.

Explore the book at
smarturl.it/HANtg

How to Be a Christian Psychic
Adrian Lee

Using the Bible as reference, historian and psychic investigator Adrian Lee, a devout Christian, digs deeply into religious beliefs that appear on the surface to denounce the work of mediums, healers, and psychics. He explains these passages clearly and in historical context, challenging Christians to understand the deeper meanings and various settings in which these passages were intended to apply, so that the Bible's true message can emerge. He also explains his work as a healer and psychic investigator, showing how Christians can safely and effectively use their own God-given psychic gifts to help others.

Explore the book at
smarturl.it/CHpsy

Making It
Ted Myers

Turn on, tune in, and ride along in the front car of the rollercoaster life of Ted Myers, as he chases his dreams of rock stardom through the '60s, '70s and '80s. Although he never quite makes it, he has many wonderful—and not-so-wonderful—adventures, and rubs shoulders with some of the true icons of folk, rock, and pop culture, including Bob Dylan, James Taylor, The Who, Procol Harum, Joni Mitchell, Graham Nash, Van Morrison, Steely Dan, Chevy Chase, Timothy Leary and even Elvira, Mistress of the Dark.

After twenty years trembling on the brink of rock stardom and fifteen years working at record companies, Ted Myers left the music business—or perhaps it was the other way around—and took a job as a copywriter at an advertising agency. This cemented his determination to make his mark as an author. Ted's nonfiction has appeared in: Working Musicians (Harper Collins), By the Time We Got to Woodstock: The Great Rock 'n' Roll Revolution of 1969 (Backbeat Books) and Popular Music and Society. His short stories have appeared online at Literally Stories, in print in the To Hull & Back Short Story Anthology 2016 and in Iconoclast magazine.

Explore the book at
smarturl.it/MAKtg

Made in the USA
Monee, IL
28 October 2022

16751060R00184